On Being a Pivot-Wise Business Leader

The Secrets of Strategic Leadership
For Successful Business Pivots

Dr. Lance B. Eliot, MBA, PhD

DEDICATION

To my wonderful daughter, Lauren, and my wonderful son, Michael.

Aut viam inveniam aut faciam (as always; find a way, or make one).

CONTENTS

Lance B. Eliot

ACKNOWLEDGMENTS

I want to thank everyone that has aided me throughout my career, and especially during times of pivoting. Like many of the founders and business leaders featured in this book, I too have had my own business pivots and personal pivots that have been instrumental during my career. I write from the heart and the head, having experienced first-hand what it means to have others around you that support you during the tough times and the good times.

To Warren Bennis, one of the greats on leadership and my doctoral advisor and ultimately a colleague, I offer my deepest thanks and appreciation, especially for his calm and insightful wisdom and support.

To William Wang, Aaron Levie, Peter Kim, Jon Kraft, Cindy Crawford, Jenny Ming, Steve Milligan, Chis Underwood, Frank Gehry, and Colonel Sanders, for allowing me to meet them and learn first-hand about their business adventures and journey. I hope that I have properly and adequately represented their stories in this book.

To Buzz Aldrin, Steve Forbes, Bill Thompson, Dave Dillon, Alan Fuerstman, Larry Ellison, Jim Sinegal, John Sperling, Mark Stevenson, Anand Nallathambi, Thomas Barrack, Jr., and many other business founders and leaders that I have met, for which I pledge that a future book that I will write on more aspects of business leadership will include them.

Thanks to Ed Trainor, Kevin Anderson, James Hickey, Wendell Jones, Ken Harris, DuWayne Peterson, Mike Brown, Jim Thornton, Abhi Beniwal, Al Biland, John Nomura, and many others for their unwavering support during my business career.

And most of all thanks as always to Lauren and Michael, for their ongoing support and for having seen me writing and heard much of this material during the many months involved in writing it. To their patience and willingness to listen.

Lance B. Eliot

INTRODUCTION

Businesses are pivoting. You hear about these pivots all of the time. In the last several years, it seems like the word "pivot" has become the darling of the business buzzwords. If you aren't doing a pivot with your business, you'd better be thinking about doing so. But what does it mean to do a business pivot? The notion is tossed around and seems to have more of a stylish value than an actual meaning. A business leader that wants to seem like they are in-the-know will hint that a pivot is on the horizon. A pivot can genuinely make a difference to a business, and it can also be used to gain attention, spark the marketplace, add to the branding of the firm, and do much more than simply change the nature of the business as a business.

One of my contentions in this book is that a business pivot is not accomplished out of thin air. In other words, we often hear that a particular company did a pivot. But, I ask, who made that happen? There had to have been a business leader or some kind of business leadership that led to the business pivot. Business pivots don't just grow on trees.

I believe and firmly assert that when looking at a business pivot, you need to look at the business <u>and</u> the business leader. Most of the time, the business leader was sparked to want to do a business pivot, and then led their organization toward the pivot. The business did not just spontaneously or amorphously decide to pivot. There in fact were business leaders that thought it through, though in some cases in a shallow manner, but nonetheless there were business leaders that were at the core of the business doing a pivot. It is a human-led endeavor.

As such, if you only examine how or when a business pivoted and ignore or not reflect upon the business leaders, you will get an incomplete picture of why the business pivot took place. This then puts confusion and misinterpretation into trying to ascertain how you as a business leader should undertake a business pivot, since you have only half the story by focusing solely on the business as an entity and not also including the business leader in the grand picture of pivoting.

1

CONTEXT OF THIS BOOK

When talking with business leaders about business pivots, I have found that there are some pretty consistent questions or issues that they offer. I have boiled down the questions into a key set of five. Each question is addressed in this book overall, and serves as my overarching basis for the book. I saw a need among my business leader colleagues and opted to put together some insights on business pivots that I hoped will address their concerns and offer an inkling of some helpful solutions. Take a look at Figure 1.

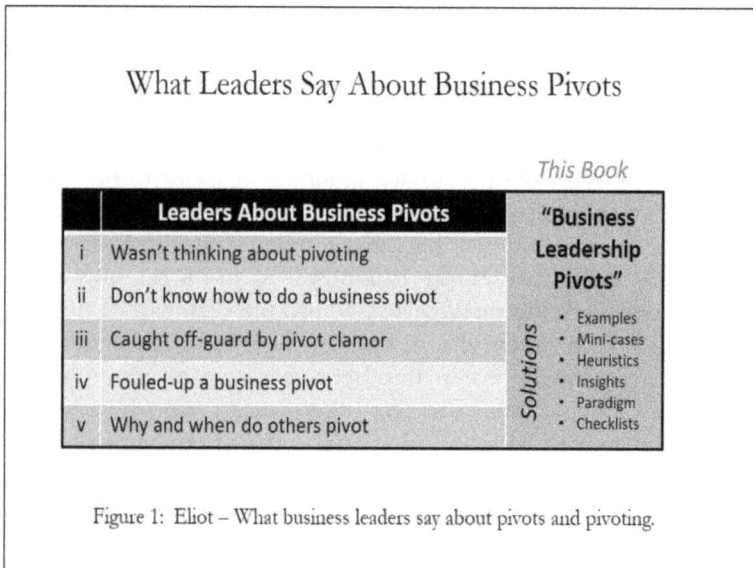

What Leaders Say About Business Pivots

This Book

	Leaders About Business Pivots	"Business Leadership Pivots"
i	Wasn't thinking about pivoting	
ii	Don't know how to do a business pivot	
iii	Caught off-guard by pivot clamor	Solutions: • Examples • Mini-cases • Heuristics • Insights • Paradigm • Checklists
iv	Fouled-up a business pivot	
v	Why and when do others pivot	

Figure 1: Eliot – What business leaders say about pivots and pivoting.

Let's tackle each of the questions briefly in this initial introduction to the topic of business leadership and pivots. First, many business leaders are hearing about business pivots, but not *thinking* about business pivots. By this I mean that they hear about other companies doing a business pivot, while they are not actively necessarily considering doing a business pivot themselves. In a sense, if one happens along then they will think about it. Otherwise, it is just kind of noise in the background and something worthy of someday getting concerned about.

For those with that question, I say it is time to start thinking about business pivots. You need to be ready for when the time comes. If you wait until the emergency arises, you might either not recognize that a business pivot is needed or you'll be scrambling and immediately behind the eight ball on how to handle the pivot that is needed.

The second question or issue is that most business leaders don't know how to do a business pivot. Even if they are wanting to do a business pivot, they are unsure of how to approach it. Indeed, there are management consulting firms that are now making their bread-and-butter by coaching business leaders on how to proceed with a business pivot.

For those business leaders wanting to be knowledgeable about business pivots, I have tried in this book to layout some of the essentials. I do so based on my twenty-five plus years of being in business, at times as a founder of a start-up, as a CEO of a small firm, as a corporate officer of a larger firm, and as a management consultant to firms both large and small.

I have been writing a popular blog (www.lance-blog.com) on business topics and was urged by many business leaders and various business leadership researchers and pundits to pull together some of my key pieces into a collective book. As you will see later on, I also was fortunate to earn my doctoral degree in business leadership under the wing of one of the foremost experts and founders of business leadership, Warren Bennis. I subsequently conducted research on the topic of business leadership and taught courses and seminars to executives.

The third question or issue that business leaders say about business pivots is that they are at times being caught off-guard by the clamor for a pivot within their organization. In other words, they are guiding their firm along, and a key stakeholder or several stakeholders have been asking them about pivots. Like the proverbial adage that if you have a hammer then everything looks like a nail, there are some Board members that have seen a pivot work elsewhere and so they want one now in your firm. Regardless of whether it makes sense for your firm or not, they want one because it seems to have cured cancer and all manner of irks in other firms.

For this aspect we'll take a look at the circumstances of when business pivots seem ripe and sensible. We'll examine the stakeholders involved and how to consider their perspectives and pressures on doing a business pivot. With a framework in hand, and some heuristics or rules to use, hopefully as a business leader you will no longer be caught off-guard. Whenever a stakeholder starts asking about a business pivot, you'll be armed with when to use a hammer, what the hammer can accomplish, and have a convincing basis for why a hammer makes sense or not to use.

The fourth question or issue involves business leaders that tell me they have done a business pivot and it did not turn out as hoped. In some cases, the pivot floundered and never actually came to fruition. In other cases it made it all the way to the pivot conclusion, but did not provide the business relief or success anticipated.

We will be taking a look at how business pivots work and what steps to take. We will also be considering how and when to do a Pivot Retreatment, backing out of the business pivot. Having a methodology and paradigm of what should take place involving business pivots should help to avoid the pitfalls that can occur. There are Pivot-Flops that you will want to steer away from.

The fifth and final key question or issue that business leaders have mentioned involves asking about other business leaders and their pivots. We often learn best as business leaders by hearing what other business leaders have done. I opted to include ten mini-case studies of business leaders that I know, and for which I was able to gain some insider insights, and cover their business careers along with both business pivots and personal pivots they've had.

My experiences include having been an advisor to many top business leaders. I was a Partner at the nation's largest executive C-suite services firm (which is also part of the world's second largest professional services company), and I also founded and ran my own management consulting firm. Thus, I have engaged with the C-suite and advised during business pivots, while in other cases observing the struggles and trials while they were doing a business pivot that I was not directly involved in. As a corporate executive, I too had been in their same seat and had to contend with and make successful various business pivots.

Seat-of-the-pants executive experiences are crucial to knowing what really goes on in enterprises, but that alone is not enough to gain a broader sense of what business pivots are all about and how they should be managed. Having an academic perspective helps to provide balance and a macroscopic look at how pivots into business. In my case, earlier in my career, I was a professor at the University of Southern California (USC) and the University of California Los Angeles (UCLA) and taught both undergraduate and graduate level courses in business. I also conducted research in these fields, and besides publishing various books and journal articles, I frequently spoke at both academic and industry conferences.

I offer the above overview of my background so that you'll be aware of my perspective on the topics at hand. This book is intended to be an interesting and decidedly useful compilation of thoughtful pieces that cover the gamut of pivots in business and especially with a focus on business leadership.

WHAT THIS BOOK PROVIDES

Many business leaders are so consumed by their day-to-day job that they do not have much chance of poking their head up and self-examining what they are doing and how innovative techniques like business pivots should be undertaken. There is a treadmill upon which business leaders are placed and with their legs and arms strenuously pumping hard, looking outward beyond the treadmill can be problematic.

For existing business leaders, I offer the essentials underlying business pivots and business leadership. Included are ten examples or mini-cases of well-known founders and CEO's. I also provide heuristics or rules, principles, insights, and an overarching framework or paradigm.

For aspiring business leaders, you should find this material equally valuable since you are at some point going to be involved in a business pivot and as a business leader need to be ready and able to do so.

For researchers that study business leadership, you likely know that the amount of substantive research on this topic is relatively light. We need more studies and deeper research to be done. I truly hope that this book will inspire you to do so.

For students studying business, the topic of business pivots is not especially covered in your classes. When it is covered, it is just an aside. I say that you should put some attention to business pivots as it is a rising tool among business leaders.

For all readers, I hope that you will find the material in this book to be stimulating. Some of it will be repetitive of things you already know. But I am pretty sure that you'll also find various "Aha!" moments whereby you'll discover a new technique or approach that you had not earlier thought of. I am also betting that there will be material that forces you to rethink some of your current practices.

I am not saying you will suddenly have an epiphany and change what you are doing. I do think though that you will reconsider or perhaps retune what you are doing.

For anyone choosing to use this book for teaching purposes, please take a look at my suggestions for doing so, as described in the Appendix. I have found the material handy in courses that I have taught, and likewise other faculty have told me that they have found the material handy, in some cases as extended readings and in other instances as a core part of their course (depending on the nature of the class).

In my writing for this book, I have tried carefully to blend both the practitioner and the academic styles of writing. It is not as dense as is typical academic journal writing, but at the same time offers depth by going into the nuances and trade-offs of various practices. The word "deep" is in vogue today, meaning getting deeply into a subject or topic, and so is the word "unpack" which means to tease out the underlying aspects of a subject or topic. I have sought to offer material that addresses an issue or topic by going relatively deeply into it and make sure that it is well unpacked.

STRUCTURE OF THIS BOOK

I have divided the material into three parts.

The first part consists of aspects that are introductory to the topic of business leadership and then business pivots. I believe it useful to start by looking at what constitutes business leadership. For some readers, this might be seemingly an academic exercise. I don't think it is solely an academic exercise and actually provides value to practitioners as a vehicle to help them think about what they are or must be to be an effective business leader.

While in the first part of the book, and after going over the foundations of business leadership, I boldly proclaim that being aware of and knowledgeable about business pivots is now a necessary and expected ingredient of business leadership. This can be debated and I am sure that some readers will not accept the idea readily; that's fine, and I offer this position to spark discussion and interest in considering the role of business pivoting as a management and business leadership element.

I expect that many of you will be eager to get to some of the stories of well-known founders and CEO's, and what they encountered as business leaders and business pivots. So, in the first part of the book there are interesting and colorful stories about notables such as Aaron Levie, founder of Box.com, Peter Kim, founder of Hudson Jeans, Jon Kraft, founder of Pandora, William Wang, founder of Vizio, and Cindy Crawford, founder of her famous beauty line and known as a supermodel.

If you aren't especially interested in the dryer material about the heuristics and paradigm of business pivots, you are welcome to read the mini-case studies of these founders and CEO's and set aside the rest of the material. Admittedly, their stories are pretty good, having all the same elements that might be found in a mystery or adventure novel. How did they get to their accomplishments? What choices did they make along the way? How did their personal lives intertwine with their businesses? These are all of incredible fascination on their own right.

The second part of the book continues with more such stories of founders and CEO's. It includes Jenny Ming, CEO of Charlotte Russe and one of the founding executives for Old Navy, Steve Milligan, CEO of the Fortune 200 publicly traded company Western Digital, Chris Underwood, CEO of the Fortune 200 privately-held Young's Market, Frank Gehry the world renowned architect and businessman, and Colonel Sanders, the founder of KFC.

The third part of the book then provides the rest of the meat underlying the business pivots paradigm, heuristics, and principles for business leaders. This can be a bit more intense than the mini-case studies, so I just want to forewarn you that the third part of the book gets a bit more detailed and technical in nature.

BUSINESS PIVOTS BY FIRMS SIZE & MATURITY

Before we move into the first part of the book, I'd like to cover some additional aspects of business pivots that will be of help to understanding the direction and nature of this book. There is handy way to think about business pivots overall, as based on considering the firm size and maturity. I suggest that there is a different way of viewing business pivots as a tool, depending upon whether you are in a start-up and acting as a founder or CEO of the start-up versus if you are a business leader in a mid-sized or larger organization of some maturity. Take a look at Figure 2.

The four-square grid provides along the vertical axis the business size and maturity, which we'll divide into two buckets. There is the start-up bucket and the mature business bucket. The horizontal axis has an indication of the magnitude of the business pivot, which we'll divide into a Minor Pivot and versus a Major Pivot. This notion of Minor versus Major is relative and so I will merely use it as an overall suggestion of magnitude as it relates to that particular business (whether start-up or whether mature).

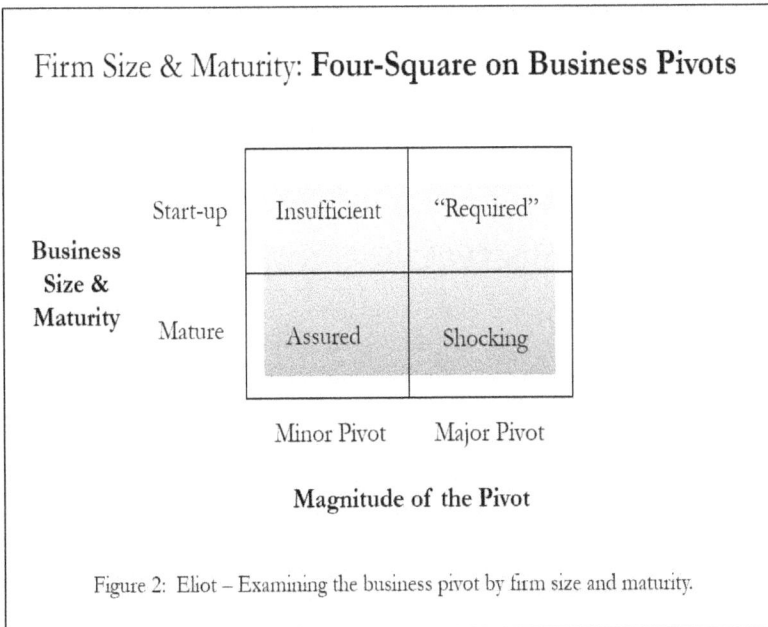

Firm Size & Maturity: **Four-Square on Business Pivots**

	Start-up	Insufficient	"Required"
Business Size & Maturity	Mature	Assured	Shocking
		Minor Pivot	Major Pivot

Magnitude of the Pivot

Figure 2: Eliot – Examining the business pivot by firm size and maturity.

For today's start-up's, it is almost de rigueur that they do a major business pivot. I have put the word "Required" in quotes into that upper right quadrant. Indeed, most Venture Capitalists currently say that they are betting on the rider more than the horse when investing in tech start-ups. By this they mean that they are betting more so on the entrepreneur than the nature of the business idea or concept, since they are expecting the business to make some significant pivots, and they believe that the consistency will be the entrepreneur as a business leader, rather than what the company does per se.

If a large and mature firm were to make a major pivot, it would be relatively shocking to the marketplace, thus the word "Shocking" in the lower right quadrant. A larger firm has such a vested interest in whatever they have already been doing that it is difficult to imagine that they could make a major pivot. Also, the view is that a larger firm is less nimble than a small start-up. Without agility or nimbleness, the thinking is that a large firm will belabor the pivot and probably kill it with bureaucracy.

In the lower left quadrant is the word "Assured" and this refers to the notion that a large business is expected to be making routinely various business pivots. These are of a minor nature though. They are expected because otherwise the firm appears to be resting on its laurels. Some competitor will come along and make a move and they will be left behind.

In the upper left quadrant is the word "Insufficient" and this refers to a start-up that is making minor pivots. Usually, the investors for a start-up want to see the firm make big swings at bat. They don't want little incremental changes. They are critical of a business leader that is not taking bold steps. Boldness and daring are thought to lead to great results and riches.

MAKING THIS FIT TO YOU

As a business leader, keep in mind which of those quadrants you fit into. If you are a start-up, the odds are that the expectation is for bold and brash major business pivots. If you are a business leader in a mature firm, be careful when proposing a major business pivot because it can make you seem perhaps overly ambitious and unrealistic.

Of course, all of these characterizations are merely generalizations and your mileage may vary, as they say, in that you could be in a large firm that is facing dramatic disruption and so the market wants to see you make a major pivot. Likewise, you could be in a start-up that has investors that liked what they saw when they first invested, and want you to stay the course, such that if you propose a major pivot it will not delight them and instead scare them silly.

PIVOT ACCEPTANCE CURVE

The last item that I'd like to cover in this introductory portion involves a Pivot Acceptance Curve that I've derived. I have found this inverted U-curve to be a handy means to depict the gaining of acceptance for a business pivot with your stakeholders. Take a look at Figure 3.

Along the vertical axis we have the **Pivotness**, which is a term I use to describe the degree of acceptance for a proposed business pivot. The horizontal axis has the perception of the business pivot, as perceived by those around you and usually key stakeholders related to the proposed pivot.

At the leftmost edge of the inverted U-curve, we have the circumstance involving stakeholders believing that the pivot is not needed. They just don't get why the business leader is wanting to have a pivot. As we will see later on in this book, communicating with stakeholders is essential to gaining acceptance for doing a pivot and likely will impact whether you can successful undertake and conclude the pivot.

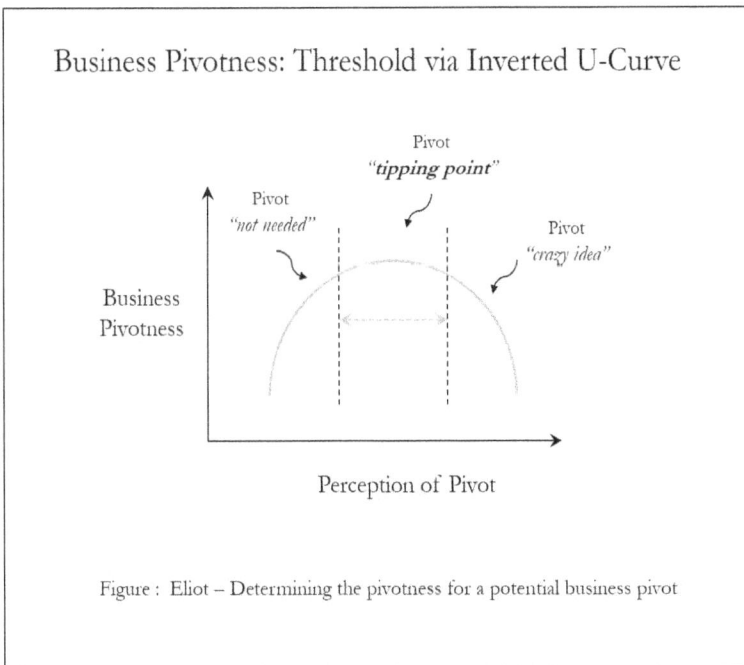

Business Pivotness: Threshold via Inverted U-Curve

Pivot
"*tipping point*"

Pivot
"*not needed*"

Pivot
"*crazy idea*"

Business
Pivotness

Perception of Pivot

Figure : Eliot – Determining the pivotness for a potential business pivot

As the stakeholders increasingly are led to believe that the business pivot is worthwhile, we step up the left part of the inverted U-curve, until we eventually reach potentially a ***Pivot Tipping Point***. Within a delicate range of acceptance, the tipping point means that now the stakeholders are willing to go along with the business pivot. I am not saying they will relish it, though in some cases they will. I am not saying they will hate it, though in some cases they will. At least while in the tipping point range, they are accepting of the notion of the business pivot and thus to whatever degree makes sense they will go along with it.

There is a third zone of this inverted U-curve, the rightmost portion. Here, the pivot has reached a point where it seems like a crazy idea. The contrasting portion of the curve was the first zone, wherein the stakeholder thought the business pivot was mundane and unneeded. At this other extreme, the stakeholders are increasingly against the business pivot and so the acceptance curves downward.

In short, as a business leader, you will need to find the sweet spot in which the stakeholders are accepting of the business pivot that you propose. You might not be able to get all stakeholders into the sweet spot, in fact it is unlikely you can, but for those stakeholders that are especially crucial and can nix the business pivot, you'll need to try and get them into that sweet spot. For those stakeholders in the leftmost and rightmost zones of the curve, you might not get them to a level of acceptance, and so should be on the wary for a fight or attempts to undermine the business pivot. We will cover more of these kinds of facets throughout this book.

For now, let's move into what makes a business leader and business leadership, and consider how business pivots and personal pivots come to play. Following that aspect, we'll then have the fun or cake of our meal and get into the stories of the founders and CEO's.

CHAPTER 1

ON THE KEY INGREDIENTS OF BEING A BUSINESS LEADER

Lance B. Eliot

CHAPTER 1

ON THE KEY INGREDIENTS OF BEING A BUSINESS LEADER

PREFACE

In this chapter, I explore the aspects of being or becoming a business leader. There are quite a myriad of opinions about what kinds of ingredients are needed to be a business leader. There are some opinions that are well reasoned and carefully based on thoughtful research. There are some opinions that are politely characterized as being at-best off-the-cuff and lack much other than a strong voice and brash claims. Into this seemingly endless pool of business leadership definitions we will focus here on what many learned and serious thinkers would likely agree is one of the most robust such definitions, authored by Warren Bennis and one of the field's foremost experts -- a founder of the business leadership field of study.

It is not by random chance that I happen to use as a starting place the work of Warren Bennis. I will next provide some context for my choice. As you will see, I was a disciple of Warren's and later a colleague. His work particularly resonated with me. He had always urged me and others around him to continue his efforts, seeking to extend it, refine it, and even question it. I not only thought about business leadership as a researcher and professor, but also when I became a corporate officer and experienced first-hand the demands, strains, and joys of being a business leader. For this confluence of reasons, I offer next a rapid expedition through the world of business leadership to set the stage for the essence of this book, namely a particular emphasis on business leadership and business pivots.

———

13

CHAPTER 1: ON THE KEY INGRDIENTS OF BEING A BUSINESS LEADER

Warren Bennis was considered one of the greats on the topic of business leadership and became particularly known for his groundbreaking book published in 1989 entitled "On Becoming a Leader." In his book and for much of his research, he tended to examine specific business leaders and attempted to surface the aspects that made them notable as leaders. He had real-world experience as a leader, having served as the provost of the State University of New York (SUNY) in Buffalo and served as the President of the University of Cincinnati, and cleverly integrated his own experiences into his analyses of business leaders. His scholarly efforts earned him the rightful nickname of "the dean of leadership gurus" (coined by Forbes magazine), and his cornerstone 1989 book became an essential text for any business school student studying business leadership and required reading for any business executive wanting to enhance their leadership acumen.

I was fortunate and undeniably lucky to have had Warren on my doctoral committee. He also was a faithful colleague and friend for many years after I had completed my doctoral degree. Allow me a moment of reflection. I recall the first time I met Warren. I had been admitted into the doctoral program and was "shopping" for the appropriate professors to serve on my doctoral committee. This can be a daunting task and will greatly shape the research that you do and your chances of actually completing the degree. I knew well of Warren's incredible reputation as a scholar and how busy he was, doing his writing, researching, teaching, and doing consulting work. He consulted with many of the Rushmore-stature CEO's of the day and routinely mingled with the founders of mega-businesses. I had serious doubts that he would see me, and even if he did that he would only say hello and then dispense with me. Furthermore, assuming I even spoke with him, asking him to be on my committee was like asking for the moon, given that he already was overloaded and had similar requests coming out his ears.

It turns out that upon first meeting him, and thereafter, he was just as he had said business leaders were supposed to be, namely, he listened to me, he made me feel valued, and he engaged in an open dialogue. He could have taken a decidedly different approach, acting in his senior capacity and opted to belittle me and not listen to a word I said (which some other faculty, less in stature, did do). Not only did we meet, he quickly altered his schedule after the first few minutes to allow us more than the abrupt fifteen minutes that I had hoped to claim with him, and we went and had coffee, sitting and talking one-on-one for a quite a while. He then made his mind up, decisively, and accepted enthusiastically my invitation to serve on my doctoral committee. During the years I spent doing my dissertation research and working with my committee, he always came to my aid when needed and miraculously somehow found the time to do so. I later on become a fellow faculty member and he continued consistently and unabashedly the same way throughout the days that followed.

BASIS FOR BUSINESS LEADERSHIP ANALYSIS

I indicated the aforementioned background for several purposes.

First, I am herein going to cover many of the important principles identified by Warren in his 1989 book, and then augment and in some cases seemingly go against some of the points he made. Do not become alarmed when I say that I will be going against some of his points, which might seem like heresy. Over the years, many of his views were modified and refined, and this can be seen in his thirty or so other books and hundreds of articles and bylines. Furthermore, he actually welcomed a Socratic dialogue on his work and we had many a debate on the topic of business leadership (often while sipping a fine beverage and overlooking the beaches of Santa Monica in California, from his sky high plush adobe).

Business leadership, as will be explained next, consists of as much art as science. If we were confined to only a science, it might be clearer as to who is "right versus wrong" on the issues at hand, but the behavioral sciences or the so-called "soft sciences" are not quite the same as studying say atoms. Of course, even pure "hard" science has its own debates, and we have seen time and again in the pure sciences that new theories evolve, they are tested and our understanding of even core principles change and get refined. For those of you that attended school some forty years ago, take a look at a physics or chemistry book of that era, explaining what the smallest particles are, and in comparison to today it is quite a changed matter.

Secondly, I provided the context about Warren to make another point, namely that he walked the talk. There are some scholars on business leadership that have never stepped one foot into the job of being a business leader. I am not suggesting that they don't have something valuable to contribute, which they do indeed can be very valuable as studiers of business leadership, but I am also saying that there are at times certain insights and certain gleam-of-the-eye revelations that can be a big plus if one has been a bona fide business leader writing about business leadership. At the opposite extreme, there is now a plethora of business leadership books, given that Warren's book in 1989 helped open the floodgates, and yet even those books written by actual business leaders can often be somewhat vacuous. The seasoned business leader that writes about their personal experiences can be entertaining as to what they did and why, though their attempts to then lift themselves out of the fray and offer useful business principles on leadership can be readily questioned.

Third, Warren walked the talk in another way too. On a personal basis, he was just like the person that he was in his work-related role as a leader, and which was precisely like the person he described as to being or becoming a leader. Let me unpack that. Sometimes a business leader exhibits one kind of persona at work, and when you meet them after-hours in a non-work setting they seem like a completely different person. This Dr. Jekyll and Mr. Hyde kind of personality split can be Okay, though from Warren's perspective we'll see that he frowned upon this kind of difference in persona. Someone that is an authentic leader is most likely to be an authentic person, I believe he would assert, and so the non-work person and the work-setting person should be about the same.

This is an important point by many that study business leaders. Is the business leader an actor that while on stage acts one way, and then is someone completely different while off-stage? Note that we are not saying that you cannot be different in some obvious respects, such as while at work you might be projecting an aura of strength that if done while also on your off-time would be exhausting and make you overwrought. It is the core that should be the same in either context, whether at work or not. As mentioned earlier in my telling of how Warren received me when I first met him, he was a listener, he valued the viewpoints of others, he made a decisive decision, and so on. Those characteristics, regardless of whether standing in an office or being out on the golf course, remain true for someone that is a business leader, based on the nature described by his becoming a leader analysis.

Let's next examine several of the stated principles and consider them in light of the world today and what else we know or think we know about business leadership at the moment.

PRINCIPLES OF BUSINESS LEADERSHIP

Intertwining of personal persona and business Leadership persona

"The process of becoming a leader is, if not identical, certainly similar to the process of becoming a fully integrated human being."

This principle of the intertwining of the person and how they are as a business leader is considered a core principle in the quest of becoming a leader. Presumably, the further you are as a gap between your business leadership persona as compared to your personal persona, the less likely you can carry off the role of business leadership in any authentic fashion. Those around you at work will ultimately realize you are two people trying to act as one. This can cause suspicion as to whether your leadership is sincere or simply an act. If it is an act, then those that see it as such will be wary of following you as a leader. They will assume that on a whim or for whatever else compels you to act as you do, you will potentially change overnight. As they say, you can fool some of the people, some of the time, but not all of the people, all of the time. You will be considered coreless and without a stability that can be relied upon.

Below is a chart depicting this aspect of business leadership, along with other facets that we'll be covering in this chapter.

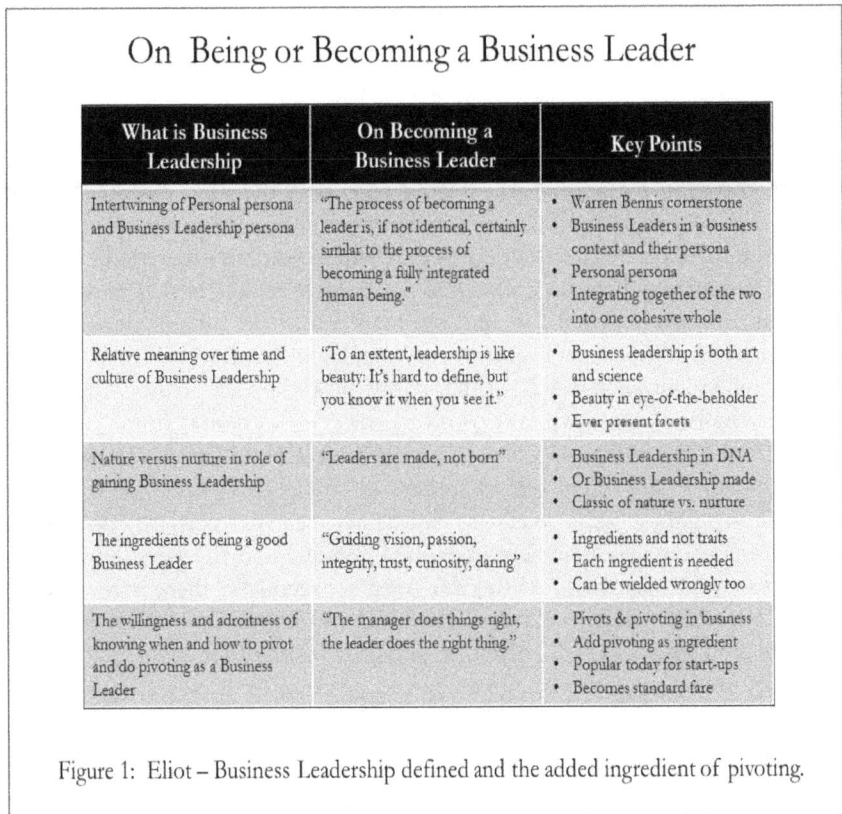

On Being or Becoming a Business Leader

What is Business Leadership	On Becoming a Business Leader	Key Points
Intertwining of Personal persona and Business Leadership persona	"The process of becoming a leader is, if not identical, certainly similar to the process of becoming a fully integrated human being."	• Warren Bennis cornerstone • Business Leaders in a business context and their persona • Personal persona • Integrating together of the two into one cohesive whole
Relative meaning over time and culture of Business Leadership	"To an extent, leadership is like beauty: It's hard to define, but you know it when you see it."	• Business leadership is both art and science • Beauty in eye-of-the-beholder • Ever present facets
Nature versus nurture in role of gaining Business Leadership	"Leaders are made, not born"	• Business Leadership in DNA • Or Business Leadership made • Classic of nature vs. nurture
The ingredients of being a good Business Leader	"Guiding vision, passion, integrity, trust, curiosity, daring"	• Ingredients and not traits • Each ingredient is needed • Can be wielded wrongly too
The willingness and adroitness of knowing when and how to pivot and do pivoting as a Business Leader	"The manager does things right, the leader does the right thing."	• Pivots & pivoting in business • Add pivoting as ingredient • Popular today for start-ups • Becomes standard fare

Figure 1: Eliot – Business Leadership defined and the added ingredient of pivoting.

Continuing the discussion about the gap between the personal persona and the leadership persona in the workplace, in the short-term a business leader can possibly get away with this gap, since it usually takes time for those "following" the leader to discern that there are two very different personas going on. Also, if you are a leader that essentially hides when not in the eyes of the workforce, it is conceivable that your other persona might not ever be witnessed or known to those that follow you. This can be especially tricky in today's age, given the advent of social media and being on-show much more than we were some twenty years ago. Especially for any prominent business leader that heads a large firm or even a small firm that perhaps has some excitement attached to its prospects. Via Facebook or Twitter, or blogs or vlogs, the odds are that the contemporary business leader of any prominence will be detected and dissected within work and outside of work.

There is also the energy factor involved in trying to keep two personas straight and apart. While at work, a business leader might put in many more hours than simply 40 hours per week. There are early morning meetings, dinner time meetings, late night crisis meetings, and the weekend is bound to have meetings and leadership decisions and actions. Having to switch constantly from being person A to being business leader B can be difficult, it wears you down, it distracts attention, it consumes personal and work energy, and generally is not likely to be effectual in the long run. One minute you take a personal call during your day, the next minute a work call, and so on, requiring a fast switch from being one person to another. It is not like the days of Leave It To Beaver where you are one person from 8 a.m. to 5 p.m. in the office, devoted exclusively to the office and nary a moment of work before 8 a.m. and nor after 5 p.m. Work and personal life have encroached upon each other, increasingly, and indeed we see the trend of the millennials that fret rightfully about how they are to find a balance between the two.

In brief, the business leader is a successful business leader as based on their character and their self-awareness of their character. If you find yourself struggling as a business leader, it can be partially due to a misalignment between your core personal persona and the persona you are trying to project at work. You will need to reconcile these two. Some business leaders undergo a transformation, shifting their work style more towards their personal style, often triggered by some other event that makes the pivot necessary to remain grounded. For example, a major health scare such as a heart attack, or a car crash that veered toward disaster, these are the kinds of events that can give pause for thought. The business leader reflects upon what they are doing, what their life means, what direction they are headed on a personal basis and on a work basis. It is then a catalyst for change in business leadership, especially if there has been a significant gap between the personal persona and the business leadership persona.

We must also consider that when discussing business leadership that it is the kind of art that one is always seeking to improve upon. It is like a master painting that is never quite finished. There is always some other nuance or trick of being a really good business leader that can be learned and used. In that sense, the gap between the personal persona and the business leadership persona can be simply as a result of being in the throes of progressing toward greater business leadership. A more junior business leader is bound to have a greater than a seasoned business leader, primarily because they are still trying on "for proper fit" the business leadership suit, so to speak. Over time, the fit should become more refined.

This begs the question about the business leader that has an utterly rotten personal persona. If a business leader needs to align their personal persona and business leadership persona, and if they are destined to shift their business leadership closer to their personal persona, this would seem to suggest that they will essentially become an equally rotten business leader. Years ago, when the more autocratic and dictatorial business leadership style was common and accepted, shifting the business leadership persona into an ogre-like personal persona was pretty much allowed and somewhat common. In today's world, the ogre-like business leader will have a harder time lasting. The likely Human Resources issues that it will cause, the potential for lawsuits by employees which is much more commonly accepted these days, and the going against the grain of the political correctness of what we view as proper business leadership will make it a rough ride for such a business leader to exist and subsist.

In fact, it is well accepted today that many business leaders often are provided with a life coach or similar kind of guiding counselor. It could be said that this is not due so much as a result of their business leadership style, but perhaps more so due to their personal persona. The life coach at times focuses on the rebooting of the personal persona, which then will naturally be forthcoming into the business leadership persona, over time and by a striving approach. In other words, the change in the business leadership persona can be sometimes more readily undertaken by going at the personal persona, and then transmuting the business leadership.

Relative meaning over time and culture of business leadership

"To an extent, leadership is like beauty: It's hard to define, but you know it when you see it."

In becoming a leader, it is said that even defining what a good business leader is can be confounding and not readily done. The moment you think you've gotten yourself a viable definition, it seems to escape and wither away. Some say we only can know good business leadership when it happens, when we experience it, when we see it in action. There are several aspects about this that are helpfully revealing.

First, think of an analogy to art. What is good art? Some would say that art is timeless and that good art will always be good art. Others would say that art and our taste for what is considered good art changes. It changes over time. It changes over cultures. As such, if business leadership is akin to art and we only know it when we see it, we are then dependent upon what our views are at that particular time and in that particular culture. Splashes of paint on a canvas can be the highest form of art in one time period for a certain culture, and be considered junk by another culture or in another time period. A business leader that acts in a certain way might be heralded as the greatest ever business leader, and yet in a different culture be reviled as a business leader, and in another time period be considered a dopey business leader.

Next, the eye of the beholder comes to play. Let's hold static time and culture, for a moment. We have two people looking at the same piece or art. Will they both necessarily agree that the art is wonderful and truly artistic? Not necessarily, as each will have a beholder's respective viewpoint about what is good art and what is bad art. When looking at a business leader, your viewpoint matters; if you are a follower, versus if you are on the outside looking in, the vantage point can radically change whether you believe that business leader is good or not. Even two people of nearly identical nature and standing in the same vantage point still might have radically different beliefs about whether a particular business leader is good or not.

As we shall cover shortly, there are alleged characteristics by which we can measure a business leader to assess whether they are good or not as a business leader. This availability of metrics might help move us away from the "you know it when you see it," since we can now have in-common ways to gauge the matter. With art, we might use metrics like whether a painting seems to have used light in a certain way, colors in a certain way, whether it tells a story, and so on. Likewise, we can try to use metrics to be more definitive in what we mean by good business leadership.

I have purposely been using the word "good" when discussing business leadership in this context, since without some kind of qualifier then we might be left with just referring to business leadership per se. If we were only discussing vanilla business leadership of any kind, then the definition would seem relatively easy since we could say that anyone in business that serves in a leadership capacity is a business leader. Haggling over that definition is possible, but not very productive. Meanwhile, haggling over what is a good business leader is more instructive since it forces us to consider the mysterious element(s) that make one business leader good at it while others flounder. How can one business leader be touted as stupendous and another business leader be considered pedestrian or worse? We want to know what makes that difference, and for which we could then presumably all be better business leaders because of knowing the secret sauce. We will shortly visit the measures and assess them for viability of being the secret sauce, but first, let's discuss another underpinning that some feel very strongly about, namely the dilemma of nature versus nurture.

Nature versus nurture in role of gaining business leadership

"Leaders are made, not born"

I am sure you've likely heard the heated discussion on whether good business leaders are born that way, or whether they are manufactured into being good business leaders. There are some that say that you must be born with whatever secret sauce there is, you must have it in your bones, in your heart, in your DNA. If you aren't biologically predisposed with the business leadership genes, you are not ever going to be a good business leader. You either got darned lucky and by birth have the right stuff, or you were regrettably unlucky and did not. Take yourself out of the game, no sense in fighting against nature; you are the business leader that quacks like a duck, walks like a duck, because you happen to be born as a duck.

There are others and including the viewpoint of becoming a leader that business leaders are made, not born. Business leadership is nurtured. You grow into it. Progressively, over time, by experience, and potentially by the addition of education or coaching, you become a good business leader. That being said, even the most extreme believers of the nurture will usually say that by education alone you are not going to be a good business leader. You need experience too. In fact, they would suggest experience alone might be sufficient, but education alone is definitely not sufficient.

Some say that you need to be born with some semblance of business leadership and then the nurturing can bring it out and make it blossom. As such, you could have it hidden within you, forever, a predisposition towards business leadership, but never have the reason or occurrence of it being found and allowed to flourish. Thus, the nature related position that you are born with business leadership is only revealed by happenstance or possibly by an inner drive that takes you there and yet will not gain traction until you have also had some appropriate dose of nurturing of it. Likewise, you can nurture the heck out of someone, but if they don't have an inkling of the nature inherent in them that is requisite for business leadership, you will maybe be able to make a stilted business leader but they will be always less than what a true business leader is all about. They will be a somewhat hollow business leader that knows the right moves but cannot make those moves in any fluid or fluent fashion.

We have then the postures of nature-only (you are born as a good business leader), the nurture-only (you are made into being a good business leader), and a combination of the two that involves a quantity of both nature-and-nurture (you are born with embers that can be stoked into becoming a good business leader). Let's consider these postures when we next examine the metrics of a good business leader.

The ingredients of being a good business leader

"Guiding vision, passion, integrity, trust, curiosity, daring"

According to the tenets of becoming a leader there are certain "ingredients" that are necessary to be a proper leader. The ingredients are that you must have a guiding vision, you must have passion, you must have integrity, you must have trust (that other's will trust in you), you must have curiosity, and you must have daring. We will take a close look at each of these ingredients.

The use of the word "ingredients" is very intentional. Your initial reaction might be that I have listed "traits," which is word commonly used to depict personal aspects such as passion, integrity, curiosity, and daring. The awkwardness of using the word "traits" is that it instantly dives us right back into the whole debate about nature versus nurture. For most people, hearing the word "traits" causes them to immediately assume that this is a characteristic you are born with. Thus, if I listed the elements of guiding vision, passion, integrity, trust, curiosity, daring and referred to them as traits, it might inadvertently lean you toward assuming that you have these qualities only as a result of your DNA. We can somewhat sidestep falling into that trap by simply calling those qualities as ingredients. Let's leave for a separate debate how those ingredients came to arise, and so avoid the distraction of that separate argument.

Guiding Vision

Guiding vision is considered a cornerstone of business leadership. It implies that you have the ability to create a sense of purpose and image of the future that others can also envision. You cannot readily rally others to a cause if they don't have a picture of what that cause is. The business vision will inspire those that are following to grasp what they are trying to follow. The vision will unify them; else they might all be headed in disparate directions. The vision gives them a sense of belonging, an uplifting perspective that will carry them toward goals and keep them going during hard times. It is not just any vision, but one that is a "guiding" vision, such that it also offers a kind of roadmap of where things are going. When hearing the guiding vision spoken by the business leader, the business leader must do so well enough that it resonates with others and sparks them.

There are of course gradients to this guiding vision notion. If I am a business leader asking someone to perform a perfunctory task, perhaps the guiding vision in that instance is rather plain. If I am a business leader that oversees thousands of business people, and the business itself is very diverse in what it does, the guiding vision must be wider in scope and more abstract in its portrayal. The key though is that a business leader must have the ability, however arrived at, which enables them to create, describe, and essentially promote a guiding vision.

This does not imply that the business leader does this solo. They do not have to sit on the top of some mountain like the proverbial guru and conjure a guiding vision from thin air. They do have to be able to somehow craft a guiding vision and often done in collaboration with others, and then be a communicator of that guiding vision. Some business leaders are adept at the crafting side of things, and less able to communicate it. Some business leaders are adept at the communicating side of things, but less able to craft it. And there are some that are adept at both the crafting and the communicating, though that's not considered a requirement per se and just perhaps an added bonus.

There are downsides to having this particular superpower and can lead others astray. Suppose the guiding vision is compelling, but it is going to lead to ruin. There have been many business start-ups that had an incredibly rich sounding guiding vision that was composed by a business leader, and communicated by the business leader, and yet in the end the guiding vision led to a brick wall. The point is that having the ability to be able to create and communicate a guiding vision is indeed an essential element of being a business leader, though having just any guiding vision, or worse still a crummy guiding vision, should be considered part of the aspects of whether you are a good business leader or a poor one.

Passion

Passion is another ingredient. Passion refers to the emotional verve that the business leader exhibits. They are not a robot. They are a human being that has a sense of energy and excitement about what they are doing and what they hope to have others do. This passion inspires others to follow. It is contagious and carries the business leader forward by engaging more and more to want to be associated with the business leader. People instinctively get the feeling that the business leader intensely believes in what they are saying and doing. A heartfelt expression gets others to look up, pay attention, and they also then believe that the business leader will really do what they say. Coupling passion with the guiding vision, the passion element convinces others that the business leader truly believes the vision and will see it through enactment.

Once again, though, this element can be a superpower for good or one that goes awry. An infectious business leader that has just amazing passion does not also necessarily imply that the passion will be well utilized. Some business leaders get very passionate about a particular new business model or new product, and their personal demeanor of passion can be very convincing. The passion can cloud judgement and defy logic. Many of the top entertainment studios have co-chairs heading the studio, one co-chair that focuses on the story of a movie and has passion for the nature of telling of a story, while the other co-chair is the finance or administrative head. The presumably logic-based co-chair will help to contend with circumstances involving the story-focused passionate co-chair becoming overcome by passion. When you greenlight a $100 million movie, there should be passion, and a lot more.

Integrity

Integrity is another ingredient. Honor, ethics, honesty, these are the elements of a business leader. The more recent buzzword has become authenticity. An authentic business leader is one that has integrity. Their word is their bond. They are transparent about what they are doing. They uphold the highest of ethical standards. They want the business to be one of respect to those that work in the company. They want the business to have respect in the marketplace. Their integrity as a business leader will encourage those around them to be comfortable in believing what they hear the business leader say. Integrity includes walking the talk.

Within integrity, there are additional components, consisting of self-knowledge, candor, and maturity. Self-knowledge means that the business leader knows of them, they know what they can do, they know their limits, and they use this self-knowledge to be a better business leader. They have candor in that when you interact with the business leader you feel that you are getting the true scoop. You don't feel like you are being hoodwinked or lied to. Maturity refers to having a seasoned demeanor and that you over time accumulated your business experiences, which then come to the forefront in what you do and are an integral part of how you conduct business today.

There are other sides of the integrity coin. How much candor is too much candor? Should a business leader tell all to their people, including if the company is faltering? If so, perhaps the act of telling others about this will ensure that it collapses; versus if the business leader held-back that it might not lead to panic or downfall. Suppose a firm is having secret discussions about merging with another company. Does a business leader need to inform everyone else in the company about these discussions? If they don't, aren't they then undermining their integrity by the lack of candor? The point to these questions is that it is not quite so apparent as to how far and to what extent these aspects of integrity can be pushed. There is a balance required and that's the mark of a good business leader, knowing how to strike that balance.

Trust

Trust is another ingredient. A business leader needs to instill in others a sense of trust, namely, those around them must come to trust the business leader and will abide by the wishes or follow their course because of that trust. If I don't trust you, I am likely to be suspicious of any business direction you provide. Your guiding vision might be scrutinized as something more likely evil rather than good, if you are not trustworthy. Trust usually takes time to build. People see you act, again and again, over and over, and gradually build-up a sense of trust for whom you are and what you do. One act alone is usually not enough to gain much trust. There is trust when the business leader demonstrates a consistency of making good judgments and so others can more easily accept and adopt what the business leader does next. A substantive pattern and history of being reliable usually breeds that trust.

When we see a business leader that seems to have a magic touch, being successful in what they do, it ingrains trust in them. If the business leader comes up with some wacky guiding vision, others might accept the guiding vision simply due to the trust they have in that business leader. Indeed, many venture capitalists often bet more on the business leader than the business idea or concept that is pitched. This so-called "betting on the rider rather than the horse" is prompted by the trust that they have in the business leader. They figure that the business idea or concept is probably going to change anyway, and that the key is to have a business leader that will shape it and drive it ultimately towards something that will be successful.

Trust, it is said, takes a while to build, but can be destroyed quickly. I think that we all have a visceral sense of that adage. Somebody might be a great business leader and we might have built-up trust for them over many years. Then, one day, they make a stupid move, sometimes small, sometimes big, and that one bad act alone is enough to have them lose nearly all the trust they once had. We've seen this in today's news, wherein a top CEO or company founder has gotten caught making an under-the-table deal or using a company for their own personal expenses, and all of a sudden they drop from heroic business leader to tainted business leader.

Curiosity

Curiosity is another ingredient. A business leader must be inquisitive. They must be questioning of what they see and hear. Are we aiming at the right customer base? Why do some customers love us and others do not? How can we improve our revenue? What are our competitors doing? How can we be doing better? How are our products faring against our competition? The business leader is constantly probing, looking, searching, and seeking new avenues, seeking better ways to do things. This kind of curiosity is fueled by a desire to always be on the watch and assume that there are other aspects to be found. Business leaders that lack a sense of curiosity are often complacent. Wherever the business is, that's fine. No desire to look further. No burning curiosity of what might else be accomplished.

That being said, there is the other side of this superpower. Remember the adage of how curiosity killed the cat? If the business leader is overly curious and unbridled in their curiosity, it can lead a company to become confused. He or she keeps asking questions, so there must be something inherently wrong. He or she seems obsessed with asking questions. This over-the-top kind of curiosity can be a burnout to people. They feel that the business leader is somehow never quite satisfied. No matter how hard the workers work, and how much they do to answer the questions, the questions still come at them in a shotgun, unrelenting fashion. Indeed, a good business leader knowns how and when to let their curiosity come out on the surface.

Daring

Daring is another ingredient and the last of the list. Last, but not least. A business leader must be bold. They must be willing to take risks. They must show that they are willing to go against the status quo. Maybe they opt to be the first into a new business or adopt a new technology. Perhaps they bring out a product that the market has not known, and do so in a daring fashion, akin to the Apple Macintosh launch that Steve Jobs is so famous for. Others around the business leader see the business leader as not complacent and not wedded to the conventional.

Daring is definitely another two-sided sword. We have seen repeatedly where a daring business leader jumps into a market, perhaps overly early, and cannot sustain the jump. The business falters and bleeds. Being imbued with their daring ingredient, they might continue to persist in the bad position. They continue to dare, challenging sheer business death and destruction in its face. This might in some cases win out, but much of the time it will be an overage of daring at the wrong time. A good business leaders judges well the use of their daring ingredient and in what circumstances and what ways to utilize it.

The Key Ingredients of a Business Leader

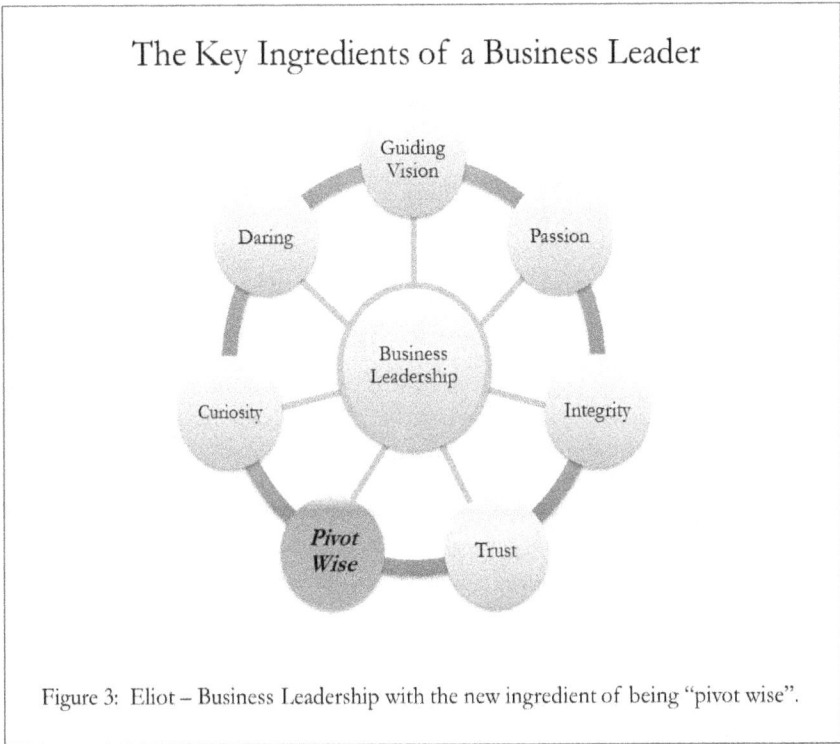

Figure 3: Eliot – Business Leadership with the new ingredient of being "pivot wise".

PIVOTS AND PIVOTING

The willingness and adroitness of knowing when and how to pivot and do pivoting

"The manager does things right, the leader does the right thing."

I'd like to add the word "pivoting" to the list of the key ingredients of being or becoming a business leader. The ingredients then read as this: Guiding vision, passion, integrity, trust, curiosity, daring, pivoting. I've opted to place the word at the end of the list, keeping the original list intact. Being at the end of the list does not connote anything about the importance or value in comparison to the others in the list. I consider it on essentially equal footing with the other ingredients.

Why would "pivoting" be added to the list, you might ask? How does it warrant being included? I am certainly glad that you ask that question. The purpose of this book is all about business leadership pivots and pivoting. I hope to show that pivots and pivoting are crucial to a business leader and being or becoming a business leader. Over the course of this material in this book, I aim to provide examples of how pivots by business leaders occur, and that it is an essential ingredient for business leadership.

Today, the word "pivot" is used quite a bit in business. We hear all the time about how a start-up decided to pivot. The same notion has made its way throughout our society. A student doing their homework essay opts to "pivot" and chooses a different topic. A country that was going toward democracy "pivots" away to another approach. The president of a nation "pivots" their position on healthcare to a different viewpoint on the matter. The use of the word "pivot" has become a darling of our vocabulary and well accepted in everyday language.

One of the more popular uses of the pivoting notion in start-ups was especially publicized by Eric Ries in his "The Lean Startup" approach. Others have of course also covered that ground, such as a piece in the Harvard Business Review in 2011 by Caroline O'Connor and Perry Klebhan on the use of pivots by entrepreneurs and other innovators. According to these kinds of approaches, a business start-up must be ready to pivot. There will be needed structural course corrections to the start-up as it evolves and finds its niche. If you take a look at most any of the famous tech start-ups, you will see that they all had a whopper of a pivot. Groupon was initially a social advocacy site and then pivoted to become a daily deals site. Instagram, Pinterest, Snapchat, and so on, they all did pivots. It has almost become a standard assumption that you must do a pivot eventually, as a start-up, regardless of whether one is needed, simply because that's what other highly noticeable and highly successful tech firms have done. Do the pivot, you'll love it, some say.

Should the pivot notion apply only to start-ups? No, and indeed all other businesses today are on the look for a potential pivot. Should just any pivot be taken? No, the pivot should be one that makes business sense, which we'll take a closer look at. According to many of the Lean Startup pundits, the pivot should come in your strategy, but not usually in your vision. In other words, your vision for the firm is supposed to remain as it had been stated, but the strategy of how to achieve that vision can be pivoted. I don't want to get into the debate on that aspect herein, since it takes us down quite a rabbit hole. Some would say that everything is on the table for a pivot, including the vision, and the kitchen sink. Others would vehemently disagree.

A pivot is usually characterized as keeping one foot firmly in place, while moving the other foot and heading to a new direction. This is a handy form of imagery of the pivot. You stay grounded in some sense, and turn in another direction, while still keeping to some degree in where you were. The business methodology to do this is often described as re-imagining your assets and talents of the business. You aren't likely going to chuck out all of what you already have, and instead leverage it, but do so in some new direction that hopefully is better than the direction that you were heading.

The ways in which you might pivot are somewhat endless, but let's consider the usual suspects. As a business, you are usually concerned with some key aspects, such as customers, products, markets, competitors, and so on. Thus, here are business types of pivots that you might do:

- Pivot into a new market
- Pivot toward a new set of customers
- Pivot by embracing some new technology
- Pivot by opening a new sales channel
- Pivot by shifting against a new set of competitors
- Pivot by crafting a new business revenue model
- Pivot by altering your products with new capabilities
- Etc.

I assert that one of the common omissions or oversights of the business pivot gurus is that they frequently seem to treat the business leader and the business as separate and distinct from each other. In other words, we hear about or read about the Widget business that did a pivot. In this case, it is as though the firm acted as a creature with its own beating heart. Did the Widget business gain human-like sentience? I think not. I would argue that there was a business leader that was involved in the pivot and caused the firm (an entity) to proceed to make that pivot. It is like saying that the computer did something bad, as though the computer has its own sentience, when in fact it was the programmer that wrote the code that caused the computer to do what it did. We cannot let off-the-hook the underlying human behind these actions. Furthermore, we should acknowledge that there was an underlying human and not some mystical entity that did this on its own.

The other extreme of this separation of business entity and business leader in pivots involves the instance where the attention goes only to the business leader alone. An entrepreneur is credited with having done a pivot, but in our context here, a business context, we need to also see whether or how that pivot impacted the business. Did the pivot by the business leader lead to a pivoting of the business?

This brings me to a four-square portrayal of this particular topic.

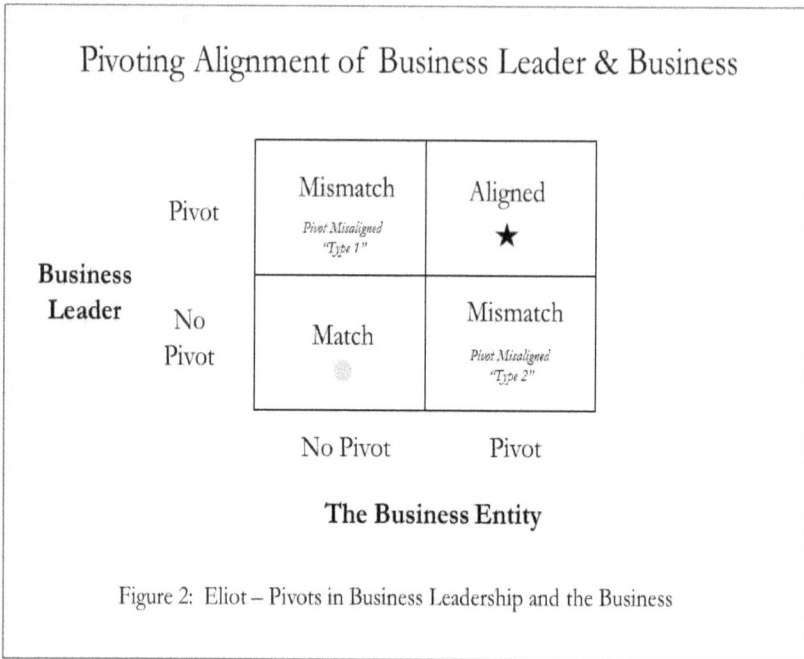

Figure 2: Eliot – Pivots in Business Leadership and the Business

We have the business leader as one side of the four-square, and the business entity at the other side. We can imagine that there are circumstances involving pivoting, and circumstances involving not pivoting.

If the business leader opts to pivot then we would likely assume this means that the business is going to pivot, and that's an aligned circumstance. If the business leader decides to pivot, but the business does not pivot, we are left to wonder what this implies. What kind of a pivot did the business leader do? Why didn't the business pivot correspondingly? I consider this to be a mismatch or misalignment and refer to it as a Type 1.

If the business entity decides to pivot, but the business leader does not, this is equally of concern as to why the business leader has not pivoted with the business. I refer to this case as a Type 2 misalignment or mismatch. This case has been seen often when "a business" changes course, but the head of the business has done so reluctantly and just really doesn't want to go in the new direction. As a result, they stay mired in where they were before, providing only a half-hearted or even less supportive weight to the business pivot.

One of Warren Bennis's most famous sayings was that "The manager does things right, the leader does the right thing." I well concur with this statement and use it time and again when working with executives and business leaders. I would also claim that the notion of doing the right thing by the business leader encompasses the ingredient of pivoting. A business leader needs to know when a pivot is warranted. The business leader needs to know how to enact the pivot. Firms invariably face the possibility of pivoting, and especially in the world today of disruptive innovation and business transformation. The ability to do a pivot must become a standard tool for the business leader. We need to have a fuller understanding of what business pivoting is all about.

If you believe that business leaders are made or at least that the making of a business leader is an aspect of becoming a business leader, an essential and integral aspect to that making must involve understanding of, familiarity with, and being proficient with pivoting. We are in a new business world where pivots are rife, and business leaders that don't know what a pivot is, and nor how to undertake one, will find themselves being forced into a pivot that will likely become disastrous. Such a disaster is bad for all. It can lead to the downfall of the business and the ruin of the business leader.

I have written this business book to help encourage business leaders to become more learned and practiced in the art and science of business pivots. I have used relevant and illustrative examples of various business leaders to showcase how business leadership pivots occur, and provided an initial paradigm or framework for understanding the pivots. This can also be used for further research on the topic, in addition to being used for business practice.

One of the leaders described in this book is Frank Gehry, the world renowned architect. In talking with him about his business career and perspective as a business leader, I found his phrasing of what he has done in architect to be very helpful here. Specifically, he says that in his architecture, he has tried to create a new language for which new forms of architect itself can be expressed and understood. Some that don't "get" his architect are, according to him, often bewildered because they either don't know the language or have never learned the language. I am hopeful that this book provides an akin new language for business pivots, and will help us all to better express, understand, and carry out business pivoting.

CHAPTER 2

THE ESSENTIALS OF BUSINESS PIVOTING

CHAPTER 2

THE ESSENTIALS OF BUSINESS PIVOTING

PREFACE

Now that we have discussed the foundations of business leadership in the prior chapter, and we have made the case that pivoting and business pivots are an essential ingredient for modern day business leaders, let's lay the groundwork for what business pivots are really about.

We will unpack, as they say, the underlying aspects of business pivots. In order to readily analyze pivoting, a diagrammatic language will be introduced, along with terminology to accompany it. Via the use of these diagrams, we can more easily take a "big picture" view of pivoting. This will allow business leaders to become familiar with pivoting, and serve as a communication vehicle when examining past business pivots and when crafting and executing successfully possible future business pivots.

CHAPTER 2: THE ESSENTIALS OF BUSINESS PIVOTING

Let's start with one of the most popular examples of a business pivot, involving Starbucks (and, maybe you are drinking your favorite Starbucks drink right now anyway, while reading this book). We will use four such examples in this chapter, consisting of two that are tech related, namely Groupon and Twitter, and two that are not tech related, namely Starbucks and Avon. I purposely have chosen to include two non-tech related examples since I want to emphasize that it is not only tech companies that do business pivots. Though tech companies seem to get the most attention about business pivots, and we have an expectation inbred that they will do a pivot, as discussed in the prior chapter it is not a technique confined to just tech related companies. For these four chosen examples, I will be brief and cover just highlights of their stories. I mention this because they each offer a quite enriching indication of the various mechanizations of business pivots, and the full set of details are interesting, so at your leisure you might want to research them further. Here, we will cover them to the degree needed to spark a discussion about the essentials of pivoting.

Howard Schultz joined a small seller of coffee beans called Starbucks as a marketer at the firm. After working there, he envisioned that they could become an expresso bar and coffeehouse. The owners rebuffed him. He left. Howard started his own coffeehouse and expresso bar called Il Giornale. Later, he buys Starbucks and rebrands his Il Giornale to become ultimately the Starbucks chain that we know today.

Fascinating story and one of those heartwarming business tales. What can we glean out of it? A business leader senses the need for a business pivot. The business leader is personally ready for and enthused about it. The business pivot is pitched, and gets turned down. Other stakeholders do not grasp the vision and feel it is unwarranted. All of this is taking place in what I will call the **Pre-Pivot** stage. The Pre-Pivot is not an actual pivot per se, but the various wrangling's leading up to a potential actual pivot.

The business leader continues to pursue the business pivot, even though the pivot notion has been dashed. Ultimately, through determination and doggedness of the pivot pursuit, the **Pivot Point** comes. In this example, the Il Giornale is pivoted into becoming Starbucks. The Pivot Point is achieved. When I refer to the Pivot Point, I am not suggesting it is one instantaneous moment in time. A Pivot Point can take place over days, weeks, or even months. Do not think of it as a light switch whereby there is an instantaneous occurrence almost as though a miracle occurred. We often read stories about pivots that seem to come across in that fashion, leading us to believe that there was a split second of an "Aha!" eureka moment that was the pivot point. That's not the notion here. The Pivot Point is a stage of the business pivot during which the actual pivot is undertaken and might last briefly or be quite lengthy.

After completing the Pivot Point, there is an unspoken and often undocumented follow-on that takes place. The **Post-Pivot** stage involves carrying forward from the Pivot Point. It is all of the likely hard work needed to ensure that the pivot truly takes hold and won't falter.

There is often a tendency to fall back to the circumstances that existed prior to the Pivot Point, which is what I call the **Gravitational Force** acting upon a pivot. Essentially, the business pivot is a process of change, consisting of aspects preceding the change itself, then the enacting of the change, and then the cementing of the change into place. This is akin to the well-known Kurt Lewin model of change, whereby there are three steps, the unfreeze, the change, and the unfreeze. There are many such models, and they usually involve either 3 steps, 4 steps, or 5 steps. This use of a 3-5 steps process is a handy number of steps because it is relatively easy to remember and comprehend. If we listed a process that had say a dozen major steps, it would be overly cumbersome and awkward to remember and use.

Take a look at Figure 1 to see a diagram depicting the three stages of a business pivot, consisting of the Pre-Pivot, the Pivot Point, and the Post-Pivot. I have purposely slightly overlapped them in the diagram. I do this because there is not necessarily a sharp demarcation between each of the stages per se. They do not need to formally end and the next formally begin in any strict back-to-back basis. When preparing a project chart like say a Gantt chart to depict the stages, you can show them as the end of one stage linked to the start of the other stage, but even in that case you can still overlap them in time, if that makes sense for your particular business pivot.

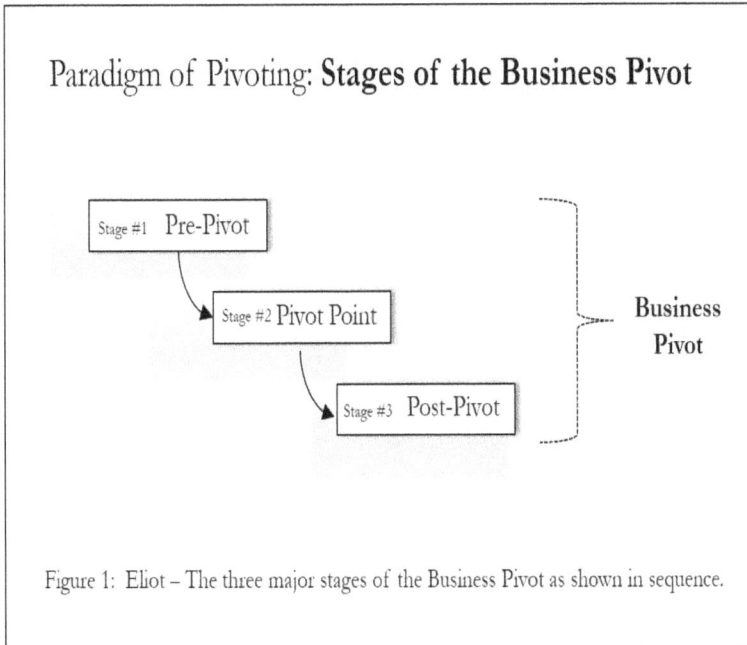

Paradigm of Pivoting: **Stages of the Business Pivot**

Stage #1 Pre-Pivot

Stage #2 Pivot Point

Stage #3 Post-Pivot

Business Pivot

Figure 1: Eliot – The three major stages of the Business Pivot as shown in sequence.

We will be using this fundamental model throughout the exploration of business pivots. It provides a useful way to discuss business pivots. Without this model, you might not understand what stage of the business pivot I am referring to. Also, when examining a particular business pivot, it is helpful to find clues as to what was the Pre-Pivot, the Pivot Point, and the Post-Pivot. This is like Sherlock Holmes trying to figure out a mystery by looking for telltale signs of what has happened. We will build upon this model and be able to use it to not only diagnose a business pivot, but use it too for planning toward doing a business pivot.

When I say that we will be planning toward doing a business pivot, this statement is worthy of a moment of reflection. Many and perhaps most business pivots have been done by ad hoc aspects. It usually just emerges over time. That's great, and we are grateful to know about them. But, as they say, it's not necessarily a good way to run a railroad. This means that if you are thinking about doing a business pivot, you would be wise to plan it out and try to do so in a systematic fashion. The odds that the pivot will happen and happen properly are increased (I would so contend). That does not mean that a planned pivot is a guaranteed pivot. It just means that the chances of success for the pivot and the ability to rectify a pivot that has gone sour is enhanced.

As shown in Figure 2, I have annotated the three stages to provide an indication of the nature of each stage.

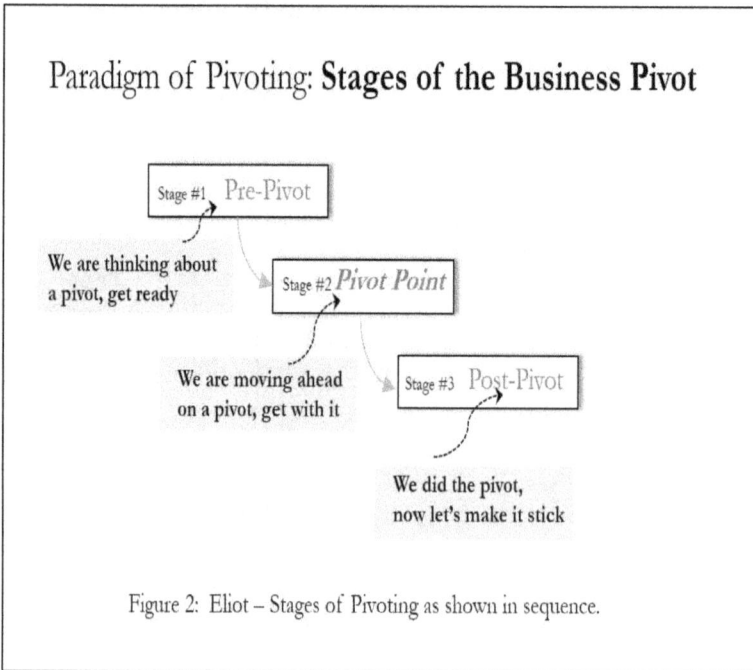

Paradigm of Pivoting: **Stages of the Business Pivot**

Stage #1 Pre-Pivot

We are thinking about a pivot, get ready

Stage #2 *Pivot Point*

We are moving ahead on a pivot, get with it

Stage #3 Post-Pivot

We did the pivot, now let's make it stick

Figure 2: Eliot – Stages of Pivoting as shown in sequence.

Let's revisit each of the stages, one at a time. The Pre-Pivot is the underbelly of the pivoting (see Figure 3 for a highlight of this stage). It is the rumination that takes place leading up to the pivot. It can be agonizing and tortuous. It can be filled with dreams and fantasies of what will become. It can be pragmatic and serious. It can be done ad hoc and on a whim.

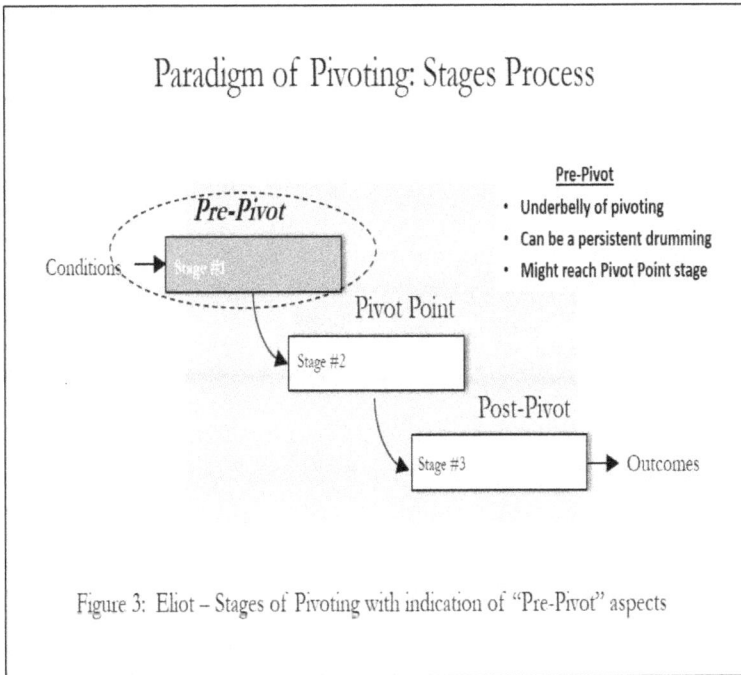

Paradigm of Pivoting: Stages Process

Pre-Pivot

Conditions → Stage #1

Pre-Pivot
- Underbelly of pivoting
- Can be a persistent drumming
- Might reach Pivot Point stage

Pivot Point

Stage #2

Post-Pivot

Stage #3 → Outcomes

Figure 3: Eliot – Stages of Pivoting with indication of "Pre-Pivot" aspects

In the case of Howard Schultz, we saw that he had a vision of what he thought Starbucks should become. Turns out that this vision was sparked by a visit he made to Italy and he saw the popularity of coffeehouses there. He sensed that this would be applicable in the US market. It became for him a constant drumming in his mind. Often, it takes that kind of business leadership to prevail. There are going to be naysayers. Sometimes the naysayers are wrong, while sometimes they are right. You cannot ignore the naysayers since they might have aspects that makes the pivot untenable. Or, they might have naysaying that causes you to adjust the nature of the pivot, doing so hopefully during the Pre-Pivot, prior to making a firmer commitment to the pivot and then having to deal with radical changes once you are in the Pivot Point itself (we will see how this can be costly and arduous to contend with).

Notice that the diagram also shows that there are **Conditions** entering into the Pre-Pivot stage. We will be looking more closely later on at the conditions that tend to spark the possibility of doing a business pivot. You should also note that at the end of the Post-Pivot there is the word **Outcomes** listed. These are the outcomes arising as a result of the pivot.

We will explore this more in-depth later on in terms the outcomes of a pivot. Generally, keep in mind that the outcomes can arise throughout the entire pivot and do not need to only occur after the pivot is concluded. I realize that on the diagram it might suggest that the outcomes only come after the pivot is done, but this is just an easier way to show things more succinctly on the diagram. Outcomes can occur at any time during the pivot. Furthermore, the outcomes can be good and can be bad. A pivot is not a silver bullet that solves all ilk's. There will be both positive and adverse consequences usually due to a pivot. One hopes to of course maximize the positive outcomes and minimize the adverse outcomes.

Next, let's consider the Pivot Point. This is the second stage of the business pivot process. Take a look at Figure 4.

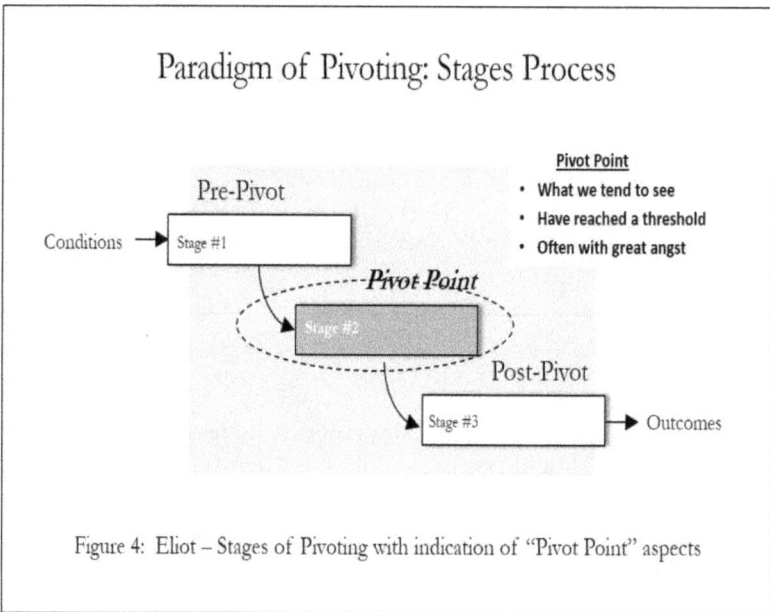

Paradigm of Pivoting: Stages Process

Pivot Point
• What we tend to see
• Have reached a threshold
• Often with great angst

Pre-Pivot

Conditions → Stage #1

Pivot Point

Stage #2

Post-Pivot

Stage #3 → Outcomes

Figure 4: Eliot – Stages of Pivoting with indication of "Pivot Point" aspects

The Pivot Point is the part of the business pivot that often gets the most attention and is the most visible. Usually, once a threshold has been reached, the business leader and the business undertake the actual pivot. Whether they know it or not, they were in the Pre-Pivot prior to the Pivot Point. Many business leaders to not consciously think about the Pre-Pivot and consider instead that the Pivot Point is one long monolith. I assert that it is better to differentiate the Pivot Point and divide out those aspects that usually precede it, and those aspects that need to follow it.

I realize that there are those business leaders that have little patience for what they consider overly complicated schemes and approaches. For them, the idea of having three stages might seem like overkill. Why not just call it a day and say that the pivot is the Pivot Point? I argue that it is wiser to separate out the Pre-Pivot and the Post-Pivot, so that they can each get their own due attention. Without realizing distinctly there is a Pre-Pivot, you can fall right into a Pivot Point and be completely ill-prepared for it. Likewise, without the explicit Post-Pivot, once the Pivot Point has been finished there is a really good chance that there won't be distinct attention to keeping the pivot in place. All three stages have a useful purpose. All three stages help us to comprehend what needs to be done for a business pivot.

Let's take a look at the last stage, the Post-Pivot. See Figure 5.

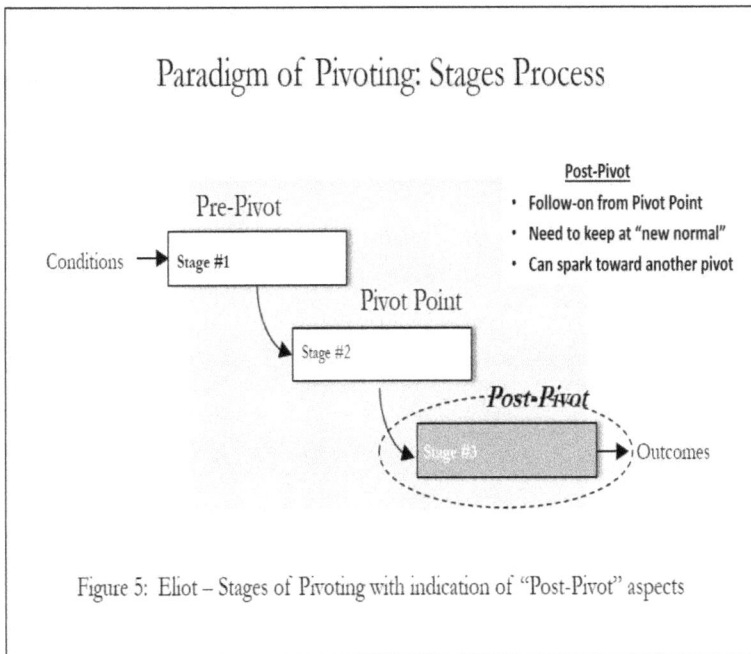

Figure 5: Eliot – Stages of Pivoting with indication of "Post-Pivot" aspects

As you can see, the Post-Pivot is there to help ensure that the pivot takes hold. Furthermore, the Post-Pivot is a timely occasion to think about what happened during the Pre-Pivot and Pivot-Point. Are there lessons to be learned that will help with the next pivot? I say this because the odds are high that whatever pivot you have just done, another one is heading along soon enough. It might be weeks away, months away, or in some cases years away, but it nonetheless is a likely chance that the business leader and/or the business will experience another business pivot, thus, try to do better the next time by gauging what you can from this pivot.

I'd like to take a short tangent, a related one, and comment about business leaders and organizations that refer to the lessons learned as a post-mortem. I know that it is an easy way to phrase things, but I avoid it like the plague. The reason is that the connotation of a "post-mortem" is that something died. You are examining a corpse. If we had a successful pivot, why should we be implying it is dead? Words matter, and the use of the post-mortem moniker to me is wrong. Even if the pivot was a disaster, I still would not call the examination a post-mortem. It gets people into a defensive mode. A post-mortem looks for the cause of death, and then however that happened maybe it means that someone should go to jail for causing the death. Looking for those to blame about a pivot is likely to be painful and distract from the completion of the pivot. With lessons learned, I avoid trying to find culprits, and focus instead on what can we do better the next time around.

Next, let's take a look again at the Conditions and Outcomes. Take a look at Figure 6.

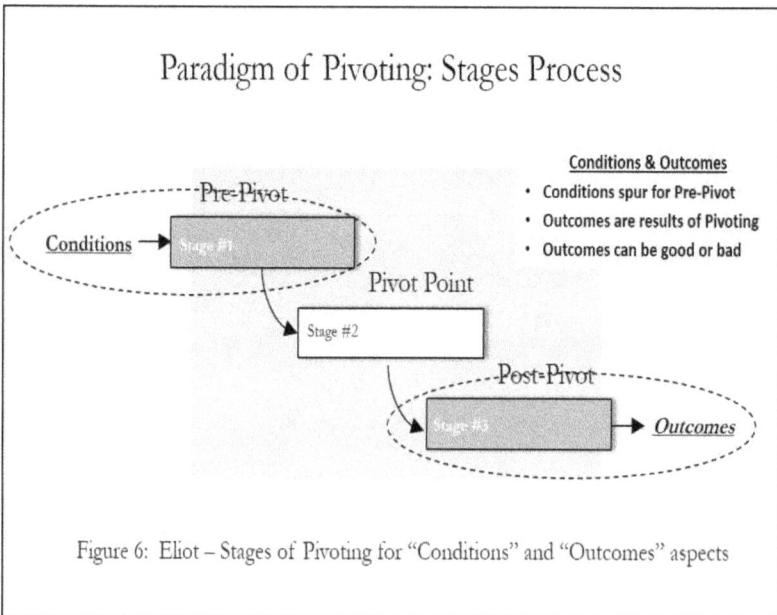

Figure 6: Eliot – Stages of Pivoting for "Conditions" and "Outcomes" aspects

As shown, the conditions spur the pivot. Some conditions will drive us toward the Pivot Point. Some conditions will block progress toward the Pivot Point. Earlier it was mentioned that the Outcomes are throughout the process. You should think of the Conditions as also occurring through the process. This is sensible because the entire duration of the pivot can be weeks or months in length, and so the Conditions under which the business pivot is taking place can likely shift and change during that time. We cannot put the conditions into a bottle and keep a cap on it for the duration of the pivot.

Speaking of duration, take a look at Figure 7.

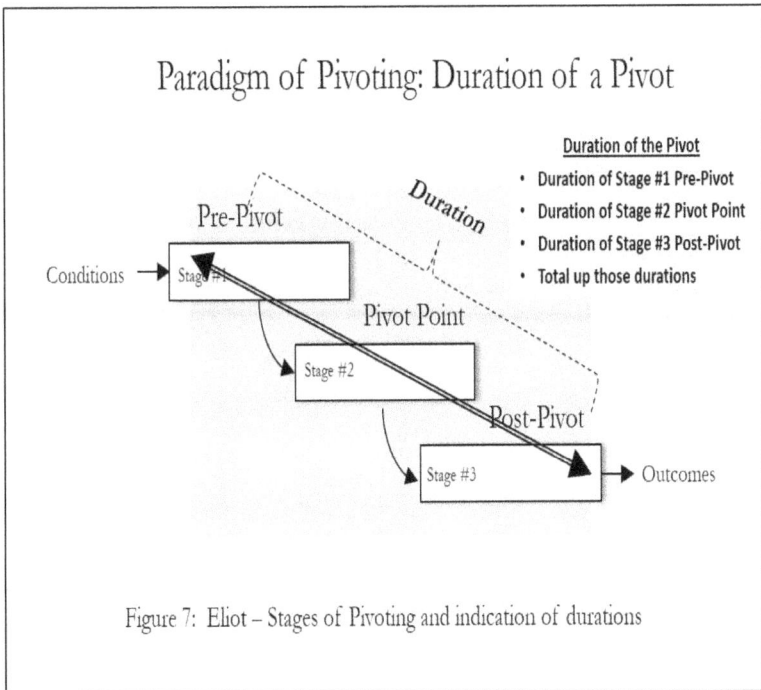

Figure 7: Eliot – Stages of Pivoting and indication of durations

The total duration of the pivot is the length of time for the Pre-Pivot plus the Pivot Point plus the Post-Pivot. Since we have already noted that many only look at the Pivot Point as the business pivot, for them the duration of the pivot is solely the duration of the Pivot Point. We will consider that the length of the entire pivot is the total of the three stages durations. When referring to the duration of a business pivot, I will customarily be referring to that grand total. When referring to the duration of a particular stage, such as the Pivot Point, I will specifically indicate that I am referring to that stage's particular duration. Just clarifying so that we are all on the same page.

The diagram shows a rectangular box to represent each of the three stages. Each box appears to be the same length. This might cause you to think that each stage is the same duration. We know that stages can vary in length. Howard Schultz spent years trying to get the pivot to Starbucks to happen. I will visually alter the length of the boxes in the diagrams to help suggest the duration of a stage for a particular case of a business pivot.

Take a look at Figure 8 to see how we'll be adjusting the box lengths.

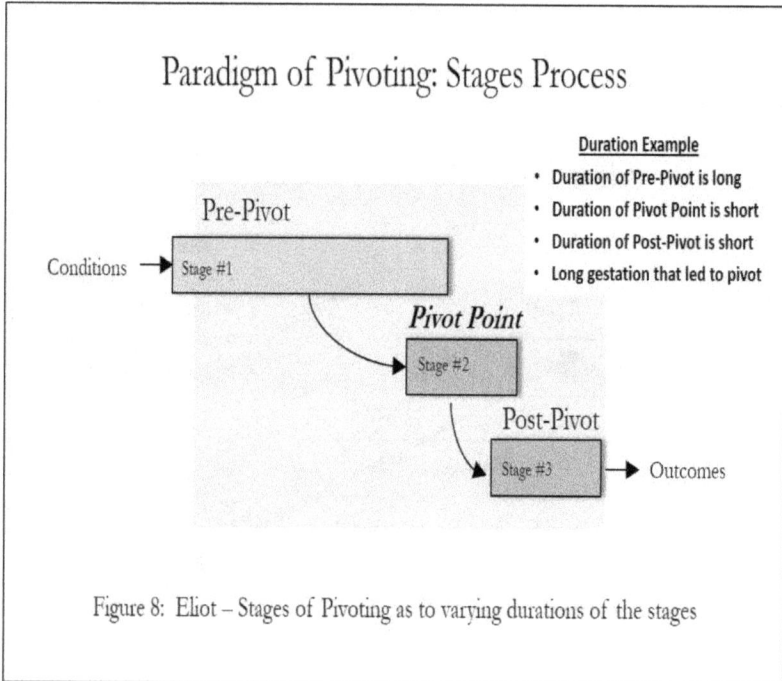

Paradigm of Pivoting: Stages Process

Duration Example
- Duration of Pre-Pivot is long
- Duration of Pivot Point is short
- Duration of Post-Pivot is short
- Long gestation that led to pivot

Conditions → Pre-Pivot — Stage #1

Pivot Point — Stage #2

Post-Pivot — Stage #3 → Outcomes

Figure 8: Eliot – Stages of Pivoting as to varying durations of the stages

As shown, in this particular example, we have a lengthy Pre-Pivot, a relatively shorter Pivot Point, and a relatively short Post-Pivot that is about the same duration as the Pivot Point. This is a pretty common circumstance. It could be said that the Starbucks example is like this.

We can argue about the durations and where the start and stop of each stage really is, but I think we are wiser to simply acknowledge that each stage can be its own duration. The diagrams now can reflect that difference in duration overall. When planning a business pivot, we can then keep in mind that the duration of each stage will depend upon the particulars of that case.

If you pause for a moment and reflect on this notion that each stage can be its own duration, we realize that there are a number of such combinations possible. Any duration can be any length of time. For sake of simplicity and ease of strategically thinking about a business pivot, we will opt to suggest that a duration is either **Long** or **Short**. This sense of time will be with respect to the business pivot at hand. I will not use these metrics as meaning an absolute or fixed time period. A business pivot might take say two months, and the Pre-Pivot takes 1 ½ months of that time, while the Pivot Point is a week and the Post-Pivot is a week. On a relative basis, the Pre-Pivot is Long, the Pivot Point is Short, and the Post-Pivot is Short.

Suppose though we had a business pivot that was 2 years in length. And let's suppose the Pre-Pivot for this case is 6 months. That might make it a Short duration for the 2 years pivot. But you might say, it is longer than was the Pre-Pivot of the case of the pivot that was in its entirety 2 months. I realize that. I am saying that we will always consider the durations on a relative basis for that particular pivot case. Thus, be careful when comparing two different pivots in terms of how we are using the words Long and Short. You can do the comparison on a relative basis, but not on an absolute basis regarding time.

As shown in Figure 9, this is a so-called "decision tree" that shows the various combinations of Long and Short across the three stages of Pre-Pivot, Pivot Point, and Post-Pivot.

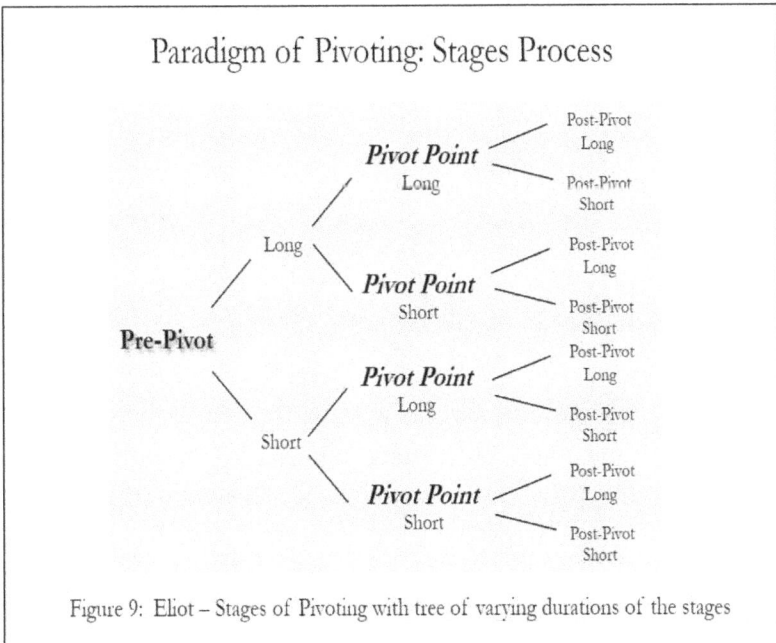

Figure 9: Eliot – Stages of Pivoting with tree of varying durations of the stages

The diagram starts with the Pre-Pivot as the root of the tree, and then shows that there are the Long Pre-Pivot and the Short Pre-Pivot possibilities. For the Long Pre-Pivot, we can have a Long or Short Pivot Point. For the Short Pre-Pivot, we can have a Long or Short Pivot Point. And so on, tree branches out, reading it from the root on the left to the final edges on the right.

It might seem laborious that we have been considering the durations of the stages and the total duration of the pivot. Why care? We are now to the icing on the cake, and I appreciate that you stayed with me during the build-up to the icing. Take a look at Figure 10.

Paradigm of Pivoting: Stages Process

Ref	Pre-Pivot	Pivot Point	Post-Pivot	Description	Phrase
i	Long	Long	Long	Long pivot	"I took my time"
ii	Long	Long	Short	Pivot lengthy with short end	"Did it and moved on"
iii	Long	Short	Long	Quick at Pivot Point with tails	"Mulled it, before & after"
iv	Long	Short	Short	Gestation, then quick to pivot	"Finally pulled the trigger"
v	Short	Long	Long	Fast into pivot, long pivoting	"Wanted to see it play out"
vi	Short	Long	Short	Long pivot with short tails	"Nearly stuck in the middle"
vii	Short	Short	Long	Upfront fast, follow-on long	"The end of it was key"
viii	Short	Short	Short	Fast pivot	"Move fast. Decide then act."

Figure 10: Eliot – Stages of Pivoting as chart of varying durations of the stages

This is an indication of each of the combinations that we saw in the decision tree. Now, I have listed each combination uniquely. Furthermore, each such instance has a brief description and a catch-phrase. These catch-phrases are very handy when discussing business pivots. During my discussions with fellow business leaders, I have found that these catch-phrases are a great shorthand to engage in a dialogue. The dialogue can be about prior business pivots, or it can be about business pivots that the business leader envisions for the future.

Rather than tediously explaining the background about the three stages and the Long and Short durations, I have found that with busy executives it is easier to focus on the catch-phrases. This makes intuitive and instant sense to them, and allows us to then consider the overarching shape of a business pivot that they might want to do.

This also awakens for them the entire set of constructs we have covered so far. Allow me a moment to elaborate. I was talking with one founder of an exciting start-up, and he was convinced that a pivot was necessary. He was the classic non-aware pivot business leader in that he really knew nothing about business pivots other than he has heard about them and wanted to do one.

In conversation and brainstorming with him, I asked whether he was anticipating it to be an elongated pivot or something quick. He indicated that he wanted it to happen nearly overnight. I then gently probed as to what would be necessary to make the pivot happen. Upon reflective thought, we sketched out that the Pre-Pivot would be relatively short, and so would the Post-Pivot. But the Pivot Point itself had something like 15 key things that would have to all occur to make the business pivot possible and getting those to happen was going to be a relatively long process.

Ultimately, I posited that this was a Short-Long-Short instance, which on the chart I use the catch-phrase of "Nearly stuck in the middle" and suggests that there is a chance that the Pivot Point might get derailed and never actually complete. When we began the conversation, whether he knew it or not, he was assuming that this was going to be a Short-Short-Short, or via catch-phrase a "Move fast. Decide then act" kind of pivot.

In other words, as a business leader, as the proponent and propellant for the business pivot, he was initially under the belief that the whole thing could happen quickly. Had he proceeded as such, and assuming that our guess of the Pivot Point being lengthy was accurate, he might have gotten caught off-guard when things bogged down during the Pivot Point. This might have created not only frustration, but in the end caused the pivot to fall apart. By starting at the end, so to speak, by using this diagram depicting the catch-phrases, I was able to introduce the rest of the aspects, such as the Pre-Pivot, the Pivot Point, the Post-Pivot, and this alerted him to the need to treat the pivot as a bona fide business action and effort that would require more than just desire to pull off successfully.

PIVOT POINT MAGINTUDE

Now that we have the foundation of the business pivot identified, let's take a deeper look. Though all the stages of the business pivot are crucial, the Pivot Point is the center stage (literally and figuratively) and gets all the spotlight. It is worthwhile to zoom in and take a closer exploration of the

Pivot Point. I will do so by first discussing the magnitude of the Pivot Point. By magnitude, I am referring to the notion that the pivot can be a radical departure from what is being done today, or it can be a mild departure. The direction of the pivot is presumably to help the firm, and essentially "elevate" it to some greater capability and success. As we shall soon see, the pivot does not necessarily come out that way. A business pivot can end-up going south or downward. Indeed, it can go bad in a big way or a small way.

Take a look at Figure 11 to see an initial example of how we will be referring to the magnitude of a Pivot Point.

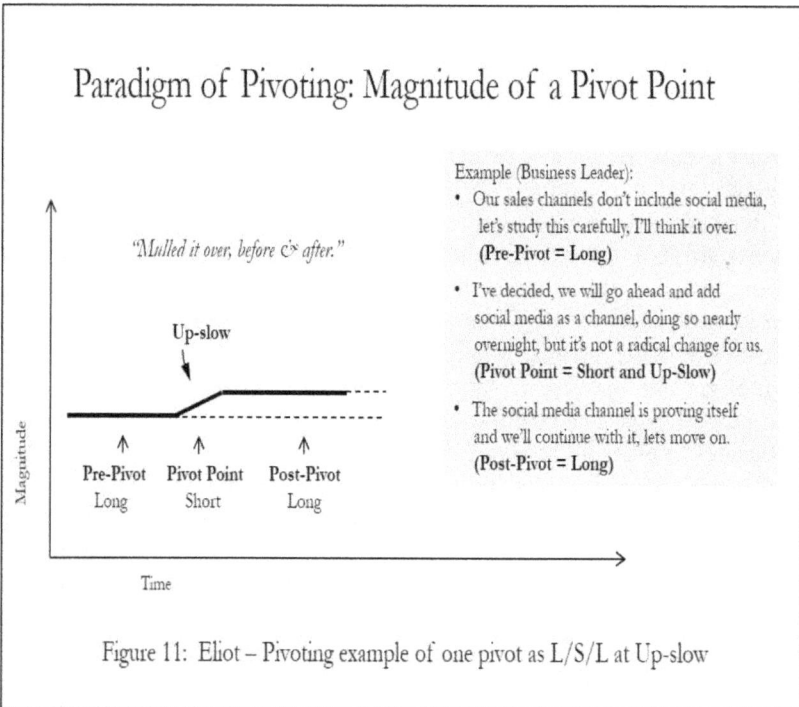

Paradigm of Pivoting: Magnitude of a Pivot Point

"Mulled it over, before & after."

Up-slow

Pre-Pivot   Pivot Point   Post-Pivot
Long   Short   Long

Magnitude

Time

Example (Business Leader):

• Our sales channels don't include social media, let's study this carefully, I'll think it over.
  (Pre-Pivot = Long)

• I've decided, we will go ahead and add social media as a channel, doing so nearly overnight, but it's not a radical change for us.
  (Pivot Point = Short and Up-Slow)

• The social media channel is proving itself and we'll continue with it, lets move on.
  (Post-Pivot = Long)

Figure 11: Eliot – Pivoting example of one pivot as L/S/L at Up-slow

In this diagram, we have a Long-Short-Long duration business pivot, consisting of a relatively long Pre-Pivot (notice the long dark line length), a relatively short Pivot Point (notice the short dark line), and a long Post-Pivot (the long dark line following the Pivot Point). This diagram also indicates the magnitude of the pivot. The Pivot Point is shown with an upward gradual rise. It has taken us from the foot of the Pre-Pivot to now a higher level which we are using to suggest that the business now has some new direction it is pursuing. The old direction is shown as a dashed line that, had we not done the Pivot Point, we would still be on.

This example is a firm that wanted to pivot its sales channels and add social media. The Pivot Point is angled as a line upward. The amount or degree of the angle will suggest how much of a radical pivot this was. In this case, the Pivot Point is shown as gently sloping upward. It is labeled as an Up-Slow to help visually understand and point out the amount of the slope of the line was modest. For this particular company and this specific pivot, their adoption of social media was considered a relatively mild pivot and so the angle or slope is accordingly displayed as modest.

Take a look next at Figure 12 to see how we will gauge the magnitude of Pivot Points overall that go well.

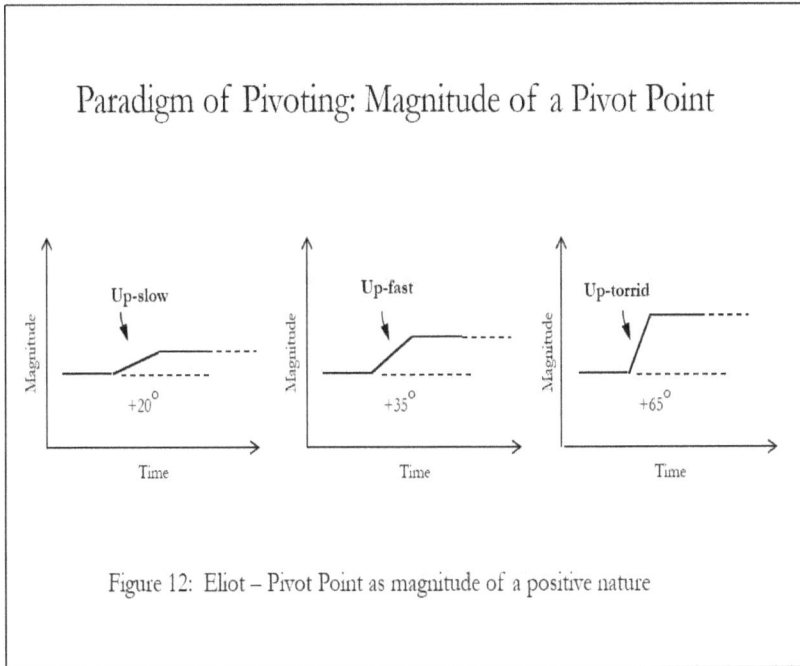

Figure 12: Eliot – Pivot Point as magnitude of a positive nature

As shown, we will divide the magnitudes into three types (again, the handy magical use of the number three). There are the **Up-Slow**, **Up-Fast**, and **Up-Torrid** indications of a positive magnitude. For those of you that are numeric nerds, I have shown that the degree of angle for Up-Slow is 20 degrees, Up-Fast is 35 degrees, and Up-Torrid is 65 degrees. Is there something special about those specific degrees? No, just wanted to use angles that could visually be interpreted readily as ranging from minimal upward slope, more acute slope, and a very strong upward slope.

The wording is also representative of the magnitude of the angle. Up-Slow is meant to suggest that the nature of the pivot is not that much of a leap for the business and the business leader. The Up-Fast means that it is a bit of a push to make the leap and will be dicey. The Up-Torrid means that it is a really challenging and big gap leap. If you see an Up-Torrid, it should hopefully convey that this is something that is a real stretch of where we were. Imagine a person physically pivoting, and having to distort themselves intensely to make the pivot.

The world is not always rosy and so we should anticipate that some pivots are going to go awry (or, we might purposely claw back). For those pivots, we'll use a downward sloping Pivot Point. Take a look at Figure 13.

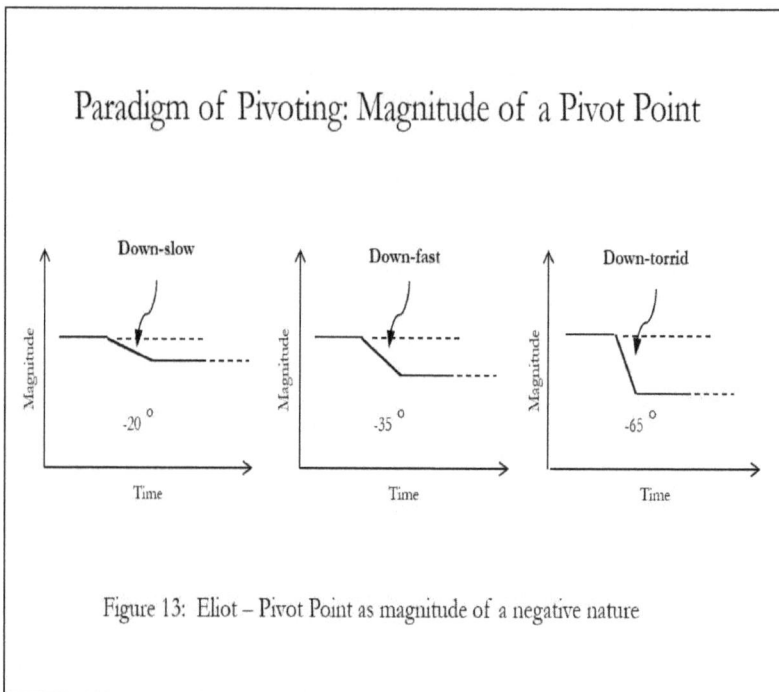

Figure 13: Eliot – Pivot Point as magnitude of a negative nature

Same as before, we'll use the angle of the slope to depict how radical the pivot is. Thus, we will have Down-Slow, Down-Fast, and Down-Torrid. If you see a Down-Torrid it means that it was quite a dramatic pivot and it went bad, really bad. We are now in a worse place than before the Pivot Point began. We have dug ourselves a hole.

There are therefore three upward angles or magnitude of a Pivot Point, consisting of the Up-Slow, Up-Fast, and Up-Torrid, and there are three corresponding but opposite direction angles or magnitudes of a Pivot Point consisting of Down-Slow, Down-Fast, and Down-Torrid.

Now that we have these tools at our beck and call, we can begin to make good use of them. We just saw an example of a business pivot that involved an Up-Slow, the case of the firm that added social media as a new sales channel. Business pivots can be looked at as one-time occurrences. Over a longer time horizon, we are likely to see that any given business leader and any given business will have multiple business pivots.

Take a look at Figure 14 to see an indication of two business pivots, both being indicated on the same diagram.

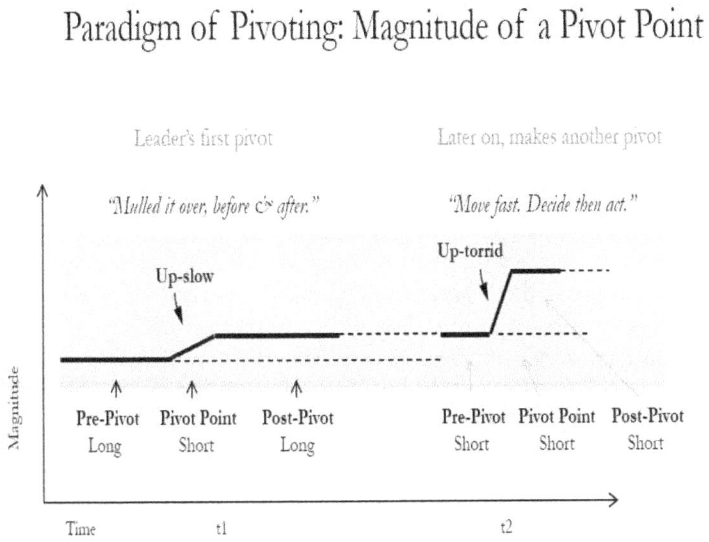

Figure 14: Eliot – Example of two pivots L/S/L Up-slow then S/S/S Up-Torrid

As shown, there was a business pivot that occurred as an Up-Slow and was a Long-Short-Long in duration (on the left side of the diagram), and then there was a second business pivot later on. The second pivot was a Short-Short-Short in duration, and was an Up-Torrid. We read these diagrams from left to right, whereby the horizontal axis is time, and time in this case of the first pivot was at time "t1" while the second pivot was at a later time indicated as "t2" (for sake of simplicity, we won't necessarily show the time on an absolute regular fixed scale, and thus the time between the two business pivots might have been lengthy, and yet the two business pivots are shown close to each other).

So, in this example diagram, the business had a first pivot that was considered by our catch-phrases as a "Mulled it over, before & after" type of pivot. Then, at some later time, a second business pivot was undertaken. It was a "Move fast. Decide then act" type of catch-phrase. Both of the business pivots were positive in that they worked out, and the first one was a modest stretch (since it is an Up-Slow), while the second pivot was a radical stretch for the firm (it is an Up-Torrid).

What does this allow us to now do or say? Well, without being excessively judgmental, it looks like the firm opted to initially do a modest business pivot and took their time about it, perhaps wanting to do so carefully and as a first foray into doing business pivots. It could be that they then realized that they needed to do something more radical. They had now under their belt the success of the first business pivot. They decided therefore to do the second business pivot and felt ready to do so of a more radical nature. They also tightened up how they do business pivots and cranked this one out, achieving a Short-Short-Short rather than the first pivot which was a Long-Short-Long.

That is quite a bit of speculation and conjecture without knowing the specific context of the company and the business leader. One should be cautious in interpreting such a diagram without having the context in mind. I can say in this case that the diagram interpretation is accurate, because it was a firm that I was working at that did indeed do two business pivots, and the diagram is reflective of what actually happened. Now that we all agree to the nature of these diagrams, I can at times streamline them by stripping off some of the explanatory info. Take a look at Figure 15, which is the same as Figure 14 but minus some of the other explanatory details.

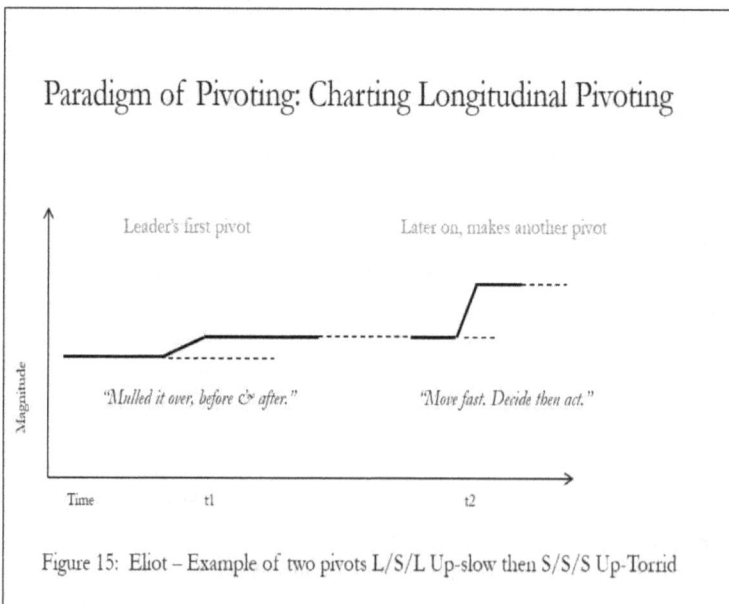

Figure 15: Eliot – Example of two pivots L/S/L Up-slow then S/S/S Up-Torrid

We can use these diagrams to portray a charting of a longitudinal nature of a series of business pivots, which we just saw an indication of two business pivots, but we can pretty much depict any number of business pivots. For example, let's take a look at Figure 16.

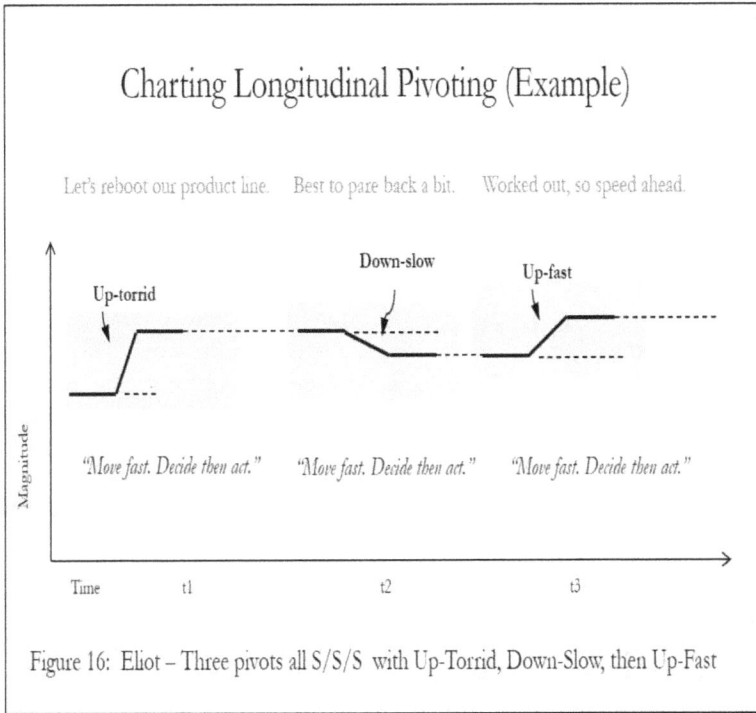

Figure 16: Eliot – Three pivots all S/S/S with Up-Torrid, Down-Slow, then Up-Fast

We now have three business pivots. The first one, on the left side of the diagram, involved rebooting the company's product line. This was considered a significant and especially challenging pivot (Up-Torrid) and happened fast. They realized they had gone too far. They ratcheted downward by undertaking a Down-Slow pivot that was relatively quick to occur. After stabilizing, they did a third pivot, rising upward again, and ending up higher than what had occurred with the first pivot.

These diagrams can help take the minutiae of business pivoting and rise them up to a more strategic and macroscopic perspective. We can use them to look for patterns in how a firm and a business leader is undertaking pivots. We can use it to diagnose whether perhaps the firm and business leader are not doing so well on their business pivots, or maybe they are doing really well and highly accomplished at it. We can try to predict what their next business pivot will be, as based on their history of doing business pivots.

We can do all of this somewhat easily via the diagrams, rather than if it was all captured solely in a written narrative of some kind. The diagrams provide the proverbial "a diagram is worth a thousand words" and now that we have a language or paradigm underlying business pivots, we can use it for analyzing business pivots.

It is also handy when working with business leaders and trying to figure out with them their interest and need for a business pivot. By charting their business pivots, it can take what they think they know and make it more readily visible. In other words, their memory of prior business pivots might be overly cheerful or overly regretful, they might distort how long it took, and so on. By putting together the diagram, it helps to rethink those prior business pivots, and be better able and more clearly be able to structure and achieve future business pivots. We will be extending all of this foundation in later chapters to arm us with even more tools and advances on this.

I promised earlier in this chapter that we'd consider four case examples of pivoting, of which we discussed Starbucks so far. A second example involves David McConnell. His name might not ring a bell (that's kind of a joke, as you'll see). He was selling books door-to-door, and provided perfume samples to try and encourage women to buy the books (this was during an era when women were predominantly at home and men were at the office, and so during the day, as a door-to-door salesman, the pitch was mainly made to women).

He found that the women wanted the perfume more than the books. So, he quit selling the books and formed a company called California Perfume Company. This still won't ring a bell for you. He then pivoted again and opted to use a multi-level marketing approach to get women to participate as sellers of the perfume and other beauty products, going door-to-door and ringing doorbells to make a sale. The name of this company became Avon. Now I know that rings a bell!

We could readily chart his business pivots. The first pivot from door-to-door salesman to selling perfume. The second pivot being the adoption of an entirely different business model of becoming a multi-level marketing firm with women being independent sales agents. There were other various details involved and we could even identify more pivots tangled in this particular business. For now, we'll just keep to the high level of things and say that at a macro level that's how this firm did its key business pivots.

For some readers, the use of Starbucks and Avon might seem like ancient history. All right, what about Jack Dorsey, a student at NYU (New York University) that was doing programming and came up with an idea about sending short messages electronically. He approached a company called Odeo. They were doing various tech related projects and aiming to have systems like one for subscribing to Podcasts. Apple iTunes was emerging into the Podcasts space and so they opted to instead pivot towards this short messages thing. That eventually became something called Twitter. Yes, Twitter is another example of business pivoting, and business leaders involved in and driving the pivots.

Another tech example is about Andrew Mason. He was developing a fundraising site for social initiatives. If enough people would sign-up for a social initiative, it would tip over, so to speak, in the Tipping Point concept approach, and get funded. That ultimately pivoted into a site that would offer local deals and if enough people signed-up, it would tip over and offer a discount for those local deals. What is that company called? Groupon.

These are examples that have been touted and told over and over again. Some of the truth of these stories has been, shall we say, massaged over time. Sometimes by design, sometimes by accident. In one sense, these stories are like having a row of people that whisper something into the ear of the person next to them. What starts at the first person and comes out at the end of the row can be quite different. The interpretations and rewordings along the way can change what the story consists of.

For this book, I have assembled case studies based on business leaders that I have met face-to-face and had an opportunity to hear their stories. I also did other research about them and their businesses. Here's a taste of what is coming next. Take a look at Figure 17.

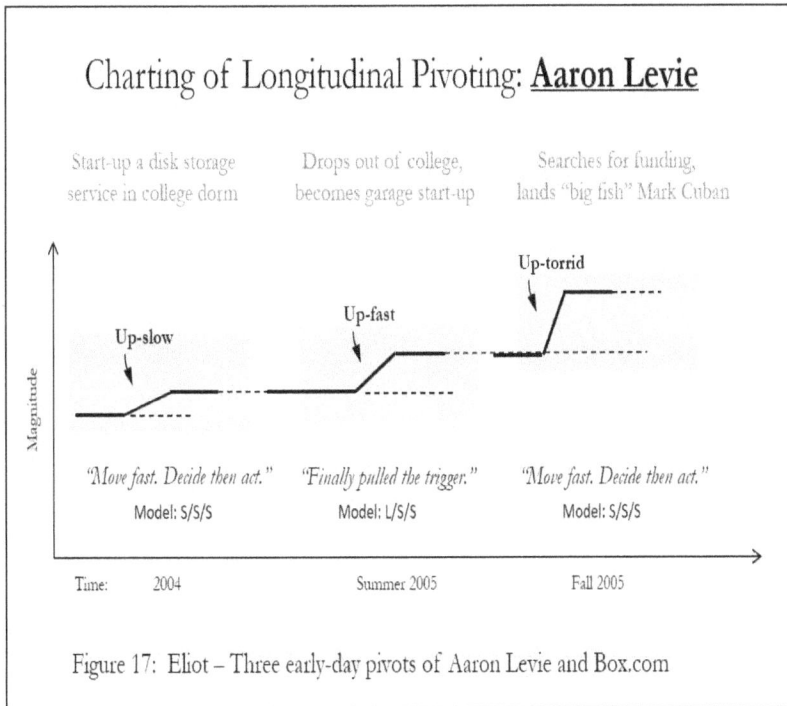

Figure 17: Eliot – Three early-day pivots of Aaron Levie and Box.com

As shown, this is a partial indication of some of the major business pivots and business leadership pivoting by Aaron Levie. He is the founder of the on-line disk storage company called Box.com. I devote a chapter to going behind-the-scenes and describe his journey as a business leader and the journey of Box.com.

In this book, I offer business leadership stories about business leaders that I have met and talked with. That will be the bulk of the next set of chapters. These stories are fascinating and instructive on their own. Read as many as you like, and read them in whatever order you might prefer.

After the case studies, we'll return to the paradigm of business pivots and build further our repertoire of business pivoting, and along the way make reference to the case studies offered for your consideration and analysis. I know that some of you might want to just read the case studies and might not be as interested in the business pivots framework. I understand that aspect and gladly encourage you to just read the case studies if you so prefer. That being said, the business pivots heuristics, insights, and paradigm might just be handy too, in case you find yourself facing a personal or business pivot.

CHAPTER 3
AARON LEVIE
(FOUNDER OF BOX.COM)

CHAPTER 3

AARON LEVIE
(FOUNDER OF BOX.COM)

PREFACE

For the first mini-case study of a business leader and the nature of business pivots, we will take a close look at Aaron Levie, a founder of the quite successful Box.com, a storage-as-a-service Internet play that took some twists and turns to get to its present position. Fittingly, like many of today's web-spurred high tech businesses, Aaron started the business while in his college dorm. I realize you might be surprised since it seems like a lot of these high tech start-ups seem to begin in someone's garage. You'll be pleased to know that shortly after gaining some success from his college dorm, he opted to take a leave of absence from college and switched to being in a garage instead. I guess he gets a prize for doing both the proverbial dorm-based start-up and the garage-based start-up.

Our interest in his story, other than seeing some fascinating under-the-hood details of how it all came together, we are also especially interested in his business pivots. As will be shown, he had several key business pivots. And, as illustration of how the business leader also needs to pivot when they pivot their business, you will be intrigued to discover that one of his initial and most important investors bowed out of the company when one of those crucial pivot moments came along. Even if the business leader wants to pivot, getting key stakeholders either within the company or outside the company to also go along can be a daunting effort to align. Later on in this book, when discussing the communications aspects of doing a business pivot, we'll revisit in greater detail this notion.

––––––––––

CHAPTER 3: AARON LEVIE
(FOUNDER OF BOX.COM)

I first met Aaron when he came to give a presentation and I was asked to walk with him to welcome him and help guide him to the location where the presentation would be given. We chatted briskly during that initial encounter.

Aaron Levie is a founder of Box.com, the cloud-based storage company that has become particularly known among businesses as a crucial system for sharing their enterprise data across their widespread operations.

When I say walk, a more apt description would be to say that we strode. Aaron walks fast, talks fast, and seems continually bursting with energy. He also has a striking sarcastic wit, which if you follow his twitter account you have witnessed time and again.

His tweets are aimed at all comers. Routinely willing to mock fellow tech entrepreneurs, he often tweets about Elon Musk to Mark Zuckerberg. He openly makes comments about politicians and celebrities. And he likes to comment about world and especially tech trends, with this tweet being a prime example of his tongue-in-cheek approach: "The future, as imagined by the tech industry, will be people wandering around their house talking to objects. My grandpa was born for this."

Whether he believes in the future of Virtual Reality and Augmented Reality, he has a healthy dose of skepticism about where tech is headed, while at the same time he is quite bullishly optimistic too. He watches what is happening in society and how tech is shaping it. Another favorite tweet of his is this one: "To anyone who has ever wondered, will Amazon enter X market? They now make their own line of diapers. So the answer is yes, they will."

In order to understand the nature of business leaders and business pivots, let's take a look at Aaron's business career path and offer insights about his leadership and the various pivots that he took while ultimately creating one of the dominant cloud-based enterprise storage companies.

Take a look at Figure 1 to get a sense of some highlights that I'll be covering.

Business Leadership Lessons

- Did web sites in high school and discovered had a knack for it

- Wandered in college, happened upon onto disk storage topic

- Took class project and coupled with students needs to do start-up

- Leave of absence from college, got his buddy to do likewise, garage start-up

- Famous email and Mark Cuban funding, much effort toward funding

- After years of struggle, pivot choice toward enterprise rather than consumers

- Converging market conditions help to aid his Return On Luck (ROL)

- Selling to enterprise, risk of being disrupted, the IPO, path to profitability

LESSONS LEARNED

Figure 1: Eliot - Lessons gleaned from the career journey of Aaron Levie

THE BEGINNING OF AARON'S STORY

While in high school, Aaron dabbled in creating various web sites. He discovered that he seemed to have a knack for it. During this time, peers were taking jobs at the local fast food restaurants, but Aaron opted instead to do web site development and pick-up what he could about how to use technology. Growing up in Seattle, Washington, his mother was a teacher and his father was a chemical engineer. Basically hailing from a middle class family, he went off to college unsure of what he wanted to do for his career.

As will be mentioned shortly, this dabbling in web site development and otherwise tinkering with technology was ultimately instrumental in how Box eventually got formed. In his high school days he had not envisioned that his web site experience was anything other than an interesting diversion and something cool to do. This aspect of later on leveraging a high school interest is an important point in that many are led down a career path later in their college days or post-college days by what took place in high school.

Some parents try to force fit their high school age children into doing efforts that they hope will drive their children in a certain direction after high school. In many cases, yes, this can work, but in other cases it can leave a foul taste in the mouth of the high schooler and they can feel as though they have no or little choice in what their future will hold. It is a tough balance for a parent since the desire is to try and provide guidance to the high schooler, and yet do so in such a manner that it opens doors later on, rather than causing the child to feel imposed upon and resentful.

THE COLLEGE YEARS AND INKLING OF BOX

Aaron went off to college on the west coast and his best friend went off to college on the east coast. They stayed in touch and shared stories of how their respective college experiences were coming along. For Aaron, he decided he would try a wide variety of classes in his initial freshman year at college. Dabbling in a diverse range of courses would allow him to make progress towards the college's General Education requirement and also give him a chance to see what academic disciplines or major area of study might be a good fit for him.

He early on had thought that film making would be a good fit for him. He attempted to get into the highly competitive and sought film school at the college, but was turned down. He even did an internship at one of the nearby major movie studios, thinking that it would give him a glimpse at the film industry and maybe increase his chances of going that direction for his career pursuits. Instead, he found the work at the movie studio as an intern to be exceedingly dull, consisting mainly of filing paperwork in conventional filing cabinets and also scanning in documents to file them electronically too. He also discovered that unless you have a connection in the film industry, via a mother or father or sibling that happens to work in the industry, it was very hard to break into it.

These facets are notable because they were all drivers away from what he thought was his destiny, namely that he had thought he would be a film maker. To this day, he is actually thankful that he did not get into the film program as he realizes in hindsight that he was not very good at it. Of course, at the time, it was quite a blow to his psyche as to smashing what was his dream at the time. Ironically, the closing of the doors toward a film career opened his mindset toward finding something else that might be his destiny.

In a grand convergence kind of way, two additional aspects arose during this same period of time in his life. One was a course that he took in business marketing, and the other was his reaction to a practice by the university as it related to student computer systems access at the college. We'll trace both of these paths and then bring these two paths and his film studio internship together to see how Box was born.

COLLEGE CLASS ON MARKETING

One of the classes that Aaron decided to take was a business class focusing on marketing. In the class, they were to do a lengthy semester-long project consisting of an analysis of a market that interested them. This would allow the students to exercise the marketing knowledge that they were learning in the class. The professor emphasized that they needed to choose an actual market and do an in-depth probing analysis, and not just pick a fake market or make-up their analysis (they had to pretend that they were real marketers conducting a real market analysis).

Aaron thought about various markets that he might do his analysis on. One particular market came to mind, the on-line storage market. Why that particular market, you might ask?

He was interested partially due to his experience during the movie studio internship, wherein he had scanned in files and shared them electronically for use within the studio. This involved making use of on-line storage. Given his prior background of building web sites, he found the on-line storage capabilities at the time to be crude to use and overly difficult for most people.

He also was irked by a practice at the university as it related to the students and access to on-line storage provided by the university. The university provided a stingy amount of on-line storage, about 50MB worth per student, and many students found this amount insufficient to house their emails, homework, class projects, and the like. Worse still was that the storage provided by the university was designed to disappear after the end of the academic year. This meant that if a freshman had all his or her files on-line at the university, when they came back in the fall as a sophomore it was all gone.

Aaron thought it was crazy that the university would not increase the amount of storage space allotted per student and equally or even crazier that the storage space would be deleted and not remain for the tenure of the student at the university. He realized that disk drives were somewhat costly, but he was also chagrined that for a private university that seemed to charge quite a bit for tuition that it could not somehow support the students better in terms of on-line storage seemed infuriating.

He dove into doing his market analysis. It revealed that the cost of disk storage would continue to be driven downward, making disk space less and less expensive. The amount of disk storage per dollar would rise and rise. The market was hot and seemed to have no end in sight. Technology was moving ahead at an incredible pace and the disk drive manufacturers were battling each other fiercely to each outdo the other in terms of increasing disk storage at decreasing prices.

The other angle was how to access and make use of that disk storage. There were companies trying to grab hold of the consumer market, such as XDrive. But he personally thought that these companies were providing access for high-tech people and not for the average non-tech person. In other words, to use these storage capabilities you needed to know arcane techie kinds of operations. He thought it should be much easier to use and not require a techie background to utilize.

He is proud to this day to say that he was ecstatic to get a B- in the class as a result of his market analysis project, which he reports was about the highest grade he ever received in college. The market analysis project gave him the impetus to do something, and that something involved the injustice of the disk storage practices at the university.

STARTING UP A BUSINESS

Aaron had tried to start other business ventures, each based on one idea or another that seemed to be interesting. As he took the diverse classes in his first year or two of college, he kept popping up ideas on a new start-up. This was during an era where the idea of creating a new business was the "in" thing to do.

In his dorm room, he decided to setup some servers and offered to fellow students at the college that they could store their files on his servers. He promised that he would not delete the files at the end of the academic year, and so the students could then reliably know that they would still have access to their files year after year. This became a hit with the students and he soon found himself buying and begging to get more servers to keep up with the demand for storage space.

He had kept in touch with his high school buddy and he too was excited about the progress of this new venture. The two of them went into it together. Needing money to buy the servers, along with paying computer programmer contractors to help write the software, his buddy was able to provide $15,000 towards the new enterprise.

This was a lot of money for them. How did his buddy come up with the $15,000? He did it via online gambling. Almost as though a script from a movie, and as incredible as it might seem, his buddy was a wiz at playing online poker and managed to wrangle his way into winning $15,000. This was a time when online gambling was generally legal to do. His friend would have a handful of computer screens going at the same time, playing multiple games at the same time, against players all around the globe. He would become the CFO for the new venture, given his skill at dealing with numbers of all kinds.

The $15,000 was crucial, but it was not a lot and they were burning up cash quickly on the new venture. They even got an $80,000 investment in their first round, of which they gave up one-fourth of the company. It was later a regret by Aaron that he gave up that sizable a chunk of the business for what turned out to not be a lot of money. That's a hindsight view, and at times during the initial evolution of a start-up, every dollar can make or break whether the business continues or not.

They still needed even more money to keep the wheels turning on the new business.

COLLEGE PITCH COMPETITION

At the college, they had a student pitch competition allowing students to propose a business or showcase a start-up and try to win cash prizes, along with gaining interest by potential investors and mentors that would come to either judge the pitches or at least hear the pitches. Aaron thought this would be a good means to get some more money for the budding business. Putting together a business plan, he went to the competition figuring that he had a solid chance of winning.

He lost. In fact, he was ranked towards the bottom of the competing student pitches. He jokes to this day that the winner was a start-up that proposed a new fire retardant capability, and which has generally gone into obscurity.

He also though acknowledges that the judges were right in that they had picked apart the business plan and offered feedback that he and his buddy needed to hear. The judges had pointed out that the disk storage market was on a wild spiral called the "race to zero" and would ultimately be a commodity market. Furthermore, the big players like Microsoft had the resources to readily take over the market and wipe out any tiny players that lacked the same capabilities of vast marketing resources and vast development resources. These were sobering words.

It was obviously disappointing to not win, and he could have either quit his now nascent business, or he could have gotten upset and insisted that the judges were wrong. Instead, he and his buddy realized they needed to make some changes and pivot the business.

This is an important characteristic of budding entrepreneurs. They need to be dogmatic enough to withstand the barrage of naysayers that they will certainly encounter along the way. They also though need to know when to listen and take good advice. Furthermore, they need to act upon that good advice and change their perspective and what their start-up is doing, otherwise the advice won't have done them much good.

THE EMAIL TO MARK CUBAN

Perhaps one of the most famous stories of trying to raise funds for a start-up is the tale told of Aaron having sent an email to Mark Cuban, the wealthy entrepreneur, asking him for seed funding for Box.

Mark Cuban had made his wealth initially in the high-tech realm, and so he was always henceforth on the look for the next hot high-tech hit. He was willing to toss around money at start-ups that the thought might have promise. For him, it was not a lot of money per start-up, and so he used a portfolio approach of realizing that some in the portfolio would do well and some would wipe out.

Aaron sent a "cold call" email to Mark Cuban, describing the new venture and requesting funding. Some people make the story a bit more exciting by saying that Mark instantly wrote a check and sent it to Aaron without any other due diligence. It makes for an especially amazing version. The reality is that Mark was intrigued by the email, and after various due diligence of finding out more about the company and Aaron and his buddy, and various contractual aspects, indeed then Mark did invest.

The point being that if a budding entrepreneur thinks that people are just going to hand them money without any kind of due diligence, well, maybe it happens, but rarely, and it did not go that way in the case of Mark Cuban and Box. Just setting the record straight. Hope that does not burst anyone's balloon.

Another facet to the story is that in the email, Aaron was asking for Mark to mention the start-up in Mark's popular blog, hoping that it would increase the visibility of the start-up, and also at the same time indicating that they were looking for funding and whether Mark would be interested. Notice that this is again a bit different from the more fanciful story often told. The request was perhaps more carefully made in that even if Mark didn't want to put money into them, the act of writing about them in his blog would have been relatively easy and with low risk to Mark. Aaron was hoping for at least the blog entry and then the outside chance of the funding by Mark.

Landing a big fish or a whale can make all the difference to a start-up, whether getting them to fund you or getting them to at least tout you.

If you can get money, and even if the money is not a lot, it nonetheless casts a positive glow to the start-up and can attract many other investors. Furthermore, those investors might be less strict in terms of scrutiny, simply because they figure that if it is good enough for that big fish that they also are willing to take a chance on it.

Another twist to this story is that Aaron sent similar emails to a wide swath of potential investors. If you don't include that aspect in the story, it seems like an incredible miracle that one email made it to the one right person and became a big hit. The reality was that he had sent out lots of such emails, on the order of hundreds of such emails. All of those were either unanswered or answered with a no thanks. He was playing the odds and hoping that one would pay-off.

I would like to emphasize that even when including the aspect that he sent out lots of emails, it is still admittedly a bit miraculous that he got even one to reply, and the one was a big fish that opted to invest. I don't want to underplay the miracle of that.

Mark invested $350,000, doing so in 2005. This is a big dollar number in that time period and for a new start-up that was existing in a college dorm. From Mark's perspective, the check wasn't overly large, since he was already worth hundreds of millions and getting into the billions. So, big deal for Aaron, just a side bet by the big fish. Now, having a big fish that invests in your start-up is a great benefit, no doubt about it. But, this also carries some downsides. Indeed, let's move ahead in time.

About a year after Mark's investment, Mark and Aaron disagreed about the future direction of Box. Aaron was worried about Google's upcoming entry into the storage market with their Gdrive. Aaron's take on things was that Box would have to go entirely the freemium route, offering disk space for free, and hope to grab up as many consumers as possible. The thought was that by getting consumers to use Box, they would not want to switch to whatever Google did, and would remain loyal to Box. Mark wanted instead to monetize each consumer that signed-up for Box.

This could have torn apart Box. Mark could have stomped on Box and made all sorts of legal troubles. He could have tried to force Aaron to go in the direction that Mark preferred. Incredibly, and mainly a testament to the perspective of Mark as a fellow entrepreneur, he opted to bow out of Box. He sold his shares in the Series A round the next year. He sold the shares at cost. If you like, you can calculate how much Mark would have profited had he simply left his $350,000 in Box, and/or how much more he could have invested and ultimately profited on. In any case, Mark did at the time what he thought was right, namely, he had helped out a start-up that he had believed in, and then when he felt it was going askew he backed out and let it continue along.

Not many big fish would have taken that stance. To me, it is nearly as big a miracle if not more so than the response to Aaron's first email. Aaron still to this day appreciates what Mark did for the start-up. And, Aaron well understands the decision that Mark made. If you are investing in something, you have a stake and want to provide guidance. It is hard and rare to make an investment in something and say that you'll just let it go in whatever direction it wants to take. Especially in the case where the investor also feels they are versed in the industry that you are aiming at. It emboldens their view of what will work and what won't work.

One might say that Aaron also learned something else from Mark. To this day, Aaron puts seed money into lots of start-ups. He does a portfolio kind of approach, just as Mark had done. I am not saying that Mark is the only start-up investor that does this, and nor that Aaron learned it only from Mark. I am just saying that it is practice that some entrepreneurs that made money from their own start-up will often pursue. Taking a look at Aaron's investments in start-ups, there are a range of ones that no one has ever heard of, and ones that made some progress, included in his portfolio is The Happy Home Company, Fundera, Hightower, Gametime, Highfive, Robinhood, Workpop, Opendoor, Instacat, Elementum, etc.

One last little tidbit to the story of Mark's investment. Mark mailed the check of $350,000 to Aaron, at his dorm address, rather than making a bank-to-bank electronic transfer. Imagine opening your dorm mailbox and finding that check for $350,000. Even if you knew it was coming, the very fact that you are now holding in your hands the $350,000, and when you have never seen that kind of money, and where you are essentially a kind of starving student and subsisting on what monies you can find to keep your business going, it would have been one of those memorable moments. Aaron says that he was just glad that the check didn't get to the wrong address and jokes about if someone else had tried to deposit it

WORKING OUT OF A GARAGE

It seems that any successful high-tech start-up has to begin in a garage. We hear those stories all the time about the nerds that could not afford an office and so worked out of the home by using their garage. Okay, well, that's true for Box too. If you are thinking of starting up a business, better make room in your garage since apparently that's the path to success (being a bit tongue-in-cheek there).

Anyway, Aaron opted to take a leave of absence from college. This is differently phrased than saying he dropped out of college. He genuinely thought that he might indeed come back to college and someday finish his degree. He wanted to take time off to see if the start-up would gain traction. Likewise, his buddy at the east college did the same. As a side note, his buddy did eventually go back and finish the degree.

He and his buddy decided that they should be in the mecca of tech start-ups so they aimed to be in Silicon Valley. Having an uncle in Berkeley, they opted to go live there, and the uncle offered them rent free space. They used the garage as their business locale. Berkeley is not quite considered

Silicon Valley and so about a year later they moved to Palo Alto. But the point is that they felt strongly that at the time they needed to be in the Silicon Valley area to be able to share in the energy and gain contacts and talent that would help them grow.

NOT AN OVERNIGHT SUCCESS AND BIG PIVOT

Many often hear about a start-up that became big time and assume that it was a quick path from the beginning to hitting it big. Rarely is that the case. Aaron speaks of the daily fear he has had about Box that someone else or something else would come along to disrupt them. It is a healthy form of paranoia that can ensure that a start-up does not get knocked out along the way of its initial growth and maturation.

Box made a big pivot around 2008, some three years or so after first being launched as a company. During the 2005 to 2008 time period, there were lots of players muscling into the on-line disk storage marketplace. Most of those players were aiming at consumers.

The consumer market can be both fun and yet tough. You try to get as many consumers to sign-up as possible. You end-up with really big numbers of sign-ups. You become known by the general populace and can become famous. At the time, it was something like an estimated $350 billion size total potential market, depending upon what you count.

The other market for online disk storage was to aim at companies. Called "the enterprise," aiming at businesses to buy your tech product or service is a whole different beast than aiming at the consumer market. It can be a long, slow sale, convincing a business to buy your product or service. There are lots of layers within the business that you need to sell and get approvals. Business often already have preferred vendors and so are reluctant to switch to someone new. They also tend to prefer established vendors over going with a new start-up that might go belly-up.

In looking at the total market size for tech spending in businesses, Aaron and his co-founder saw a $1 trillion sized market. The question was whether or not they could sell into it. Up until 2008, they were finding that their Box capabilities were nearly over-whelming in terms of features for the consumer market, and somewhat potentially under-whelming for a business market. They had to make a choice, do they strip down the product so that it is more akin to consumers, but then they become more of a commodity and cannot be differentiated from the heavy competition coming increasingly into the market, or do they go after the business market and boost their features accordingly.

The business market seemed less saturated and they thought they might be able to penetrate it. The world was changing such that firms were potentially willing to look outside their conventional tech infrastructure. It was also as the movement toward selling end-users in businesses was emerging, rather than only selling to the techs in businesses.

For various such reasons, they decided to switch away from the consumer market and go all-in toward the business market. This was not an easy decision. They could easily flounder and make no inroads to the business marketplace. Meanwhile, by taking away their attention to consumers, their market share in the consumer market would plummet and likely never be recoverable. Taking a deep breath, they went the less exotic route of the business marketplace, and looked wistfully at the consumer market as it receded in their rear view mirror.

BOX AND RETURN ON LUCK (ROL)

Box steadfastly pursued the business marketplace. In 2014, they finally released their financials to the public for the first time, as they were proposing to go public. There was a collective gasp at what was shown. The company was chewing up about $2.50 to produce each $1.00 in actual revenue. Like many of the high-tech start-ups, it was consuming vast quantities of money to try and gain a market.

Even Mark Cuban commented when the financials were revealed and said that the company could potentially combust, and some analysts said it was a house of horrors in terms of the financials and the business model. Box delayed its IPO for about a year to try and showcase better numbers. Of course, it did go public. And, by the end of 2015 it actually had over $300 million in annual revenue, along with a positive cash flow.

Aaron proclaimed that after nearly ten long years, they were finally done with fundraising. How much of the story of Box is based on skill versus luck? The term Return on Luck (ROL) has been used by various business authors and researchers to suggest that you need a certain amount of luck to succeed in business.

Usually, it is not purely luck alone, but also being ready to leverage the luck when it happens. Even as important involves knowing or recognizing when luck has occurred. Was it lucky for Aaron that his aspirations to become a film maker were dashed in his early college days? Was it lucky that he happened to take a business marketing class and then turned the class project into a personal interest that was to become the basis for his business? Was it lucky that he got Mark Cuban to make that first outside capital investment in Box? Was it lucky that they later realized they had to turn away from the consumer market and aim at the business market instead?

These each involve a mixture of both skill at recognition and leveraging, combined with being at the right place at the right time. You need to be working toward something where if luck occurs you can see that it has and make use of it. Luck alone is unlikely to make the day. Skills alone are perhaps unlikely to make the day in that a dash of luck can make the swing difference.

.

CHAPTER 4

PETER KIM

(FOUNDER HUDSON JEANS)

CHAPTER 4

PETER KIM
(FOUNDER HUDSON JEANS)

PREFACE

This next mini-case study about business leaders and business pivots involves the experiences of Peter Kim and his founding of the famous jeans company called Hudson Jeans. As you will see, his journey included several pivots along the way to success, including during his college years and post-college. Peter ultimately crafted a denim line of extremely popular designer jeans, known perhaps more so among the younger generation and considered a very "hip" pair of clothing to own and wear. His jeans carry a now universally known trademark of having triangular back pockets and with an insignia of a Union Jack logo. Britney Spears and other notable youth oriented stars often were seen wearing Hudson Jeans.

Like most of these case studies, success did not come overnight. It took years of fierce attention and determination to make Hudson Jeans into a success. After about a dozen years in business, Peter opted to sell Hudson Jeans to Joe's Jeans, interestingly Peter and Joe surf together, and Peter remained head of the firm and gained a seat on the Board of Joe's Jeans. While in college, Peter had not anticipated that he would someday be heading a clothing company and during his college years had other dreams of what he might do. Being in a family that had money, he assumed that money would always be available and that he could choose to do whatever he wanted to do. Turns out that he underwent a somewhat shocking pivot and then fell into what his career was to become.

———

CHAPTER 4: PETER KIM
(FOUNDER HUDSON JEANS)

When I first met Peter Kim, founder and CEO of Hudson Jeans, I was somewhat taken aback by his appearance. He had tattoos about his arms and sported men's earrings, and his firm handshake was accompanied by rather plainspoken language that included a multitude of rather shocking four letter words, though they were uttered in a perfunctory way that belied any harsh intention. Exceedingly friendly, he immediately had an aura as the type of person that would offer a bear hug to someone he has just met and would likewise be a loyal and caring friend for the lifetime of those that are dear to him.

After further interaction with him, I came to realize that his appearance resonated with being in the apparel business and showcased his continuous efforts to remain at the forefront of fashion. With clothing lines that aim at a younger generation, he too was visually indicative of that same fashion awareness. A father with twin daughters, he did not seem at all like a staid Leave It to Beaver kind of dad, and instead likely could well align with his children and their millennial mindset. Furthermore, in spite of the presumed wildness of the fashion industry, he was very much a well anchored person that exuded authenticity in what he says and what he does. That differs from the more traditional hollowness that one might experience when hobnobbing with the fashionista.

An astute business man, his in-depth business acumen is infused with even deeper ruminations about philosophy and the overall meaning and purpose of life. He espouses that we all need to do at least one thing each day to change someone else's life. If we could do that, if we could all do that, it would change the world, and he emphatically repeats this like a mantra that should be heard over and over again.

He sees his apparel line in the same light. For him, the clothing that he sells is all about bringing happiness to the world. Some might view his clothing as simply fabric, a mere product that hangs on store racks and awaits a buyer that wants protection from the elements. Peter sees things differently, and is providing a little bit of happiness that customers feel in their heart once they have bought one of his jeans. Each and every pair of jeans sold is his effort to bring that happiness to each and every person that he can.

Urging those around him to consider the three pillars of life, he asks each person to define their purpose, have passion for who they are and what they do, and always be seeking to push themselves and what they do to the edge. Overall, his apparel matches to his philosophy and he is continually on the lookout to drive his clothing lines to the edge of fashion.

Work is rewarding for him, but also at times all-consuming and overwhelming. He mentioned that on a recent vacation in Waikiki, Hawaii, he watched as an ice cream scooping young worker at a Haagen-Dazs created a multi-scoop topped ice cream cone, and meanwhile Peter was wishfully thinking that it would be nice to be that young again and have that kind of carefree job. Imagine it, he lamented, being able to scoop ice cream throughout the day, and at the end of the day you put your scooper into the water, you walk out the door, and you are away from work until the next time you step foot into that ice cream parlor for the next day's work.

Peter's childhood provides further indication of why he might wistfully dream of days of freedom from the daily grind and seek to avert the pressures of keeping a business going.

PARENTS AND CHILDHOOD

Before he was born, Peter's parents escaped from North Korea to South Korea, and though quite poor were able to find a means to come to the United States. They setup shop in Southern California and sold blouses that went under women's suits. Built to be virtually indestructible, the blouses at first sold like wildfire (he said they sold like cockroaches, though the metaphor of a wildfire might be more appealing). Money was everywhere. His parents bought real estate in Southern California and in Hawaii. They gave money to both near and distant relatives that needed backing, including one that needed money to get a Kawasaki dealership. It seemed that his family had a never ending supply of money and could spend wantonly.

As Peter began to near adulthood, he tried to come up with ideas of how he could make a difference for the family and find a different avenue than apparel, hoping to stake out his own turf, so to speak. He told his parents that he wanted buy and run liquor stores, but his dad said the idea stunk and that he (Peter) was a piece of you-know-what. And though you might think that Peter had a silver spoon as he grew-up, his parents limited his spending. He watched in envy and frustration as his friends whom also came from wealthy families were able to spend freely. Upon reaching college age, his parents made sure that he would go to college, which was important to them, and he found himself majoring in business.

Peter used the word affluenza a couple of times when describing his childhood.

The trendy word these days to describe wealthy young people that have a lack of motivation is affluenza. It is an overall malaise that some argue can come over a young person that is immersed in riches and can lead to them wandering aimlessly, suffering from feelings of guilt, and not knowing what they want to do and not even sure they want or need to do anything.

Peter overtly characterized his teenage years as having been overcome by affluenza.

THE PIVOT EMERGES

While in college, Peter partied and had a great time. His interest in his studies was lukewarm at best. The business classes that he took in accounting and finance were tough and he saw little value in them. He wandered from class to class, just going along for the ride. To him, going to college and studying business was mainly his parents dream and so he tried to find solace in the extracurricular aspects more than the academics.

Finally reaching his senior year of college, he continued to bump along in terms of just muddling through his classes. During his final semester, he continued to party hard and was not sure what would occur next in his life.

During spring break, and after another night of partying, he one morning suddenly got a call from his father and groggily answered the phone. His dad instantly questioned why he was asleep so late in the morning. Because it is frigging spring break, he replied. Well, get off your butt and get into the office, his father heatedly insisted.

This adamant demand by his father that he come into the office was shocking to Peter. By and large, Peter had been kept outside of the family business. He certainly was never sought to help out or step into anything about the business. He was surprised and uncertain about why he was being summoned to come to the office.

Rushing over to the office, and upon his arrival, Peter experienced the shock of his life and was later to realize that it was a pivotal moment in his career and his life. It turns out that due to a downturn in the economy, the family apparel business had been bleeding money right and left, and the unbounded family spending had been draining their personal coffers. Their real estate investments were suffering too as the real estate market had tanked. Their investment in the Kawasaki dealership soured and Kawasaki had come after them. The apparel business had relied on women desiring business oriented blouses and clothing, but even that trend had changed and women were no longer buying the clothing lines that his family was selling.

Peter had been kept in the dark about all of this. He had been enjoying his "carefree" college days and thought that the family business was booming and would last forever. And then the second shoe dropped. His father announced to Peter that the reason they sent him to college — and the reason he was majoring in business was so that he would be able to take over the family business when needed.

Now was that time. From Peter's perspective, this was entirely unexpected. He was suddenly thrust into the family business. He was not ready for this. He was also expected to magically turnaround the business. He was not ready for that either. His parents assumed that because he had taken all those formal business classes that he must be a business whiz and could make the family business become enriched once again.

A tall order for an affluenza struck college student that had been marginally paying attention to his business classes and that had been kept outside the family business throughout his upbringing.

After seeing the depth of the company woes, the financial straits, and the desperation on the faces of his family, the pressure of his having to be the savior for the family was daunting and overwhelming. He recalled that when he got into his car and drove back over to campus, he spoke to himself in the car and wondered how he could deal with it all. Soul searching, he decided that he would need to change his attitude and try to look at the circumstance as a grand opportunity.

This willingness to change his own mind and turn the seemingly insurmountable problems into opportunities is what helped him ultimately turn things around with the family business.

THE TURNAROUND

Immersing himself directly into the family business, he pored over the company books. His accounting classes which earlier had seemed like wasted time, now had use to him. He rethought all of his business classes and tried to figure out how each of the business fundamentals that he had learned could now be put to applicable use.

It was a rough road. He aided in the laying off employees, a sobering and saddening effort that ripped at his heart. Grown men that worked for the company had fist fights as tensions in the firm mounted. These were people that the family knew and had once all been the closest of friends and co-workers, but now it was all infighting and acrimonious. And, meanwhile, the company cash was being drained by an astronomical $50,000 per month that they were paying out in interest alone.

Eventually, over a multi-year period in 1990s, he helped dig the company out of $10 million in debt. Meanwhile, he harbored an intense desire to ultimately start his own apparel line, and in 1999 launched a new brand called Drunken Monkey that he later sold to the founders of Fubu.

Using those prior real-world experiences, he then realized that the premium denim market was relatively untouched and opted to start-up

Hudson Jeans. Having started the firm in 2002, he proceeded to work long weeks and days, building Hudson Jeans into a thriving powerhouse and a household name, he later sold Hudson Jeans to Joe's Jeans for nearly a $100 million in 2013. The combined firms become one a behemoth of the global denim market.

Peter is a successful entrepreneur and a generously giving philanthropist. He is also a maverick, which is equally evocative of his jeans and the rock-the-world attitude that his clothing line has become known for. One of his favorite personal motto's is that we should all hold our head high, and have your middle finger even higher.

SOME PIVOTAL LESSONS

Peter's story is a rich treasure trove of business and life lessons. Let's especially focus on the pivotal moment when his father called him during spring break of his senior year in college. This was one of those out-of-the-blue moments that can sometimes happen in life. It was not anticipated by Peter. He had no inkling that it would occur.

In his case, he was not particularly ready for the sudden thrust into the family business, but nonetheless he took what could have been a crushing moment and decided to adopt a positive mindset that it was an opportunity to be reckoned with. Imagine if he had mentally seen this pivot as ruinous. The likelihood is that he would have driven the family business further into the ground and might have personally become so despondent that he might have considered himself a lost cause and incapable of being a business man.

If the family business had gone under and if he had not been able to help aid and guide them to survival, it seems unlikely he would later have started his own first business and ultimately unlikely that he would have eventually started Hudson Jeans. Similar to a house of cards, the underpinnings that began upon that pivotal moment would never have been built.

In one sense, we can say that he was lucky to have had the opportunity, since many of us might not ever even have a circumstance where we could step into a situation and turn it around. Regardless of whether you see this as some kind of fate or happenstance, the bottom-line is that he was able to capitalize on his education, his upbringing, and the mental fortitude and courage to fight and win his way in business.

CHAPTER 5
JON KRAFT
(FOUNDER PANDORA)

CHAPTER 5

JON KRAFT (FOUNDER PANDORA)

PREFACE

Pandora has become a household name, vaulting to the stratosphere of high-tech Internet based companies that turned music streaming and automated music recommendation into something that we now nearly take for granted. Once upon a time, music streaming did not exist, and nor did automated music recommending. There were three co-founders of the company, Jon Kraft, Tim Westergren, and Will Glaser. We take a close look in this chapter at the business leadership and career of Jon Kraft, which well illustrates the nature of business pivots in his own focus and for that of Pandora.

At the start, Pandora was not an instant success. In fact, it took several years of painstaking pitches and pivots to eventually raise the funds to get the company truly underway. At one point, they began to pursue a business model pivot toward licensing to third parties their technology, rather than continue to do their own thing. They ultimately returned to their bread-and-butter of offering customized radio stations. Pivot to the right, and then pivot back to the left, so to speak. They also went back-and-forth as to whether to be a paid service or an advertising service. Many start-ups in the high-tech Internet based arena struggle to ascertain what business model will work best. They either prepare to pivot into a new business model, or sometimes just fall into a new business model nearly by happenstance.

CHAPTER 5: JON KRAFT
(FOUNDER PANDORA)

Jon Kraft is an entrepreneur extraordinaire. Having gotten to know him, I can see in his demeanor and enthusiasm that he serves as an inspiration to those aspiring to be entrepreneurs. Perhaps best known as a co-founder of Pandora, a company that went from the unknown to now becoming known worldwide and a staple of our daily vocabulary, Jon has continued to exert his entrepreneurial spirit and vibe in many other ways.

As co-founder and chairman of Thrively, a now seasoned start-up, he combines his personal devotion to his family and children into a new venture that provides a platform for helping kids to discover and pursue their passions in life. This well illustrates how every molecule of Jon is infused with an entrepreneurial zeal, taking aspects that he observed in his own personal life and then leveraging that into his business life by launching and supporting a start-up based on what he observed and what he believes (as mentioned later on herein too, in his earlier days he had helped kids in baseball and basketball at Stanford).

Some entrepreneurs are in fact "serial entrepreneurs" that push forward on one start-up after another. Not only is Jon a serial entrepreneur, he also is an entrepreneur "catalyst" that aids others in realizing their entrepreneurial dreams, doing so via his start-up accelerator called LiftOff that he co-founded and serves as a managing partner in.

Keenly reflective about what it takes to be a successful entrepreneur, Jon is what I consider to be an entrepreneur extraordinaire because he fulfills several key "extraordinary" characteristic at the same time, namely:

1) Able to envision, launch, and sustain a start-up vision into reality (a successful entrepreneur),

2) Able to do so repeatedly (serial entrepreneur) and not as a one-time fluke,

3) Able to be reflective of how he and other entrepreneurs achieve results (introspective),

4) Able to aid others in realizing their start-up dreams (as an entrepreneur catalyst)

Very few of those in the entrepreneurial world that I meet are able to embody more than say one or two of those above characteristics, let alone all four. In this chapter, I trace Jon's business career path, and then offer some remarks about business leadership and business pivots that are based on Jon's experiences and as combined with my own thoughts too.

In my own case, having been a serial entrepreneur and undertaken several business pivots, I have found it important to be reflective on what it takes to be a successful entrepreneur and especially be ready for and undertake a business pivot. Notice that I keep saying "successful entrepreneur" because there is a distinction between being an entrepreneur and being a successful one. There are lots and lots of entrepreneurs floating out there. They are being minted like so many coins. The fever toward becoming an entrepreneur seems to be once again at an ever rising tidal wave.

Regrettably, only a small percentage of those budding entrepreneurs will be successful, assuming that by success we mean that they are able to actually create a new enterprise that goes beyond the walking dead stage of progression. As Jon would attest, getting a start-up underway and have it gain traction requires relentless optimism and a willingness to pivot.

This is one of Jon's relentlessly repeated exhortations to entrepreneurs and upcoming entrepreneurs, you must be ready for and be willing to be or become relentlessly optimistic. You will see how Jon's own experiences are indicative of this needed core element. Figure 1 depicts some of the key business lessons that I want to bring to your attention.

Business Leadership Lessons

- You will need relentless optimism to be a successful entrepreneur
- Working in a large company can trigger you into going the start-up route
- Start-ups are usually about risk taking, often leaping from a secure job
- Going solo into a start-up is not the only path, can combine with friends
- Few overnight successes, be prepared to pitch endlessly, taking "no' repeatedly
- Commitment is crucial, sometimes getting family and friends invested too
- Better mousetrap does not mean entirely new, provide a variant that is better
- Intuition is required, trust your gut, but verify when feasible

Figure 1: Eliot - Lessons gleaned from the career journey of Jon Kraft

THE EARLY DAYS

Jon graduated from Stanford University with his bachelor's degree in human biology. Yes, that's right, he earned a degree in human biology, rather than getting a degree in computer science or the like. This might seem surprising, given that he is a co-founder of Pandora, and so many assume naturally that he must have gotten his degree in either computer science or perhaps music.

In my experience, there is often not much of a correlation per se between the discipline chosen for an undergraduate degree and where the person goes as an entrepreneur. Sure, there are lots that get an undergrad degree in computer science or engineering that tend toward creating mobile apps or web sites as their start-up. Likewise, there are those that say go the medical route and thus aim for some kind of medical related new product or service as their start-up. But, it seems more often that the undergrad degree is a signal that the person had the persistence to complete something that was arduous. It also created a certain sense of rigor in how to pursue something.

I know that some of you might think, wait a second, what about all that partying in college, and yes, I acknowledge that aspect, but in the end to complete four years of tons of classes and especially at a top ranked university where the classwork is especially demanding, I'd argue that's as much a crucial foundation for becoming an entrepreneur as is whatever specific major you happen to have picked.

In any case, after finishing his degree, Jon went to work at Oracle (a relatively large firm at the time that continued to grow and became larger and larger over the years).

ORACLE AS THE TRIGGER TO A START-UP

Jon was at Oracle for about 3 ½ years, and during that time he found that nothing much that he could do personally at Oracle would "move the needle" particularly. He enjoyed the job, he did his part, and he also included time to play some golf and go to the bars, all part and parcel of what a newly minted college grad would be expected to do. Feeling like there must be something more in business and in life to be accomplished, he bravely opted to leave Oracle.

I say bravely because Oracle was a pretty safe bet at the time, and relatively well paying. He could have remained there, taking in the paycheck, and gradually making his way up the ladder, but at a snail's pace in comparison to what he could become in a start-up.

His energy and desire for something more was the impetus to jump off the Oracle wagon train. He also was young enough and generally unencumbered by other of life's burdens such as not yet having a family, a mortgage, etc., making the leap not overly risky. This was his first of several business pivots. In this case, opting to pivot his own career direction and do so toward a start-up from a large company. For many that take this route, they often start in a large firm, getting used to the business world and seeing how a big company gets things done. Along the way, they often find themselves stifled and desirous of something more. A large company often has no ready means to accommodate them, and so off they go, aiming toward a start-up.

HIS FIRST START-UP

Jon made the leap with some friends of his. This can be another important factor when shifting toward a start-up. Though there are many circumstances of the solo breakout, it can be comforting to have fellow colleagues that are willing to make that same leap. Furthermore, the odds are that they might complement your strengths and weaknesses, shoring up what otherwise might be a gap in what you know or can accomplish.

Not all is necessarily rosy in such circumstances. Sometimes, the strain of a start-up causes close friends to become less close. Sadly, there are times when the friendships will completely shatter due to the stress and strain of a start-up. This can be a tough lesson to learn, gaining a company but maybe losing good friendships along the way.

He and his colleagues co-founded a company called the Stanford Technology Group. This company was to provide him with the initial experience to see and learn how start-ups work. Growing the company to over two million dollars in revenue, they were able to raise money from several venture capital firms. Cutting ones teeth on how to pitch to and get funding from angel investors and venture capital firms is an important skill that Jon was able to get initiated into.

They sold the Stanford Technology Group to Informix. A nice way to exit from the start-up and yet also keep his paychecks coming, since he then became part of Informix and did business development and product marketing for them. He once again found himself in a large firm. Constantly at trade shows and having concerns about the sales team, even his former partners opted to leave. He stuck it out for two years or so.

Meanwhile, as a side avenue, he was writing screen plays. He dreamed that maybe one of his screen plays might make it big. Outside of work hours, he was pitching agents. Akin to pitching venture capitalist, but definitely not as fun for him.

THE BIRTH OF PANDORA

A friend of Jon's from his college days was a budding composer. His friend was trying to break into the movie business as a musical composer. Jon was trying to break into the business as a screen play writer. Leaving Oracle, Jon combined with his college composer buddy, Tim Westergren, and with Will Glaser, and they formed Pandora Media in 1999.

There has been quite a bit written about the formative years of Pandora, and so I am not going to repeat that story here. Nonetheless, there are some key moments and aspects that I think are worthy of specifically mentioning and using as valued lessons learned. Let's dig into those aspects.

NOT AN OVERNIGHT SUCCESS

Notice that I mentioned that Pandora Media was started in 1999. The company went public in 2011. t hadn't gained much traction until at least several years after the company had been formed. point this out due to the aspect that some people think of Pandora as an overnight success story.

The truth is that it is more like a movie star that slaved away for years in bit parts as an unknown and never knowing whether they would ever make it big time. That's exactly what happened with Pandora, it pivoted, it languished, it teetered on going under, and otherwise required unrelenting optimism by the founders to keep trying.

For those of you that are starting up a business, if you think that you can just wave a magic wand and find yourself a year or two later with a smash hit, sure it could happen, but the odds are that it won't go that way. Expect a rough and tough battle that will potentially endure for years and years.

GETTING INVESTORS

Jon tells the engaging story about getting the initial investment for Pandora. He and his co-founders made pitch after pitch. They pitched to just about anyone that they thought might be viable to provide funding. Every single pitch involved putting their souls out there as to what they wanted to do. Well, they did this pitching for over 250+ times. Each time, they got back the same answer, no. No, no, no, no, no, no, and so on.

Most would have given up after say 20 no's, maybe 50 no's, or certainly after a hundred or more.

This is the kind of relentless optimism that Jon speaks of. They remained optimistic even though all of these potential investors said over and over that their start-up was not worth putting money into. Imagine how discouraging this would be. You would figure your idea was crazy and you should just toss in the towel. They did pivot the business slightly along the way, adjusting to feedback that they received during the pitches, but kept the core premise still intact.

THE INVESTOR REQUIREMENT

Jon also describes what happened when they got an investor that was willing to put money on the table. The investor insisted that they would need to raise like monies from family and friends. Not sure at the time why this was so important, they nonetheless contacted family and friends to raise some of the needed funds.

What Jon later realized was the incredible staying power that having an investment by family and friends would be. There were dark days at Pandora where it seemed that all was just collapsing. If they were only concerned about the money from the investor, you could kind of say to yourself that it is the risk of making an investment. Logically, the investor was risking capital and knew beforehand that the investment might payoff or might not. The entrepreneurs could walk away knowing that they gave it their all and if perchance the investor lost their money, it was unfortunate, it was not desired, but it was part of the game of business.

But, when you have your Aunt Sally investing a thousand dollars and your grandmother investing a chunk of her retirement funds, you think twice about tossing in the towel. To this day, Jon usually has a similar requirement for those budding entrepreneurs that want to get his funding and support. He wants them to go "all in" in terms of having their body and soul committed to the start-up. It could potentially be the difference between staying in the game during the rough times versus calling it quits.

THE BETTER MOUSETRAP

Some budding entrepreneurs believe they need to find some new product or service that is unheard of. They believe that their product or service must be so new that there is absolutely nothing like it in the marketplace. This can be a pretty tall order.

By-and-large, when you look at most of the now famous examples of start-ups that went big, such as Facebook, Uber, LinkedIn, etc., you would find that what they proposed was not unique and unheard of. There were other variants akin to what they had or what they wanted to do.

Jon has pointed out that for Pandora there were probably twenty other companies trying to do something similar. There was even one similar kind of approach being funded by Eric Clapton, the famous singer and songwriter. How could Pandora, a firm that had no such celebrity, no such connections, no such potential access to vast resources and funding, how could Pandora compete against that? Launch Radio emerged at the same time and it had a billion dollar valuation.

One might think that the market was already sewn up. Now, this other competition could mean that the market was already taken and so why try to reinvent the wheel. On the other hand, you could also say that it established that a market existed, and so if you could find a better way to compete in that market that at least you already knew that there was a demand for the product or service.

That's what they opted to do. They sought to find an angle that was different from and would be a better appeal to the marketplace.

When it comes to mousetraps, you are usually aiming to build a better mousetrap, realizing that there are already other mousetraps out there. It is generally okay and even good that there are other mousetraps out there because it shows that people want a mousetrap. If you were to create a trap for say aardvarks, yes, it might be new and no one else has it, but then again what market exists for it?

I am not saying that there is never a need or value in bringing out a completely new product or service for which no known market is already proven. Indeed, there is an entire business approach, often referred to as a Blue Ocean Strategy, which advocates establishing a new market (unlike trying to fight your way in a so-called Red Ocean that is bloodied by the many competitors duking it out). I am just saying that trying to create a new market can be especially challenging. Likewise, I am not saying that competing in an existing market is easy. Depending upon how entrenched the competition is, it can be challenging to break through that market and differentiate what you have.

THE PERSISTENCE

Jon indicates that Pandora nearly ran out of money. Not just once, but on several occasions, perhaps at least a half dozen such times. I relish his comment too that you are not done until the sheriff takes out the furniture. I'll let that remark sink in with you for a moment. After a comparable pause, Jon then looks you in the eye and pointedly says, furniture is probably overrated anyway.

That's the kind of persistence you have to have as an entrepreneur. When they are trying to turn out the lights, work in the dark if you need to do so.

CREATING VALUE

As mentioned earlier, Jon left Oracle, a relatively safe company to be working at. Oracle only had about 3,000 employees then (today it is around 136,000 employees), but nonetheless for Jon it was a large company that had multiple layers of management and multiple layers of waiting time. He figured that if he had waited maybe 15 years that he could have risen up the ranks. Maybe he would have gotten someday his bosses job. And then gotten his bosses bosses job. Of course, there would have been intense internal competition for those positions and it was not a foregone conclusion that he would have gotten up the ladder.

In my experience, there are some that are willing to go the conventional corporate route, aiming to move upward, or later move out to another comparable firm and move up. Someone that has that kind of mindset is often not as willing to endure the on-the-edge aspects of being an entrepreneur.

I say this because I often get those that are long-time corporate types that think they want to jump into being an entrepreneur. I don't want to dash their hopes, and I am sure that many of them will succeed in doing so, but I also have seen that it is difficult if you are used to one kind of working world to adjust to a completely different kind of working world.

I would say the same about entrepreneurs that want to leave the entrepreneurial world and go into the conventional larger corporate world. They often find that being in the conventional corporate world is hard for them to do. Jon's tenure at Informix is an example of how he really seemed to be a fish out of water, and needed to get back into the start-up pond. Sure, there are larger companies that try to instill an entrepreneurial zeal. They aim to have intrapreneurs in their company. Or, they carve out an entity or create a skunk works that they seed with those that have that entrepreneurial flavor. It can happen.

Generally, though, one tends to see those that have the entrepreneurial spirit that crave and are only satisfied when being in a start-up or equivalent, and you see the conventional corporate types that are more comfortable in the conventional larger size firms. Being bilingual and bicultural of those two kinds of entities can occur, but it tends to be somewhat rare.

THE ROLE OF INTUITION

One other aspect about business leadership is the role of intuition. For large companies, they often will have vast amounts of data about markets, they can afford to do in-depth market research, and they can run test groups to figure out what might work in a market.

Typically, a start-up won't have that kind of analytical underpinning to go with. As Jon points out, intuition is a crucial part of being an entrepreneur. What does your gut tell you? That being said, if you have data that you can also look at, don't ignore it. Some entrepreneurs blindly go only with their gut, and are unaware of what else might be taking place.

At the other extreme, there are some entrepreneurs that over-analyze, getting stuck in the classic realm of analysis paralysis. At some point you need to make a decision and move forward. It is the proverbial Goldilocks of decision making, just the right amount of intuition and the right amount of analytics. Jon's journey as a business person, leader, executive, and entrepreneur provides an opportunity to explore some important aspects about business, business leadership, and business pivoting.

CHAPTER 6
WILLIAM WANG
(FOUNDER VIZIO)

Lance B. Eliot

CHAPTER 6

WILLIAM WANG (FOUNDER VIZIO)

PREFACE

If you have ever shopped for electronics in a Costco, you have likely noticed the prominence of products produced by the company Vizio Inc. At one time a complete unknown, today most consumers are familiar with Vizio's line of affordable flat televisions and HDTV's, along with an array of other electronic goods. With startling low prices and yet reasonably good quality, the Vizio brand has become a nearly household name. Recently, it was announced that Vizio would be acquired by the Chinese company LeEco, turning the already now wealthy founder of Vizio, William Wang, into the billionaire league of founders that made it big.

The slogan of Vizio has been "beautifully simple" and that is indeed at the core of William Wang. He eschews complexity and strives for simplicity. As you will see in his career story, he made several business pivots as a business leader. He took his instincts and experiences and kept trying until he found a winning formula. William is a perpetual seeker of new ideas and new innovations. Sometimes they work out, sometimes not, but he is always on the pursuit. Like many of the founders highlighted in this book, he began working at a larger company and opted to change direction. He also endured a scary life altering experience that renewed his business determination.

———

CHAPTER 6: WILLIAM WANG
(FOUNDER VIZIO)

I was a speaker at an industry event and during a speaker's reception first met William Wang (he was the keynote speaker at the event). As founder and CEO of Vizio, he had built the company from the ground up and made it into a multi-billion dollar powerhouse that is one of the largest sellers of HDTV's.

Gracious and warm in his demeanor, it was evident right away that he also had an underlying drive to succeed. His pursuit of business and his belief in what he is doing were passionately displayed. When I learned about his personal story of business up's and down's, I realized it was jam packed with many lessons in business and showcased numerous pivots and pivotal moments that led him to where he is today.

In this chapter, I start at the beginning of his career and walk through the significant highlights and business pivots over the course of some thirty years or so. Take a look at Figure 1 as an outline of the journey you are about to read.

CRUCIAL BUSINESS ASPECTS OF WILLIAM WANG (VIZIO)

- Initial career direction shift from architect to engineering
- Seeing a better way (IBM standard monitors)
- Being bold and brave to act and start-up a business
- Getting caught-up in success and misreading market shift
- Searching for the next big thing
- Facing financial ruin by the enduring search
- Plane crash survival reshapes attitude and perspective
- New opportunity that started another path
- Path ultimately blocked so the start of something new
- Convergence of timing, sweat, luck to realize the big thing
- Sticking to your knitting, and leveraging your foundation

Figure 1: Eliot - The business pivots of William Wang, founder Vizio

INITIAL CAREER DIRECTION

William was born in Taiwan and raised there until his parents opted to move to California when he was 14 years of age. He arrived here without any knowledge of English and with little understanding or awareness of American culture.

Rapidly learning English and becoming familiar with the U.S. culture, he eventually graduated from high school and went to college. Upon entry into college, he first decided to major in architecture. When he found out that engineering jobs pay more than architectural jobs, he chose to switch majors into electrical engineering. This change in majors was significant throughout the rest of his career, providing him with the necessary electronics related background that would turn out to become essentially his career realm.

Completing his engineering degree in 1986, he was unsure of what he would do next. His GPA was so low that he realized that he had little hope of getting into a masters of engineering program. He answered a newspaper ad of a Chinese firm that was looking for someone to do tech support on the computer monitors that the firm sold. He got that job and proceeded to do customer tech support over the phone. Eventually, he shifted somewhat into the sales side of things too, and even sought to get an MBA, but with traveling for his job and other aspects he decided to drop out of the MBA program.

SEEKING A BETTER WAY

At the time, the IBM standard monitor was the mainstay of what was selling in industry. William was frustrated that the IBM standard monitors were poorly engineered, including a flickering aspect that was accepted by everyone but that he knew could be eliminated. He stared at those monitors and could see inside and beyond them, envisioning a much better monitor.

Realizing that he was not going to go much further up at his employer (the job of Vice President was not likely, he figured out), he decided that the way to proceed would be to start-up his own firm.

BEING BOLD AND BRAVE TO ACT

At the youthful age of 26, he started a company called MAG Innovision. Upon reflection, William now says that he was bold, fearless, and also quite foolish to think that he could pull off this new business. He borrowed money from his parents, got his former boss to provide $150,000, put in his own savings, got a shareholder in Asia that tossed in $150,000, and got the company underway with a total of about $350,000.

He developed new kinds of monitors and was able to use his Taiwanese connections to make them inexpensively. Market demand for computer monitors was dramatically rising at the time, and he was able to grow from

2 people to 400 people in six years, landing at an annual revenue of $600 million.

By his early 30s, it seemed that he had managed to hit the big win. Furthermore, Gateway (popular at the time and a purveyor of computer hardware) was one of his key customers and he came to know Ted Waitt, co-founder and Chairman. Ted helped mentor William and provide guidance throughout the growth of MAG. Ted himself became a billionaire and known for being one of the Forbes "40 under 40," being a top business success before the age of 40.

GETTING CAUGHT UP IN SUCCESS

Shortly after peaking at an annual revenue over $600 million, the revenue at MAG started to decline. In 1998, it had dropped to $470 million, a decrease of nearly 20% and which was stunning too given that rising growth had been the forecast and expectation for the firm. William now says that he was over his head in terms of the leadership needed to pull the firm out of its downward spiral.

The marketplace had shifted from a technology-driven focus to instead considering computer monitors as a commodity. He did not adjust, and nor did he adjust his firm. He believes he spent the company resources on the wrong things and should have focused on getting the right people into place. Finally, after deciding that it was hopeless to continue, he sold the firm to the manufacturer of the monitors and got out.

SEARCHING FOR THE NEXT BIG THING

He was not down for the count, though. He knew that there were new opportunities to be discovered. He started up a new firm called Princeton Graphics Systems. Yet again a computer monitor firm. This was a business he knew well and had an established track record in. He had all the contacts and the knowledge to try and do something new and great.

But what would that new and great thing be? He started an R&D group in Asia and explored HD TVs. He dabbled with Internet-enabled TVs, which was a hot idea at the time.

During this same time period, Congress had indicated that they were going to impose a mandate on TVs to shift from analog to digital. Most digital TVs were quite expensive, often in the $8,000 to $10,000 range and beyond what an average consumer would be able to afford. William realized that with a legislated mandate that there would have to be a market for digital TVs, and that those firms that got into the market first with reasonably priced digital TVs could take ahold of the market.

FACING FINANCIAL RUIN

He doggedly pursued this next big thing. He was utterly convinced that he could develop the right product for the right time at the right price. Unfortunately, he was spending money right and left to get there. Step by step, his firm was bleeding dry of funds. Creditors were complaining and worried that the whole thing would collapse like a house of cards. William himself was under incredible stress and strain. Everyone was looking to him to find a way toward success, and he had tasted success before, so why could he not get there now? He was tormented by wanting to show that he could keep the firm going, that it would work out, and that he would also not let down his family and friends that had all supported him.

He flew over to Taiwan to have a serious and heart wrenching meeting with his creditors there.

After the meeting, and being as despondent or more so than when he had arrived for the meeting, he sat on the plane at the airport and waited to go back to Los Angeles, deep in thought about what to do next. He was seated toward the front of the plane. The large plane, a fully loaded 747 with fuel to the brim to make the long journey, went on the runway as William sat in his seat contemplating the future.

PLANE CRASH SURVIVAL IS RESHAPING

The pilot had been told to use runway 5-L, but mistakenly used runway 5-R. Turns out that runway 5-R was under various construction and there was construction equipment sitting toward the end of the runway. As the plane tried to liftoff, the underbelly struck some of the construction equipment.

The plane rammed back down to the ground, splitting into half. The fuel ignited and fire seethed throughout the parts of the plane. The front half of the plane continued forward on its own momentum. The back half of the plane was wiped out. After terrifying moments that seemed an eternity, the front of the plane came to a rest. Acrid and toxic smoke filled what remained of the plane. William struggled to get out, breathing in the fumes and incurring carbon monoxide poisoning.

Overall, he got out and made it safely away from the wreckage. About half of the passengers died and all of the crew perished in the crash. This was a pivotal moment in his life and it was then that he began to realize how lucky it is to be alive.

His first thoughts as the plane careened down the runway was about his family. He recalls even thinking that since it was coming up to Halloween that he wouldn't be home to take his 3-4 year-old daughter out for Halloween. These are the kinds of thoughts that many facing death have expressed, seemingly simple thoughts that bely the overarching severity of the moment per se.

It took him about a year or two to recover overall from the incident, and during that time he changed his attitude and perspective. He closed down the business. He had lost nearly $48 million from 1996 to 2001. But he was alive, he had his family, and was restructuring his business outlook.

NEW OPPORTUNITY FOR A NEW PATH

In 2001, Gateway had discussions with him about TVs. Ted Waitt wanted to sell additional products in their popular Gateway computer stores. The thinking was that rather than being typecast as only selling PC's, they could branch out to other electronics like TVs. Working together, they came up with a proposed $2,999 42-inch plasma TV. Plasma TVs were much more expensive at the time and only purchased by a somewhat wealthier customer. Not many plasma TVs were being sold due to the high price. If the price could be brought down, the expectation was that the market could be huge.

William tapped again into his base of overseas contacts and manufacturers. They made the plasma TVs and they sold pretty well in the Gateway stores. Customers in the store were amazed at the low price and yet incredible clarity and color of the picture. Things went well.

PATH ULTIMATELY BLOCKED

Gateway though was undergoing big changes. The marketplace was no longer hot for computer stores, and so Gateway decided it wanted out of being into retail stores. Without an ability to sell the plasma TVs in a store, whereby the prospective customer could see the TV, the sales began to dry up. William decided it was time to start a new business.

He started a company called V Inc. with some colleagues in 2002. He thought it made sense to get into this same business, aiming now at HDTVs, and mortgaged his home to raise $600,000 for the firm. He once again got money from his parents and friends. He eventually got some venture capital funds too. And, he gave some ownership to manufacturers to get them on-board.

Some thought he was crazy to think that he got enter into the fierce market of HDTVs.

That market was dominated by household name brands such as Sony, Sharp, and Zenith. How could an unknown name possibly break into the market? He even found that few seemed to be able to say or like the company name V, so he changed the company name to Vizio.

CONVERGENCE OF TIMING, SWEAT, LUCK

William had previously worked with Costco and sold monitors via Costco. The housing bubble in the U.S. was skyrocketing demand for affordable flat-screen TVs. Costco is universally known for having quality goods at affordable prices. William pitched that he could provide just that in the flat-screen TV niche.

For the Christmas season of 2013, Vizio put its 46-inch flat-screen TVs on sale in Costco. The price was about half of what other vendors were charging. The rest, as they say, is history.

Consumers were willing to buy an unknown brand because they trusted Costco. Costco found themselves with a big winner on their hands. The sales were so great that Costco even created a new profit center for this niche. Eventually, Vizio branched out beyond Costco and even provided product for one of Costco's arch rivals, Sam's Club. Vizio to this day continues to flourish and expand.

STICK TO YOUR KNITTING

As might be evident throughout the career of William, he always came back to what he knew. He also leveraged his foundations, utilizing for example his Gateway contacts at a later point in his career, and likewise utilizing his Costco contacts later in his career, and his contacts in Taiwan, etc.

He had been careful to forge good relationships over time, and strive to become a trusted business partner during his career, creating goodwill for later tapping into when needed. The largest pivot in his business career occurred as a result of the horrific plane crash.

He also had other pivots throughout his career, including when his MAG Innovision plummeted, and later when Gateway pulled out of the retail store business. William has always remained determined to continue moving forward.

CHAPTER 7

CINDY CRAWFORD
(FOUNDER BEAUTY LINE,
SUPERMODEL)

CHAPTER 7

CINDY CRAWFORD
(FOUNDER BEAUTY LINE,
SUPERMODEL)

PREFACE

Unless you've been living in a cave for the last 30 years or so, you have undoubtedly heard of Cindy Crawford and likely have seen pictures of her (or, perhaps seen her TV infomercial spots). Her supermodel fame is well known, and some would say that she was one of the founders of the realm of being a supermodel. Forbes magazine notably lists her as one of the founding five, and also in the 1990's had said that she was the highest paid model on planet Earth. She has graced the cover of hundreds of beauty and consumer magazines.

You might not be aware that she is also a beauty line magnate and has turned her supermodel career into a long lasting business. Touting the web site link of simply www.cindy.com (who else could it be, but of course Cindy Crawford), her beauty line was at first an extension of her modeling, and then once her modeling began to reduce, the beauty line became her mainstay. Not many models are astute enough to realize that someday their beauty will fade, which I realize sounds harsh but it is akin to anyone that relies upon their body for their career, whether it be a model or an athlete. In this chapter, we'll trace the various business up's and down's, and the business pivots of Cindy Crawford.

———

CHAPTER 7: CINDY CRAWFORD
(FOUNDER BEAUTY LINE, SUPERMODEL)

Upon recently meeting Cindy Crawford, she radiates the same incredible beauty that had been her ticket to becoming a supermodel. She mentioned that she was nearing 50 years of age, but perhaps even more surprising was the declaration that her beauty line was just hitting one billion dollars in revenue.

Unlike many models that end-up with little in the bank after their modeling careers end, Cindy has carefully and systematically made sure that her beauty fame remains a strong brand that keeps the money flowing in. Besides beauty products, she also has a line of furniture known as the Cindy Crawford Home Collection and has other extensions of her mainstay beauty products.

Cindy has that rare gift of being able to portray the alluring beauty queen and yet at the same time be a shrewd business woman that smartly launched a "side" business that would keep her going long after the beauty starts to fade or the marketplace decides in its fickle fashion that her particular beauty is no longer of interest.

This is akin to a top professional athlete that leverages their physical attributes playing say football into ongoing earnings even after their body is no longer apt for being in the sport, perhaps by going into the sporting goods business or other such avenues. Few that rely upon their physical attributes that are age dependent and get them early success are able to think far enough ahead to plan for the future.

Those that do plan for the future often find that they aren't able to make their earlier fame and prowess into having longer legs to support them in their later years. In this chapter, I trace some of the key aspects that define Cindy Crawford and illustrate her business leadership and the elements and pivots that led to her success.

HUMILITY GROUNDED IN UPBRINGING

One of the foundational aspects of Cindy is her sense of humility that was established by her upbringing in DeKalb, Illinois. Her parents taught her a work ethic that lasts until this day. She worked in the corn fields doing manual labor. She worked in other jobs in her small town and learned to save up her money. She would use the money to buy her back-to-school supplies, along with getting that new dress or those cosmetics that she had her eye on.

These Midwestern values were to keep her rooted in humanity during the time that she rocketed to the top of the modeling profession. The various temptations during those high flying years were of such that like any stratospheric international celebrity she could have become full of herself and lived for the moment only.

She also became known as a model that was willing to put in the hard work needed to get the right photos and produce the right kind of image for her and the products she was showcasing. Some might think that modeling is merely the act of showing up, but the reality of gaining true supermodel fame is that it requires meticulous attention to detail and a willingness to keep trying to find that particular pose and particular look that will keep you at the top.

AN EARLY PRANK THAT WAS A HARD LESSON

Cindy tells the story of her first alleged opportunity to do modeling and it provides insights again into the shaping of her personality and perspective on the world. During her sophomore year in high school, a call to her home by a local clothing store became an important moment for her. The clothing store reported that they wanted her to come to the store to do some modeling. Cindy had in the back of her mind the potential for some kind of modeling, but had not known whether it would ever occur and nor how to have it occur. Now was her seemingly big break into being a model.

She selected her Gloria Vanderbilt jeans and did up her hair. With uncontainable excitement, she headed to the clothing store. Telling the cashier at the store that she was there to do modeling, the clerk had no clue about what Cindy was claiming. The store manager came out and said that there was no modeling going on. As Cindy left the store in tears and confusion, she saw two girls from her high school standing nearby and laughing.

It had been a prank on Cindy. Imagine the rush of anticipation that Cindy had about her big chance into modeling that then was dashed and also a cruel joke on her.

Though this was a painful experience, and yet it also furthered Cindy sense of wholesomeness and fair play, in that she had so disliked the prank and it left such an ugly indelible impression that she was always mindful hence to be careful about being fair and upfront with others. She knew first-hand the pain that can come from trickery and tomfoolery, and that empathic aspect still resonates with her in her dealings with others today.

THE FIRST TRUE BREAK INTO MODELING

In her junior year, Cindy was able to become a brand ambassador at a different clothing store in town. She also participated in a fashion show there. These were the inklings of her modeling career that was about to get started.

A local photographer that covered the activities of DeKalb from a hometown perspective had seen her around town and wanted to have her appear in the Northern Illinois University paper. Even though she was in high school, he had been weekly providing pictures to the paper of local college girls and thought that Cindy looked the part. Cindy's parents were hesitant and naturally suspicious. They accompanied her to the photo shoot and ultimately the picture got published and became her first "cover" of her modeling career.

Though the local photographer was the trigger into modeling, Cindy credits the woman that did her hair and makeup as the catalyst for going into modeling. The woman urged Cindy to try an open call at the Midwest Beauty Show in Chicago. Cindy went, and the hairdresser there, a "big time" New York hairdresser (Cindy viewed him as such), advised her to get an agent there in Chicago, and provided some names for her to contact.

Notice that each step along the way that she had been provided with a kind of mentoring that not only provided her with advise and tips, but also that gave her handy specifics in terms of recommended next steps and contacts.

THE MOLE AND DISTINCTIVENESS

Upon meeting an agent in Chicago, she was told that her mole should be removed. For those of you that know of Cindy, you probably are well aware that her mole on the left side of her face has been a distinctive feature throughout her modeling career.

Cindy tells the story that her mole had always been of controversy for her and for others. Her sisters had told her that only a mole on the right side of a face could be considered a beauty mark, and otherwise it was just an ugly mole. On her first day in high school, some football players rattled her by telling her that she had chocolate on her face, ridiculing her about her mole.

When she was younger, she had often discussed with her mother the notion of removing the mole. Her mother had cautioned that removing the mole could leave a scar. Cindy felt trapped between the conflict of having a mole that seemed to be a disadvantage to her, but faced with the potential of an even worse disadvantage if it was removed and a hideous scar took its place.

In any case, she opted to keep the mole and the Chicago modeling agent had Cindy do a photo shoot, mole included. The hair dresser on that photo shoot then showed the pictures to a colleague at the Stewart Talent Agency in Chicago (which later became Elite Model Management). This next agent liked Cindy's look, including the mole, and set her up to be photographed with an up-and-coming modeling photographer.

Those photos and her new agent at the Stewart Talent Agency got her a newspaper ad for Marshall Field's, appearing in the Chicago Tribune, and was her first paid act as a model. Many at her high school tried to ridicule her about the ad, but she was paid a princely sum of $150, she had not been out in the hot sun picking corn, and she was breaking into modeling, so for her it was looking pretty good.

She began to find that others looking for a model would sometimes refer to her as "that one with the mole" and so it became a distinctive feature that made her stand out. After eventually landing the cover of Vogue magazine, she gradually overcame her concerns about the mole and began to accept that it was actually her trademark (and the rest of the world became enamored of it).

MENTORSHIP AND THE PARTING OF WAYS

Another important moment of Cindy's career occurred when her agent informed her that a notable high-fashion photographer in Chicago wanted to see her. Nervous about going to see him, Cindy worked up the courage and drove to his office. The studio manager took a look at Cindy and seemingly mistook the mole for a pimple. Cindy was not able to get to see the photographer and was screened out by the studio manager.

Fortunately, Cindy got called back and got included in a modeling shoot with some other well-known and New York based models that were in Chicago at the time. Cindy observed what they did and realized that there was a lot more to modeling than might at first glance seem to be. The high-fashion photographer took a liking to Cindy and became a mentor to her.

For two years, Cindy worked closely with this high-fashion photographer, doing one photo shoot after another and gradually becoming known in the modeling world, albeit in a more regional and localized way.

A point of deflection was about to emerge. She got an opportunity to do a photo shoot for a New York agency that would require her to go to Egypt for ten days. Her agent asked for permission to take some time away from the Chicago studio, and the high-fashion photographer refused to let her do so. Indeed, he said he would ex-communicate her if she dared to do so.

Imagine the anxiety for Cindy. This high-fashion photographer had taught her the ropes of the business and helped to propel her career forward. But now, upon a potential added big break, he was refusing to let her make a try for it. She hoped he wasn't completely serious and so she opted to do the photo shoot in Egypt, thinking that when she got back that he would realize that it was not such a big deal of her being gone for a few days.

Turns out that he exiled her, as he had claimed he would. This was one of several impetuses that led Cindy to decide to move to New York where she knew that if she wanted to climb the modeling ladder was the right place to be anyway. In that sense, this was another of life's painful lessons that actually helped her to progress. Had he not exiled her, she might have stayed there in Chicago and never risen up in the modeling ranks.

SMART UNLIKE THE IMAGE OF MODELS

Shifting slightly back in time about the above story of Cindy's career, one aspect that is also noteworthy to mention is that she is smart. The only reason I bring this up purposely is that most might assume that a model is an airhead. That is a relatively standard perception of models (sorry, models, but that seems to be the general perception).

While in elementary school, she got all A's and in 6th grade she made a bet for $200 with her father that she would never get less than an A throughout school. Later, as a senior in high school, she won that bet and also was named valedictorian of her graduating class.

She also won a full academic scholarship to the prestigious Northwestern University. The scholarship was for chemical engineering, which wasn't a subject that Cindy was particularly interested in, but it was a full academic scholarship and a means to getting into a great university.

During her summer after graduating from high school, she traveled throughout Europe doing modeling. Once college began, she tried to do double-duty of both attending classes and doing modeling. She found herself getting stretched into long days and nights. It seemed that she was not going to be able to do both well, school and her modeling at the same time, and instead she seemed to be sacrificing substantively each for the other.

Weighing continually on her mind of what to do, she decided to drop out of college after her first semester. It was with a heavy heart that she did so. Her logic was that modeling was "now" — this was her moment in time for breaking into modeling, while college she could later come back to, if needed and desired.

CRUCIAL BUSINESS ASPECTS

Cindy's story is filled with lots of useful business insights about how various moments, pivots, and decisions can be defining for the direction of where you will go and what you will do in your career. Look at Figure 1.

CRUCIAL BUSINESS ASPECTS OF CINDY CRAWFORD

- Humble roots leading to hard work and the value of a dollar
- Pranked about modeling, but fostered empathic nature
- Able to make connections with people and network
- Listening to others and acting on their advice
- Keeping her distinctiveness in spite of ridicule and self-doubts
- Importance of a mentor to learn the ropes
- Difficulty in breaking away from a mentor for the next step
- Having smarts and using it either explicitly or implicitly
- Able to use the perception of models to her advantage
- Able to use the perception of her for her business growth

Figure 1: Eliot - The business pivots of Cindy Crawford, supermodel & business magnate

Her humble roots and hard work as a youth were instrumental in how she treated other people and in the hard work that she put into her modeling career. Some might assume that a supermodel was probably born into luxury and lackadaisically lands into modeling. Though this might happen, in the case of Cindy she worked hard to leverage the breaks she got and was determined to push forward in modeling.

The prank that was pulled on her at the start of her modeling quest has left an indelible mark in her psyche. Though she suffered, she also likely became more empathetic to others and realized how matters that are important to people should not be lightly treated.

Notice too that the connections she was given were step-by-step crucial in her climb up the ladder. She likely would not have had these connections were she not heartfelt to others and able to befriend them. Again, the stereotypical view of a model might be that they are aloof and standoffish, but Cindy remains to this day a warm and ingratiating person, even after having achieved the incredible celebrity status that she has attained.

She carefully listened to others, and often heeded their advice. Some that walk around in their own bubble and fail to listen to others are not likely to leverage what others have to tell them. Like a sponge, she soaked up what others had to tell her about modeling and how to succeed as a model.

Her mole is one of the most important of all of the business lessons in her career. She had been urged by others to get rid of it, and that it was out of the ordinary and not in keeping with the norm. She heard this from friends, relatives, family, and even strangers. Her self-doubts about it were constant. Yet, she kept it, and it became a distinctive feature that made her standout. Instead of having her picture sit in a pile of models pictures and remain just another model, it was the "get me the one with the mole" that helped her make progress in her modeling career.

We all should keep in mind our own distinctiveness, and for which it might be unusual and considered outside the norm, but it could very well be the aspect that ultimately provides that big break or makes you memorable.

She had mentors along the way and especially the high-fashion photographer in Chicago. Having a mentor can be essential for getting good guidance and avoiding the pitfalls that lay ahead of a career as it unfolds.

Interestingly and perhaps paradoxically, a mentor can also sometimes become a trap. The mentor might see you in only a particular way and typecast you forever. Or, a mentor might relish having you in their fold, and be unwilling to give you up and let you otherwise progress. For whatever reason that the high-fashion photographer harbored when he refused to let Cindy go on the trip to Egypt, his rebuffing her was instrumental in helping Cindy break a bond that seemingly might have kept her trapped, and might not have allowed her to ultimately become the supermodel that she aspired to become.

In terms of being smart, Cindy is able to use this talent to her advantage in both implicit and explicit ways. When going into business negotiations, the other side is likely to harbor the belief that a supermodel might be empty minded and must not have any business acumen. Rather than being irritated per se by this stereotype, Cindy indicates that she often uses it as a means to lull the other side into thinking that they can bowl her over. She then strikes at the right moment, having anticipated their next move, or she can play the "I don't get what you are trying to say" and pretend to be the aloof and demanding stereotypical supermodel character to overcome whatever they are proposing.

How has Cindy parlayed her supermodel achievements into a billion-dollar enterprise? She had the smarts to know that her looks would only take her so far and that she had to have more, and do more, in order to secure her future. She credits too her husband for his partnership with her in the business endeavors. Those on the outside might look at her superficially and see just the supermodel, but upon closer exploration it is clear cut that she is also a well-rounded individual that has the business savvy instinct to leverage her own image and create a lasting brand.

CHAPTER 8

JENNY MING

(CEO CHARLOTTE RUSSE)

CHAPTER 8

JENNY MING
(CEO CHARLOTTE RUSSE)

PREFACE

Have you ever been to an Old Navy clothing store? If so, you are experiencing the handiwork of Jenny Ming, one of the founding executives of Old Navy while she was working at The Gap. After the tremendous success of Old Navy, Jenny took a small break in her career as a kind of sabbatical, and then jumped back into the business world by becoming the CEO of Charlotte Russe. Charlotte Russe is a retail clothing chain store that targets women. The main customer focus is women in their teens and in their twenties, and the store offers women's clothing, accessories, and footwear. If you are a woman in a youth oriented age bracket, you'd know about Charlotte Russe. The chain operates in nearly all of the states of the USA, having something like 600 stores worldwide. The name Charlotte Russe was chosen by the original founders and refers to a French dessert.

Jenny has had an incredible business career. She is one of those rags-to-riches kind of stories. As a female, she fought hard and smartly to overcome an often male oriented environment and showed that she was determined to make business her focus. She also managed to find ways to balance her personal life with her work life, an often delicate and difficult dance to achieve. We will take a look at the various business pivots she's encountered and undertaken along the way of her business successes.

———

CHAPTER 8: JENNY MING
(CEO CHARLOTTE RUSSE)

Jenny Ming is a dynamo. Former president of Old Navy and one of its founding executives, and today the CEO of Charlotte Russe, the women's fashion clothing retailer that operates over 550 stores, Jenny seems to continually be moving at a frenetic pace.

In person, she is quite warm and charming. Quick to get to the point and a straight shooter when it comes to dialogue, she has had one of those incredible life and business stories in a rag-to-riches kind of way. In this chapter, I trace aspects of Jenny's career and glean insights from her business efforts, business pivots, and the legacy that she has already established. Take a look at Figure 1.

BUSINESS LEADERSHIP LESSONS

- Bilingual and bicultural upbringing valuable for global business
- Leveraging college studies into a career direction

LESSONS LEARNED

- Turning a first-time manager failing into how to best manage others
- Importance of being forthright with employees and transparent with them
- Defining what it means to be tough in business, and appearing as such
- Value of having a mentor and riding the wave of the mentor
- Spin-offs and the crucial nature of entity naming
- Consultants as advisers, while management still as the decision makers
- Showcasing ambition, dealing with stereotypes that others hold against you
- Overcoming the class ceiling and aiming for a work-life balance

Figure 1: Eliot – Business leadership insights as gleaned from the career of Jenny Ming

THE BEGINNING

At the age of 9, her parents brought her to the United States, settling in the San Francisco area. She was in 4th grade at the time. Not yet conversant in English, she was put into an English as a Second Language (ESL)

curriculum at school. She found that watching TV was one of the best ways to pick-up English and was glued to the set whenever she could do so.

Her mother simultaneously insisted that Jenny learn Chinese. Jenny thought this was an absurd notion at the time and that her focus should be on becoming truly fluent in English. Nonetheless, at her mother's insistence, Jenny made the trek into Chinatown to learn Chinese.

This aspect of learning Chinese was actually later in life proven to be a stroke of good fortune. Jenny later in her career was able to make a big splash in business by negotiating with various manufacturers and distributors overseas due to her fluency in Chinese. Had she not been forced into learning Chinese at this earlier age, she probably would not have had been able to leverage capability that then stoked her career path.

COLLEGE AND HER MAJOR

Going to college at San Jose State University, Jenny was unsure of what to choose as her major. Somewhat to her surprise, she discovered that there was a major in home economics and she gravitated in that direction. She figured that perhaps she might teach home economics, especially to middle school students.

Her boyfriend at the time, and later to become her husband, prompted her to consider taking some business classes. She did so and got a minor in business. Graduating in 1978, she proceeded to work at various jobs, most notably working at Mervyn's, the department store.

In some ways, working at Mervyn's readily leveraged her home economics degree. Working out on the floor of the store, she performed as a sales associate, working directly with customers and getting a sense of what was selling and what was not selling. She was able to interact with customers and offer tips and suggestions about selections for home use.

Jenny was eventually promoted into becoming the departmental manager in domestics, which included home related items such as towels, bed sheets, pillow cases, and the like.

A FIRST-TIME MANAGER BUSINESS LESSON

It was during the first month of her becoming a manager that she learned a valuable business lesson. Having come up the ranks, many of her now subordinates had previously been her peers. They were all a friendly lot and were used to the kind of comradery that goes along with being co-workers. Now, though, she was their boss. They continued to interact with her as though she was a co-worker, and she treated them as co-workers rather than being "the big boss," so to speak.

In her first month as a newly minted manager, one day her boss brought her into the office and confided in her about a potential issue. The sense was that Jenny was not willing to play the tough role of making sure the sales associates were properly doing their job. They were at times chatting when they should be providing assistance to customers. Her manager told her that she was perhaps too nice to be a manager and should reconsider whether it was really what she wanted to be.

This often happens to an individual contributor that is first promoted into a supervisory or managerial role, and especially when they remain in the same functional area that they had while working as an individual contributor. It can be very hard to switch hats and become the boss. There are friendships that were formed with co-workers that can become stressed in such circumstances. The frivolity that one had as a co-worker must now be set aside and the heavy responsibility of overseeing others needs to take root.

A first-time supervisor or manager can react to this awareness in one of several ways. There are some that immediately become the bulldog and start bossing around their subordinates. This typically creates ill will and can be bewildering to the former co-workers that perhaps believe the job of supervisory role has gone to the person's head.

Another approach involves trying to break-up the chit chatting co-workers and parcel them out to other supervisors, hoping that the friendliness among the co-workers will be diminished in terms of impacting on the job performance. This is also not usually very satisfactory and creates other adverse consequences for the other supervisors too.

After her manager essentially reprimanded her, Jenny went home that night after work and contemplated what she should do about her bosses' admonishment. One option was that she could retreat back into a sales associate role. Maybe she wasn't fit for a manager's job. Or, maybe she needed more time to get seasoned and be better prepared for the manager's job. Doubts flowed through her mind that night.

The next morning at work, she gathered her subordinates. She told them what had happened, deciding to be direct with them. She explained that they were going to need to refocus on the customer and curtail the chit chatting. Jenny offered that she could schedule their breaks so that they would have time to go on chit-chats throughout the day, if that would help. And, she pointed out that if they weren't willing to find a means to deal with the problem with her as their boss, Jenny herself might get replaced by someone else that would be a lot less accommodating as a boss and maybe be a real ogre in comparison.

Her former co-workers appreciated Jenny being so forthright. They indeed reduced the chit chatting and were able to shift their attention back to the customer and worked more seriously as sales associates. For Jenny, this incident had several important business lessons.

She realized that the perception of her by her boss was that she didn't seem tough enough to be in management, and so she opted to ensure that she would showcase a stronger impression. She also decided that being forthright with her employees was better than trying to hide issues from them or sneakily trying to fool them into changing. It is this business lesson that seems to have stayed with her all these years, including today that she still prizes being open with her employees.

She also realized that as a manager she had not set expectations with her team. She should have made it clear from the start as to what she wanted them to do as sales associates. Without having set expectations, the team was able to wander aimlessly and one could say innocently did not realize that they were not living up to what was expected of them (since they didn't know what the expectations were).

COMING TO THE GAP

In 1986, Millard "Mickey" Drexler at The Gap recruited Jenny to come on-board at The Gap. He had been in merchandising throughout most of his career. Beginning his career at Bloomingdale's, he had eventually served as CEO at Ann Taylor, and was a rising star at The Gap, destined to soon become President and then later on become CEO.

She was asked to be a buyer. This was a crucial step in her career and would ultimately show her ability to gauge what styles were in, and find ways to get good deals for the goods to be displayed in stores. Drexler was a crucial mentor for her. Providing key guidance to her, she was able to perform and provide ongoing validation of having her come to The Gap.

After three years as a buyer and merchandising manager, she was promoted to vice president. Then, about four years later, she was promoted to senior vice president. She describes those years as ones of back breaking hard work and great devotion to The Gap.

GAP WAREHOUSE EMERGES

Target stores had noticed the rise of The Gap, which during the 1990s had a particularly hot clothing line that was seemingly insatiably sought by consumers. Target sent signals that it was going to copy The Gap and mimic their clothing line. Worse still, Target was going to provide the clothing line at lower prices than The Gap.

Drexler gathered his top executives, which included Jenny at that time, and they brainstormed what to do about the potential competition from Target. If they did nothing, it could mean that The Gap would see its sales radically diminished once Target grabbed a chunk of the marketplace that wanted lower prices for the same kind of gear. On the other hand, if they were to lower their prices at The Gap, it could undermine their profits, and create a perception that The Gap was no longer a haughty line of clothing.

They decided that they might was well do the same thing that Target was threatening to do, namely provide The Gap style clothing at lower prices, but they would establish a whole new business that would do so. In this manner, they would hopefully not create any stench for the conventional perception of The Gap, and yet could also get some of the glow from The Gap as its say little sister or little brother.

What to call this new entity? They decided to go with the name of Gap Warehouses. It was pretty common at that time to think of warehouse stores as offering lower prices. By putting the word warehouse after the word Gap, they expected that consumers would realize that this was an entity of The Gap but that it was a discounted version.

To try and inexpensively launch the Gap Warehouses, they decided to take existing Gap stores that were under performing and convert them into Gap Warehouses. This seemed like a good way to approach the new entity, avoiding distributing any well working stores of the Gap and dealing with stores that anyway were struggling.

Jenny became part of that start-up team of the Gap Warehouses. After some discussion and bickering about how many such Gap Warehouses there ought to be at the start, Drexler said he would go for a round number of 50 such Gap Warehouse stores. They then looked at the under performers of The Gap stores, picked 49 of those, and tossed one brand new Gap Warehouse into the count of 50.

Opening in August of 1993, within about 6 weeks they had ample evidence that they had picked a winner of an idea. Revenue was looking good. The store locations that had previously done poorly were now performing well. Consumers seemed to like the Gap Warehouses.

For Jenny, this was an exciting period of time. She was involved in essentially a brand new start-up. At the same time, unlike a from-scratch start-up, they had all of the infrastructure of The Gap to borrow from to get the new chain underway. This also had downsides as there were occasional difficulties of taking attention from The Gap, and some within the Gap that either resisted the Gap Warehouses or felt that it was diverting precious resources away from their rightful place at The Gap.

Unlike a conventional The Gap store, these Gap Warehouses were devised to have a warehouse-like feel to them. There were barren floors of cement, metal shelves rather than stylish racks, and other elements that said these were warehouses. They also had large aisles, put impulse purchase items at the front, and even had gaudy shopping carts that were more accepted in grocery stores than in a clothing line shopping store.

OLD NAVY EMERGES FROM GAP WAREHOUSES

One aspect that they had not anticipated was confusion about the name of the new entity. Many consumers were confused by the new name. Was this something associated with The Gap? Was it something different or just The Gap with a different name? What made a The Gap different from a Gap Warehouse?

Rather than trying to fight this battle and attempt to further brand the Gap Warehouse name per se, top management decided they would try to find a different name for the Gap Warehouse. Jenny tells the story of how they sought to identify a better name for the Gap Warehouse.

Apparently, a high priced consultant was brought in, and studied in-depth what the Gap Warehouse was. They interviewed everyone on the top management team. They did surveys of consumers. They researched and researched. Finally, the vaunted consultant asked to have the top management team assembled so that a short list of new names for the entity could be shared and discussed.

At the start of the presentation, the consultant announced that there were three solid names that had been carefully and systematically identified. With baited breath, Jenny and her fellow executives excitedly waited to hear what the three names were. The first name presented, and which was done with great flourish, consisted of one word, Forklift.

Jenny was stunned. The thought that they might christen the Gap Warehouse as the Forklift just seemed crazy. Imagine consumers saying that today they are going over to the Forklift to get a new shirt or pants. The reaction of the top team was one of hesitation and certainly not of enthusiasm, but they also knew that there were two names left to go.

The second name announced was Elevator. At this point, I am sure some of the top executives might have thought they were getting pranked. After paying the big bucks to this consultant and consulting firm, they so far had two words, Forklift and Elevator. Perhaps the third word was the charmer. Maybe it was the new name they were waiting for. Cutting the suspense, the consultant then announced the third name, Monorail.

The assembled executives were nearly speechless. After excusing the consultant to exit from the room, they sat around trying to decide what to do next. Should they hire someone else? Should they have the consultant try harder? Should they give up and not try to do a renaming?

Suddenly, Drexler spoke up and offered a potential new name. What about Old Navy, he asked the group? He explained that he used to enjoy going to a pub in Paris that had the name of Old Navy. He had often thought it would make a good name for a another business someday.

Everyone at the table was already a bit shell shocked from the Forklift, Elevator, and Monorail names, and so they agreed to think over the idea of using Old Navy. They asked the marketing team to put together something to show what a logo of Old Navy might look like. When they all got back together to revisit the naming options, marketing showed-off some mugs and T-shirts that had the Old Navy name and logo. They decided it sounded and looked pretty cool. To be safe, they made sure that no one was already using that name, and they even bought the name from the Paris pub.

Of course, today, the name of Old Navy seems just perfect and we all have come to accept it. At the time, though, it was a gamble as to whether the marketplace would think it acceptable, and whether it would do better than the Gap Warehouse name.

This story also illustrates some other facets of business lessons. High priced consultants aren't necessarily always going to provide the best of advice. Furthermore, the advice by consultants is just that, it is advice, and so it is still up to management to decide whether to accept or reject the advice. Another facet was the kind of instinct that one sometimes has, including that Drexler just seemed to believe that the Old Navy name had a ring to it.

TAKING A LEAP FORWARD OR NOT

By 1996, Jenny was promoted to Executive Vice President of merchandising for the spin-off. She had come quite a long way from her days as a sales associate on the store floor of Mervyn's. In the early days of her career, she had been passed over for a promotion. She was confused and upset that she had been skipped. She worked up the courage to go see her boss and find out why she had not even been considered for the promotion.

Upon discussing the situation with boss, he told her that he did not know that she sought the promotion had not thought she was that ambitious. Jenny felt that because she had children and that because she was a woman that her boss had made an assumption that she would not be seeking higher and higher positions.

She vowed that henceforth she would make it abundantly clear that she was interested and eager to progress in her career. And that regardless of having children this was true. And regardless of being a woman that this was true. She also realized that there was a glass ceiling that she needed to be watchful of.

To this day, she explicitly tries to help women to advance in their business careers. She asks all on her team to think about what they want to achieve. What is the dream job they wish to someday get. She also pays attention to work-life balance. For example, on weekends, she tries to get herself and her teams to shut off work and focus on their personal lives. She believes that the "time lost" of working on weekends is gained by having happier workers that are more satisfied in their work and that are loyal to the company for aiding them in achieving a work-life balance.

Around 1998, she was approached about moving from being the EVP at Old Navy to become the president of the company. At first, she politely declined the notion. There were various personal reasons and other factors that led her to do so.

Eventually, she changed her mind and indicated that she would like to become president. Indeed, in 1999 she became president of Old Navy and remained in that position for seven years.

A NEXT STEP

Taking about a year off, Jenny traveled and contemplated what she would do next. Having gotten on the cover of Business Week and being named as one of the top fifty women in business, she was hunted by many of the top executive recruiters. Eventually, Charlotte Russe was brought to her attention. It was essentially in the same line of business that she already knew well, and it had a kind of start-up appeal to it in that it was still in a growth and maturing stage.

She has established a casual kind of environment there, encouraging those at all ranks to speak up. She purposely does skip level touch bases, ensuring that she hears what is going on from those lower in the company. Having ten direct reports, which is more than what normally might be expected, she believes that in a smaller firm it is doable to have that many direct reports, and perhaps even necessary.

A believer of surrounding yourself with others that can complement your own strengths and weaknesses, she indicates that for example it is important to her to have a strong CFO since she is somewhat less versed in the financials side of the business.

She still relishes knowing what is selling and what is not selling in the stores. They routinely have meetings where they bring in a rack against a wall of what is selling, and another rack of what is not selling. They then figure out what is making the selling stuff sell, and try to do more of that. For the stuff not selling, they try to figure how to convert it into something that will sell or otherwise remove it from their line. She travels extensively and always makes sure to visit their stores wherever she goes.

.

CHAPTER 9
STEVE MILLIGAN
(CEO WESTERN DIGITAL)

Lance B. Eliot

CHAPTER 9

STEVE MILLIGAN
(CEO WESTERN DIGITAL)

PREFACE

Western Digital Corporation is in the Fortune 200 ranking of companies, and yet most people have probably not heard of the company, or perhaps the name of the firm seems vaguely familiar but just not one that you can readily remember what they do. They are actually one of the largest hard disk drive manufacturers in the world and you probably have one of their storage devices in your electronics at work or at home. They don't do the over-the-top Intel-inside kind of marketing campaigns that some other electronics makers are fond of doing. Nonetheless, their products are known for being high quality and constantly at the leading edge of new technology. Interestingly, they began in the 1970's by making computer chips for calculators, and then when their "cash cow" calculator customer went bankrupt during the oil crisis, Western Digital also declared Chapter 11. They've come a long way since then.

Stephen Milligan is the CEO of Western Digital and has a long history with the company. I am fascinated Steve's business leadership and the pivots he made, since it involves going away from Western Digital and later coming back into the company. Many of us have likely had circumstances where we thought we had a good career going with a firm, and then for whatever reason things turned the other way. As you will see, Steve had this happen to him, and then he later came back and became CEO.

———

CHAPTER 9: STEVE MILLIGAN
(CEO WESTERN DIGITAL)

Steve Milligan's spartan office is evocative of his down-to-earth style as a business leader. Having his roots in the Midwest, you instantly get a firm handshake and a look straight in the eye upon meeting him. Indeed, he is a straight shooter when it comes to business dealings, namely he says what he means and you know that his word is his bond.

His career path provides a fascinating journey that illustrates the importance of handling pivots. Overall, his career was coming along just fine, and then a jolt out of the blue caused him to swerve. Turns out that in the act of swerving, he ultimately came back onto the road he was headed and ultimately successfully achieved the vaunted CEO seat at Western Digital.

Many readers might not be instantly familiar with Western Digital Corporation (WDC), since WDC is hot a household name per se. Their name recognition is akin to how most people were unfamiliar with the Intel company until Intel itself went on a bent of trying to brainwash us that "Intel inside" was crucial to the PC's that we buy.

Western Digital is a preeminent provider of disk drives and other storage devices. You likely have one or more of their products in an electronic device that you own or are using, perhaps in your DVR or your PC or maybe even in that cloud-based storage you are using, though you probably aren't aware that it was WDC that made your storage possible.

Comfortably ensconced in the Fortune 500, Western Digital has approximately 100,000 employees worldwide. Given the ongoing rise of demand for storage space by our digital age, WD prides itself on enabling consumers and businesses to readily store, collect, and utilize digital data and information. In this chapter, I will trace the path of Steve and offer some business pivot insights that can be gleaned from his business journey.

THE EARLY DAYS

Having grown-up in the Midwest, Steve opted to go to Ohio State University after graduating from high school. He majored in accounting. Now, you might find it unusual that someone that majored in accounting was eventually to become a CEO (since the path of accountant-to-CEO is pretty rare). And, perhaps equally seemingly unusual is that he rose to be the CEO at a high-tech firm. As you will see, the progression does make sense.

After graduating from Ohio State, he went to work at Price Waterhouse. That certainly is a relatively standard and prudent first step for someone in accounting. While at Price Waterhouse, he came to be one of the auditors for IBM's disk drive business. Doing so gave him a great deal of exposure to what makes a disk drive business work. He saw the numbers underlying the business. He learned the vocabulary of the disk drive business. He was savvy enough to pay attention beyond just the numbers and observe how the business was run and the trends taking place in the disk drive industry.

After a dozen years at Price Waterhouse, he went over to Dell. This kept him in the electronics industry and was a logical progression. Often, accounting grads will cut their teeth in a major accounting firm, and then their next step involves going to a firm that potentially was akin to clients when they were at the accounting firm.

His next move was into Western Digital, doing so in 2002. He had been in the finance area at Dell and so came into Western Digital as a vice president of finance. Fairly rapidly distinguishing himself, he rose quickly to the CFO slot. In 2007, he seemed successfully immersed at Western Digital, known for his astute financial perspective of the company and was considered a sound CFO. The industry knew him and the market watchers knew him. He was considered universally as trustworthy, factual, and commanding of where the company was and where it was going.

JOLT TO THE CAREER

Like many things in life, the road ahead will sometimes have potholes or obstructions that suddenly appear around the bend, often not seen until the curve itself is traversed. Another executive at Western Digital moved into the CEO slot in 2007. As often happens when there is a new CEO in a company, the newly anointed CEO in this instance had other preferences for some of the executive slots, and for the CFO slot he asked Steve to step aside.

You can imagine the shocking impact this might have. Should he remain in the same industry or try to shift to another industry? Should he reassess his career direction? Should he maybe aim to work at a smaller company, one with upside potential, or continue at a larger sized firm?

There was also the quandary that there were really only three major disk drive makers at the time, WDC, Seagate and Toshiba. So the choices for him in terms of staying in his industry was either go to one of the other two majors, or find something smaller.

Going to one of the other majors though would be tough because top executive positions don't just appear when you want them to. It would likely be a wait to hope that a slot would open and that he would be chosen versus say an internal candidate. He conferred with his wife, family, friends, and colleagues, trying to ascertain what his next step should be.

A DICEY MOVE THAT SEEMED WORTHWHILE

It turns out that WDC had previously been exploring potential acquisition targets in their industry, one of them being Hitachi Global Storage Technologies (HGST). HGST has been a marriage between IBM and Hitachi of their storage technology business units. HGST was in pretty bad shape in 2007. When first created in 2003, the share price was around $25 a share, and by 2005 it had risen to nearly $40 per share. But, after 2005, the stock tanked. By 2007 it was pretty much flat lining at near 0.

Would you be willing to go into a company that you knew was hemorrhaging? He had been a successful CFO at a company that was growing and rising, and so it might seem backward to now switch to a company that was drowning. Perhaps he would enter into the sinking ship and ride it to the bottom of the sea. How would that look if he then tried to get another job after HGST went completely under? He could get the blame for the demise of HGST, perhaps becoming an outcast of the disk drive industry.

Furthermore, if he then tried to step outside of the disk drive industry, he would be potentially held culpable for the HGST collapse and be poisoned by it. Plus, he might have consumed more years of his career in the disk drive industry, and so making it even harder to try and switch over to another industry. Of course, there was some chance that he might be able to help HGST get back on its feet. Those kinds of turnarounds are rare, and it is dicey to make a big bet at a crucial juncture in your career on such a hope.

Steve decided he would go ahead and aim at HGST, figuring that he could contribute towards a turnaround and with his in-depth knowledge of the industry he envisioned that HGST could be doing well, if it was willing to transform. He was willing to give it his all.

MAKING THE PIVOT

Coming on-board to HGST as the CFO in 2007, he immediately got to work. He traveled extensively, worked long hours, and had to sacrifice a lot of time and attention away from his family. This would be similar to doing a start-up, though at least a start-up usually begins fresh and there is enthusiasm for what might someday come to fruition. Trying to turnaround a company is harder in that the company already feels beat down. It can be difficult to rally the troops when they already feel so under trodden.

Wasting no time, Steve and his fellow executives at HGST proceeded to do a large-scale footprint consolidation. They also bumped up their investment and attention to R&D, which for a disk storage business is a true make-or-break (everyone wants the latest in disk storage technology, and if you can't offer it then they will find someone else that can).

By 2009, Steve had been named president of HGST. The company was triaging their financial circumstances and undergoing rapid and significant management and organization changes. Steve was seen as vital to the turnaround. After rebranding and shifting toward being a market maker, the share price began crawling upward, reaching about $10-$20 per share by 2010-2011, pushing up toward the $30s as 2011 emerged. This was a turnaround in record time. Steve had helped to orchestrate a companywide transformation in just two years. An amazing and remarkable feat. Well worth noticing.

ACQUISITION TARGET

Noticed indeed it was. HGST had become such an incredible turnaround that suitors to buy it began to appear. Sure enough, one of those suitors was Western Digital. After various negotiations, WDC acquired HGST for $50 a share in 2011. The acquisition was formally completed by March 2012.

BECOMING THE CEO

Shortly thereafter, in January 2013, the existing CEO at WDC retired (the same one that had been appointed CEO in 2007), and it was announced that Steve would become the new CEO of the now combined WDC and HGST.

The marketplace liked this choice and knew that Steve had the industry experience for the job. He had been considered a leader on cost-optimized platforms and knew WDC inside and out. Besides undertaking his duties as CEO, he also serves on the board of directors for Ross Stores, Inc., and manages to find time to support Ohio State, his beloved Alma mater.

BUSINESS LEADERSHIP LESSONS

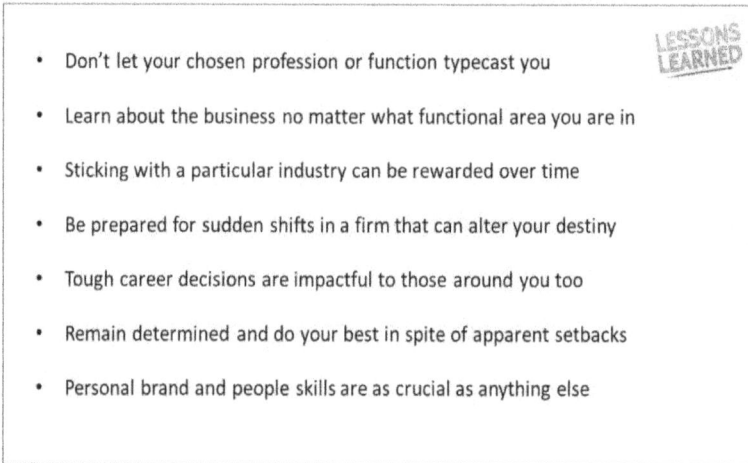

In exploring Steve's journey, there are some insightful business leadership lessons to consider. Take a look at Figure 1.

Business Leadership Lessons

- Don't let your chosen profession or function typecast you

- Learn about the business no matter what functional area you are in

- Sticking with a particular industry can be rewarded over time

- Be prepared for sudden shifts in a firm that can alter your destiny

- Tough career decisions are impactful to those around you too

- Remain determined and do your best in spite of apparent setbacks

- Personal brand and people skills are as crucial as anything else

LESSONS LEARNED

Figure 1: Eliot - Lessons gleaned from the career journey of Steve Milligan

1) Don't let your chosen profession or function typecast you

Even though Steve started out as essentially "an accountant" and though (without wanting to make any jokes about accountants) that's a perfectly fine profession, you just don't see many accountants that rise up to become a CEO.

That being said, you do see a lot of CFO's that make the jump to CEO. Steve was able to shift outside of the accounting branding and make his way up the finance ladder. A wise choice.

2) Learn about the business no matter what functional area you are in

A so-called "bean counter" (that's a derogatory term for accountants and sometimes even finance professionals), can become so enamored of the numbers and figures that they lose sight of what the business is all about.

Some even don't really learn anything about the business at all. Steve was someone that sought to learn the ins and outs of the business. He not only had command of the numbers but also understood what made the business tick.

3) *Sticking with a particular industry can be rewarded over time*

It used to be somewhat common that you would stick with your profession more so than stick with a particular industry. In other words, if you were an accountant, you would be able to go to any firm in any industry and be an accountant there. Gradually, business has shifted such that now for most professions the notion is that you need to know the particulars of a specific industry.

For example, if you are in the entertainment industry, the accounting practices are so arcane and specialized that you need to know those specifics to do well in that industry. Likewise for say oil and gas, or for banking, and so on. In that sense, you need nowadays to establish yourself in a specific industry and then ride forward with that chosen industry.

This can be a daunting choice since if you pick an industry that ultimately had dead-ends then you are stuck. You can try to switch to another industry, but you then are behind everyone else that already has years of intense experience in that industry. Steve opted to make a bet that he would stick with the disk drive storage industry. For him, this bet worked out. That industry has continued to do well over the years.

4) *Be prepared for sudden shifts in a firm that can alter your destiny*

Steve was confronted with the same nightmare possibility that we all face. He had been in a company and done his job. He had done his job well, in fact exemplary performance. It is easy to think and assume that your hard work in building up goodwill in a company will be rewarded by longevity at that firm. Then, suddenly, a change can alter that whole notion.

A new CEO comes in, such as in the case of what happened to Steve. Or, maybe a firm gets acquired and the acquiring firm guts the executive team of the acquired firm. And so on. The bottom-line is that for today's careers, you need to be resilient and be prepared for a shocker that knocks you out of your comfort zone and throws you for a loop.

5) *Tough career decisions are impactful to those around you too*

I am guessing we all realize that whenever a big career choice needs to be made that it is likely to impact not just that particular person, but also impact those around you. Your spouse or other partner. Your children.

Your friends. Your colleagues. All kinds of stakeholders that are part of your network are going to be impacted by whatever impacts your career path.

Steve had some quite tough and serious conversations with those around him, seeking their counsel and also trying to gauge the impacts that whatever choice he made would have on them too.

6) *Remain determined and do your best in spite of apparent setbacks*

Any kind of career setback or pivot point can be upsetting. The shock of the setback can lead one to becoming despondent. Do you not have what it takes to succeed? Are you a failure? Can you get back up on your feet? It is hard to contend with. Steve demonstrated his determination to continue moving forward in his career.

He even went perhaps the harder route of opting to take on a turnaround situation. As is evident, his raw determination and persistence, along with a vision of what the future could be, played a crucial role in his getting back into the game and showing his muster.

7) *Personal brand and people skills are as crucial as anything else*

Most accountants are typified as numbers oriented and not people oriented. They are considered by some to be rude when it comes to interpersonal skills, almost say Spock-like in being logical and maybe abrasive to some. Though Steve is a quite modest person when you meet him, it is immediately evident that he is able to create warmth with other people and he would likely downplay how adept he is at being personable. Steve had over many years been able to create a personal brand that helped him carry the day throughout his career.

His people skills gained the trust and support that was needed for the turnaround at HGST. Those same skills still to this day are crucial in his day-to-day role as CEO. Keep in mind that for whatever profession or functional area you select and pursue, in the end the business world consists of people interacting with people. You need to hone your people skills as much as and maybe even more so than any particular functional skills.

.

CHAPTER 10

CHRIS UNDERWOOD
(CEO YOUNG'S MARKET)

CHAPTER 10

CHRIS UNDERWOOD
(CEO YOUNG'S MARKET)

PREFACE

Do you sometimes find yourself having a glass of Jack Daniels or a fine selection from Sutter Home? If so, you might not realize that Young's Market Company might have had a role in getting that beverage to you. As one of America's largest privately held firms, they are a kind of middleman, serving as a major wholesaler and distributor of wines, spirits, and other select beverages. Focusing on the western part of the United States, they are especially recognizable by their red colored trucks. Founded in 1888, they are one of the oldest continuously running companies in the US.

They are a family owned business. As you will see in this chapter, Chris Underwood is the CEO and has focused his business career at Young's Market. Following in the footsteps of his father, Vern, whom previously was CEO and now serves as Chairman of the Board of Young's Holdings, parent company of Young's Market, Chris has not only kept the legacy going but also strives to further extend the firm and decidedly keep the company at the forefront of its industry. Chris was a top-rated volleyball player in his youth, and today often uses a sports analogy when discussing his business leadership style and approach. I've found that when discussing business pivots that a sports analogy can be instructive and instrumental to readily exploring the nature and impacts of doing a business pivot.

———

CHAPTER 10: CHRIS UNDERWOOD
(YOUNG'S MARKET)

Towering at 6 feet 5 inches in height, meeting Chris Underwood, CEO of Young's Market Company, can at first be daunting. He maintains his trim figure that gained him fame as a top volleyball player in high school and college. A friendly handshake and a hearty hello though immediately puts you at ease.

As CEO of one of America's largest privately held companies as listed on the Forbes 200 List, he oversees a $3.2 billion dollar firm that began in 1888. Known more so in the Western part of the United States, they distribute wine and spirits to states such as California, Oregon, Alaska, Washington, Montana, Utah, Arizona, Idaho, and other locales.

You might be more familiar with the brands of alcoholic beverages that they distribute, including notables such as Jack Daniels, Fireball, Cakebread Cellers, and Sutter Home. For those of you that have seen their famous red trucks on the road, you have perhaps been side-by-side with one of those trucks and noticed the emblazoned name of Young's Market on the side of the truck.

Young's Market is a privately owned firm and Chris follows in his father's footsteps as the CEO now of the company. As the fifth generation tapped to run the firm, Chris feels directly the enormous weight of upholding the tradition of the company, while simultaneously ensuring that the enterprise continues to flourish and adapt as society and markets change. The Underwood family bought out the other shareholders in 1990, and opted to focus on wine and spirits, nixing other aspects of the firm that included food, meat, and gourmet.

Having become the President and COO of the firm in 2007, Chris later achieved the position of CEO in 2011. He has devoted his career to the company and even worked there during his summers while in high school and college. Young's Market is a great passion for him.

In this chapter, I take a look at various business lessons to be learned in the business career of Chris. Take a look at Figure 1 to see some of the highlighted aspects that I will be covering.

Business Leadership Lessons

- Avid and accomplished volleyball athlete in high school and college

- Applies sports insights to business leadership and guidance

- Being an owner's son had pluses and minuses, "owner's boy" aspects

- Competitors also reacted, aiming to "kick his butt"

- Challenge of uniting the firm as one holistic company

- Build the brands they distribute versus build their own brand per se

- The share-of-stomach when selling wine and spirits

- Family based firm and industry changes in an age of disintermediation

Figure 1: Eliot - Lessons gleaned from the career journey of Chris Underwood

SPORTS AS A METAPHOR OF BUSINESS

Chris was an outstanding athlete in high school and college. His record of accomplishments in volleyball reads like a who's who of awards and successes. Volleyball Monthly magazine named him part of the "Fab 50" of top volleyball players. He was considered a major force for Team USA, and competed in the Pan American Games and the World League. His kill shots were lethal and his opponents cowered as the volleyball rocketed at them. In fact, he earned the nickname of "Thunderwood" as a result of his thunderous like shots and as a mash-up with his last name.

A sports background can be instrumental in ultimately shaping a leader and business manager. In Chris's case, he attributes much of his belief in working as a team and ensuring team chemistry in business as based on his experiences growing up in sports. He saw first-hand during his volleyball days that if the team did not work together, in unison, and even if one member was off-target, the results could not only be less than optimal but could be even much worse.

In the sense of sports analogies, when discussing business pivots I often find it helpful to characterize a business pivot as analogous to pivoting in sports. For example, a volleyball player needs to be able to pivot at the right time to get to the ball. Arriving late means that you'll miss being able to keep the ball in play. Making not enough of a pivot means that you might only partially strike the ball and fail to get it where it needs to go. This is a literal way of understanding the notion of pivoting. An entire volleyball team might also need to pivot, shifting how they are competing and the strategies they are using. This is another analogous use of pivoting, though one of a more abstract level than the portrayal of a player that physically is pivoting.

Let's return back to Chris. Today, as CEO, he strives to gain team cohesion, similar to what he had seen as successful in sports. The company fosters team bonding among the employees. This is undertaken at work and outside of work too, extending the family notion of the business to include the families of the employees.

Chris sees himself now in a coaching role. Similar to some of the great volleyball coaches that he once had guide him, he today tries to provide that same kind of coaching to his employees. As he says, he tirelessly watches their backs. The use of sports as a means of guiding a business philosophy and day-to-day practice is ingrained in Chris. Besides shaping his executive demeanor and character, it also is used to inspire his employees.

By the use of sports related vocabulary and analogies, executives are often able to communicate with their employees in a manner that is especially inspirational. Rallying the troops can be easier when sprinkling sports terminology into your business phrasing and urging them to win one for the Gipper, so to speak (the famous line said to Knute Rockne, football coach of Notre Dame).

GROWING UP IN THE BUSINESS

Chris started working at Young's Market during his summers in high school and then continued during his summers while in college. He had an opportunity to work a wide range of jobs, including working in the warehouses and at all levels of the firm. This grounding provided an understanding at the foot soldier level of what the firm does. He also came to see how hard working the employees were. Today, as CEO, he is able to relate to all levels of the firm by his having been in their shoes at one point during his summer work efforts.

You might at first assume that being the owner's son made everything rosy. Turns out there were both pluses and minuses associated with being considered the "owner's boy" as his calling card. Some of his fellow employees tried to treat him differently, at times shielding from him the true aspects of the work or hesitant to reveal any difficulties or concerns.

Chris realized that without knowing the full extent of what the work was like, he would potentially get a partial and perhaps false impression of the realities of the firm. He found himself having to try and break through that filtering and screening, doing so in a gentle way, wanting to foster relationships and build a rapport that would be long lasting since he knew that his future would depend upon it at the firm.

He also found himself sometimes as the recipient of practical jokes. Seasoned workers sometimes would have him do something at their instruction that would be silly to do, but that seemed like he should do as based on their urging. Or, they would set him up in a circumstance where he would get stuck as to what to do next.

He could have reacted like a classical owner's son and exploded, being upset and angry to these gestures, but instead he opted to take the good natured jabbing in stride. This gained a positive reputation for him among the employees. He demonstrated that he could be a normal everyday person and that he realized his special status, but that in spite of his special status that he was there to learn the business and be an ally of the employees.

Even his managers often were worried about providing any feedback to him. They might have assumed that if they were to criticize his actions or offer recommendations to him about his budding business experiences that they would get in trouble. You can imagine that some of them figured that he would walk straight to his father as CEO and possibly complain or point them out for retribution.

Chris attempted to put his managers at ease that he did seek their feedback. He wanted them to showcase how to manage, which he then could learn from. He wanted to get their insights about how he could improve. Over time, due to his adaptation, he gained respect from the employees and managers of the firm, building up goodwill that to this day aids him in his efforts.

THE MERCHANDISING JOB

At one point, he worked in an entry level position in merchandising at the firm. This consisted of getting up at 4:00 a.m. and going out to businesses where Young's Market distributes their goods, including grocery stores, liquor stores, and the like. He wanted to show that he could do the job and was determined to do the best that he could in it. This could be contrasted to the again classical owner's son perspective, whereby an owner's son might normally think "why should I bust myself when I can just lazily do the job" kind of thinking.

He discovered that the competition, once they realized who he was, opted to play hardball with him. They purposely put some of their best people against him and put the squeeze on clients that he was assigned. They were determined to "kick his butt."

Notice that this was more pronounced than had it been any other "typical" employee in the merchandising role. In that sense, he had it tougher doing that job since the competition was gunning for him specifically. Fortunately, with hard work, and with his fellow work teammates also supporting him, he was able to do well in the job. It left a strong impression on him and made him a better leader because of the experience.

As one of the most respected wholesale distributors of alcoholic beverages in the United States, Chris was able to learn the business from the ground up. Carrying over 3,700 brands and on the order of about 14,000 SKUs, he now oversees approximately 3,500 employees. Yet, the firm is relatively unknown to most consumers.

STRATEGIC PERSPECTIVE

Chris acknowledges freely that the firm is often not known to consumers, and indeed he would say that this is by design in that they actually seek to build the brands that they distribute, rather than their own brand. They essentially rent the product that they are selling. They don't own what they sell. They have no rights as to what they put onto their trucks.

And, the firm had traditionally been known by other names in many of the states that they operate in, operating in businesses that Young's Market bought or in divisions that were setup to have their own distinct identity in the local markets. Chris is today leveraging the long-term relationships that they have with their suppliers, often dating back to the days of prohibition, and evolving those relationships in today's world. He is seeking to unite the company as one.

In his industry, the metric of share-of-stomach is used to consider how well a firm is doing. They provide three key products, beer, wine, and spirits. Wine continues to be doing well and has seen an upswing in popularity. Consumers are increasingly educated about wines and their wine selections. Meanwhile, retailers and producers seek higher margins in the alcoholic beverages that they are selling.

As a kind of middle man in their distribution role, Young's Market gets faced with tight margins, and the slightest hiccup in delivering the product can harm their relationship with the retailers and the producers. Plus, the major producers have tended to consolidate over the years, giving them added leverage.

At the same time, the distributors also consolidated, providing somewhat a matching strength to the producer's consolidations. Unlike say bottled water or facial tissues, the industry is one dominated by national brands and there has not been much of an influx of private labels. Consumers seem to exhibit ardent brand loyalty when it comes to wine and spirits. They have a pre-dispositional commitment to a chosen brand.
It's what keeps the industry going.

DISINTERMEDIATION

Some analysts have suggested that the industry will undergo radical changes as the direct-to-consumer market increases and brick-and-mortar stores fade away. This would of course have a tremendous adverse impact on the business of Young's Market as it stands today. Chris is quick to point out that they aren't selling books.

In other words, they are selling a very special kind of product. By selling alcoholic beverages, they and the industry and consumers are all bound by rather stringent regulations. The minimum age for purchase in the United States is the age of 21. Imagine if FedEx drivers had to check ID when they deliver a package of alcohol to the door of a consumer. Is that a fake mustache or a real one? Figuring out how to properly control and abide by the regulations of these products is a crucial element toward reshaping how the product is sold.

The idea of drones flying such beverages to consumer's homes seems equally farfetched. The laws about alcohol were put in place as a protective mechanism. And as an important means of collecting taxes. The three tiered system was put in place for a reason. This structure is relatively solidified and not easily disturbed or disrupted. Presumably, significant changes in regulations at the federal and state levels would be needed to upset the status quo.

Overall, disintermediation does not seem to be on the horizon for their industry. That being said, we have of course seen disintermediation radically shake-up travel agencies, an industry which was once huge and today barely hangs on. Bookstores are another industry shaken at the roots by disintermediation. Uber and other car riding firms have shaken up the taxi cab and limo industry. Hotels are being shaken by Airbnb and similar firms.

All of this is to suggest that some form of shake-up might well occur in the alcoholic beverages industry too. If regulations and practices shift, Chris indicates they are ready to pivot as needed. He certainly keeps his eyes wide open and they are watching and anticipating what might happen next. Just like he would watch for the volleyball that might come smashing over the net at him, he stands tall today as CEO of Young's Market and keeps on his toes for whatever might come next in his industry.

So, the next time that you see one of their signature red trucks on the highways, it might make you think about Chris, and even more so, from his perspective, remind you to perhaps seek to enjoy one of the many beverage products that they distribute.

.

CHAPTER 11

FRANK GEHRY

(RENOWNED ARCHITECT)

CHAPTER 11

FRANK GEHRY
(RENOWNED ARCHITECT)

PREFACE

If you are an admirer of architecture, you might be familiar with some notable buildings such as the Walt Disney Concert Hall in Los Angeles, the Guggenheim Museum Bilbao in Spain, the Dancing House in Prague, or the Louis Vuitton Foundation building in Paris. What do all of these have in common? They all have Frank Gehry, renowned architect, as their mastermind, maestro, and designer extraordinaire. *Vanity Fair* magazine said he is one of the important architects of our age, and he has received countless medals and honors for his architectural work, including the prestigious Pritzker Prize amongst other awards.

You might not know that Frank is also a businessman. He started an architectural firm in 1967 that then later pivoted into becoming Gehry Partners in 2001. Rather than tolling away in someone else's architectural firm, Frank opted to put out his own shingle, so to speak. He runs the business while also doing his architecture. This duality of being both architect and business person can be quite stressful. Some would prefer to be one or the other, but not both at the same time. In this chapter, we take a look at the various business pivots that Frank has undergone. He is a dynamo, even now when presumably he should be retired and taking it easy.

———

CHAPTER 11: FRANK GEHRY
(RENOWNED ARCHITECT)

Though nearing the age of 90, Frank Gehry is still the same spirited iconoclast that he has always been and that is evidenced in his linage of extraordinary architectural designs. In talking with him, you are instantly aware of his modesty, which is surprising given his incredible accomplishments and acclaim. Yet, beneath the modesty sits a strong willed and adamant architect and business man that knows what he likes and what he does not like. Don't let the modesty lull you into thinking he is a wallflower, instead he has the inner strength of an ox.

When asked what he does, he politely says he's an architect, and after a moment of reflection he adds that he likes to do buildings. And buildings he does. On Wikipedia, they devote an entire lengthy page to just listing his buildings alone, and the magazine Architectural Digest has paid homage to his works by providing a compilation of his most striking designs.

Considered one of the most outstanding architects of our times, his business career has shaped the world of architecture forever and buildings of all sizes and types are often designed with the Gehry touch in mind.

Controversy has been both his boon and his adversary. There are some that love his work and praise every inch. Meanwhile, there are others that deride his work and accuse him of being a "starchitect," which is a blanket term for architects that do designs that are intended to gain their own notoriety and that the buildings so guided are considered overly flashy and like something one would do to fulfill the whims of a movie star.

Shrugging off the derisive title, Frank knows that not everyone will like his work. Indeed, he is in a fortunate position that unless a prospective client expresses overtly that they want a "Gehry design" then he won't take them on as a client.

His reputation and brand precede him, providing a form of self-selection in that companies wanting to use his architectural services already know what they are going to get. A few firms sometimes approach his firm based on simply the prominence of his name, but by-and-large they should already be aware of what they are getting themselves into as a result of the now famous instantiations of Frank's vision and approach.

The firm that he founded in 1962, Gehry Partners, LLP, continues to grow and flourish. Numbering around 150 employees, Frank is not only an architect but also essentially a CEO. The ability to express himself architecturally is dependent upon being able to run a business that entails doing architectural work for companies. He is a craftsman at heart, and a business man in wanting to make sure that he and his partners can continue to keep the engine running of designing buildings again and again. Like any such business, they are at the whim of the flow of projects, which come and go, and a constant effort is required to fill the pipeline with new work to be done.

In this chapter, I trace his career and provide highlights that illustrate some of the key business pivots that led to his amazing success. Take a look at Figure 1 to see an indication of the major points and insights that will be covered.

Business Leadership Lessons

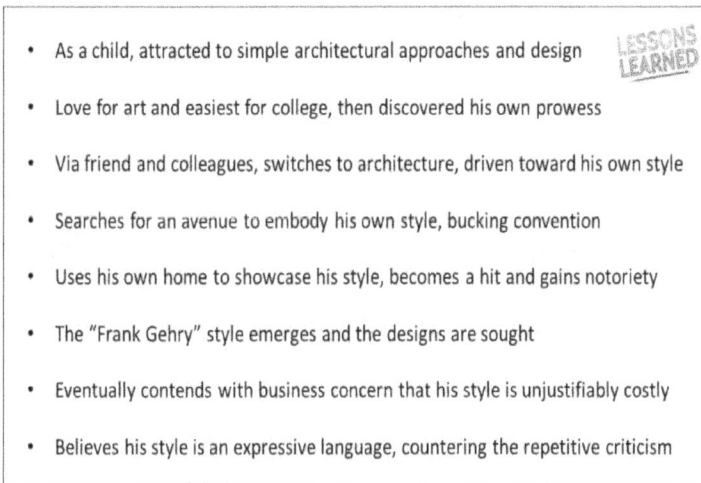

- As a child, attracted to simple architectural approaches and design

- Love for art and easiest for college, then discovered his own prowess

- Via friend and colleagues, switches to architecture, driven toward his own style

- Searches for an avenue to embody his own style, bucking convention

- Uses his own home to showcase his style, becomes a hit and gains notoriety

- The "Frank Gehry" style emerges and the designs are sought

- Eventually contends with business concern that his style is unjustifiably costly

- Believes his style is an expressive language, countering the repetitive criticism

Figure 1: Eliot - Lessons gleaned from the career journey of Frank Gehry

THE BEGINNING

Frank was born as Frank Goldberg, later changing his last name due to concerns about how he (and at the urging of his first wife) and his work might be perceived simply due to a last name that denoted his religious beliefs (his father was born to Russian Jewish parents and his mother to Polish Jewish parents).

He purposely changed his name to Gehry, doing so to keep the same initials and so that the flow of his signature would look roughly equivalent to his original last name. In that sense, he has been throughout his life faced with discriminatory facets that have shaped not only his career but one could say even his architecture. Some see him as a Woody Allen like figure, creating his work tirelessly and with exceedingly high quality, and yet also with an edge and a message based on his life and upbringing.

He was born and raised in Toronto. During his childhood, there were four notable aspects that one could say were precursors to what his future was to eventually become.

First, his grandmother would regularly come over to see him when he was young and would bring along a bag filled with scrap pieces of wood that she got at a local woodshop. He recalls that he would play with these wood scraps for hours on end. He made imaginary buildings, bridges, and even tried to create entire cities from whatever odds and ends that he had to play with.

To be clear, this was not at the time anything notable per se. It wasn't as though he or his parents somehow saw a flash of the future and knew that he would become an architect. In looking back and using hindsight, Frank realized later on that doing architectural kinds of tasks was something that he happened to enjoy as a child. As will be seen in this analysis of his career, it is the same interest and passion that subtly subsequently drove him toward the field of architecture.

Second, his grandmother would occasionally bring over live fish, specifically carp, used to make a special dish for dinner. She would place the fish into the bathtub, filled with water, in order to keep them going until the dinner time cooking was to begin. Frank would sit outside the tub and watch the fish swimming back and forth. Mesmerized by the movement, he found it visually appealing.

If you take a look at the overall style of Frank's architecture, you will see that it has a flowing series of shapes. Some say they look like waves. Using hindsight, Frank suggests that the observing of the moving fish were instrumental to his later attraction to and desire to design buildings with the same kind of shape. In fact, one architectural philosophy that he relishes is the idea that buildings should not look as though they are completed per se, but instead seem to be always unfinished and unending. This is a particular school of architectural belief. The movement of fish swimming back and forth in a tub, creating a kind of infinite looping effect, can be considered the same underpinning for much of Frank's architectural masterpieces.

Third, while in high school, Frank would wander over to the nearby University of Toronto to attend the Friday night lecture series. Some at the time thought it strange that a young man age 17 would spend his Friday evenings in such pursuits, and instead should be out partying and such. His intellectual curiosity was of such a draw that for at least some Friday nights he relished going to the lectures. At one of the lectures, he happened to hear Alvar Aalto, a famous architect from Helsinki.

Alvar described architecture in a way that resonated with Frank. Indeed,

Alvar was not only an architect but also a sculptor and a painter, and brought along a chair that reflected his approach to combining art with furniture. The unusual shape of the chair caught Frank's attention. This led him to do some experimentation with plywood and chairs, bending familiar shapes to create a strikingly new looking type of chair.

Fourth, when nearing the completion of high school, Frank was encouraged to consider what vocation he might pursue after high school. In looking at a shelf filled with books on various vocations, he recalls looking at several and in particular one that was on architecture.

Now, at this point in the telling of his upbringing, you might be assuming that he saw the vocational book on architecture and that when combined with his earlier joy of playing with wood scraps and with the watching of the movement of fish and with the inspiration by Alvar that he must have at that moment realized that architecture was his fate.

Well, you'd be wrong.

The vocational book depicted the field of architecture by showing little cottages, made of stone and nestled in an English countryside. This was not the architecture that Frank was interested in. If the vocational book was saying that's what an architect does, he wanted nothing to do with it. So, he put down the vocational book and made a mental note, don't become an architect.

There is a vital lesson hidden in this turn of events. Children can be led, intentionally or accidentally, away from or toward a particular profession or career based on what they come across during their childhood. This is maybe a common sense aspect that seems obvious, but it is perhaps not quite so apparent and certainly not well considered.

If a child is shown that a particular profession seems a kilter, regardless of whether that is the truth about that profession or not, it can become a lasting impression. Imagine that you are aiming to go to a faraway location and that at the start of your trip you are aimed off by even just a few degrees. The few degrees at the start become magnified over time and you might not ever reach that final destination accordingly.

It is for these reasons that making sure that high school children especially are made aware of various professions, and a realistic understanding of those professions, allows them to have a better chance at aiming toward a profession that is a fit for their interests and abilities.

Back to Frank, you might be wondering that if he realized upon seeing the vocational book that architecture was not for him, how did he eventually come back to architecture? Let's continue the career analysis to see how this occurred.

COLLEGE DAYS

Frank's father had been abusive toward him throughout his upbringing. When in high school, Frank one day struck back at his father. After hitting his father, Frank ran frantically and fearfully out of the house, unsure of what would next happen. When Frank returned home, he discovered that his father had suffered a heart attack and then was hospitalized. This weighed on Frank as to whether he had caused his father to have the heart attack and it became an added nightmare to some of the familial aspects of his upbringing.

The doctors eventually advised his father that he needed to find a climate that would be more conducive to his health conditions, and so the family immigrated to the United States, opting to come to the Los Angeles area. To help ends meet, Frank became a truck driver delivering breakfast nooks. Meanwhile, he started taking college classes at the Los Angeles City College, a community college program, and took the traditional general education courses such as history, literature, and the like.

He took a course in Perspective and got an F. This was irksome to Frank and so he repeated the course and earned an A the second time around. This demonstrated his determination to succeed and also that he learned that he should not take lightly his courses, which he had been somewhat inclined to do for the Perspective class since he felt that he already pretty much knew what was being covered.

For various personal reasons and in order to aim toward a Bachelor's degree, he enrolled at the University of Southern California. He once again started by taking more of the needed general education classes, earning mainly C's and D's.

He took Art Appreciation and earned a B, which was the best grade yet that he had received at USC and encouraged him to consider that perhaps art was his forte. He then declared his major as Fine Arts, partially due to his interest, partially due to his grades, and partially due to the requirements for entry into the major were the least of any other major that he thought he might pursue and the most likely that he would get admitted into.

An important pivotal moment occurred when he opted to take a Ceramics class. The professor took a liking to Frank and was impressed with Frank's skills. At one point, Frank made a beautiful ceramic pot, and upon explaining how it came out so well, Frank told the professor that it was the result of the material and the kiln. The professor corrected Frank and emphasized that it was him, it was Frank, and that it was the mastery of the artistry that led to the successful end result.

This had a long lasting impact on Frank. As mentioned earlier, he is a modest person and also one that has a tendency to second guess his own abilities. Having a professor express such confidence in him and that he should believe in himself was a factor that led Frank to later on believe that he could accomplish things that otherwise he would have doubted he could do. The importance of having a mentor or a respected figure that can recognize talent and also make someone aware of that talent cannot be overstated.

TURN TOWARD ARCHITECTURE

While in college, Frank met a young budding architect from Montreal. The two became fast friends. The friend was working for Lloyd Wright, son of the famous architect Frank Lloyd Wright. Frank and his friend decided to start studying houses in Los Angeles, and would drive all around town trying to see different architectural styles. His friend introduced him to a well-known architectural photographer, which then plugged Frank into the larger community of architects throughout the Los Angeles area and beyond.

Frank's ceramics professor could see that Frank was enchanted by architecture. With his professor's blessing, Frank switched his major to architecture. The university admitted him into the major as a second year student rather than what would have been his first year in the major. To this day, Frank is not sure how this happened but believes that his ceramics professor helped pull those strings, and indeed even the paying of his tuition was somehow he believes undertaken by the professor (since Frank and his family could not have afforded the full-time tuition).

The USC architecture degree was a five year program, and he was lucky that he landed into the USC program which was considered the best in the area at the time, attracting many of the greats of architecture and those too that eventually became known in architecture. This occurred just after World War II, and so there were lots of people settling into the Southern California area and it created a boon to the area and also the universities in the area.

Housing was being created in Southern California at a frenetic pace to keep up with the population explosion. The housing growth fueled the building industry, which fueled the architecture business in Southern California, which fueled the university programs in architecture. It was a kind of grand convergence that Frank happened to perchance be in the midst of.

Right place at the right time. Not all was necessarily rosy. In his second semester as an architecture major, one of his professors told him he would never make it as an architect. This shaped his architectural approach and philosophy, actually emboldening him, as explained next.

At the time, most of the architects in Southern California were men, and they had tended to serve in WWII, and had been in the Pacific Region. After having seen the homes and buildings of Japan, they were impressed by the architecture and so they tended to carry that same perspective into the homes and buildings they were architecting in Southern California during that time period.

This became somewhat known as the minimalist approach to architecture, which also carried over into art at the time too. Frank was not a believer in this approach. He quickly learned that there were particular philosophies in architecture and that depending upon whom you preferred, you would either be considered embraced if you bought into the particular philosophy or be considered an outcast by that philosophy if you were unwilling to embrace it.

His willingness to go against the tide was demonstrated in other ways too. He joined the Alpha Epsilon Pi fraternity and was later asked to leave when he tried to put forth a pledge that was Black (this occurring during the time when such an idea was nearly unthinkable).

POST-COLLEGE EFFORTS

Frank completed his architecture college degree in 1954. He was married and had a child, and so he realized that he needed to be gainfully employed to support his budding family. At one point, he applied to be an apprentice architect at a firm that was led by a famous architect. The interview with the famous architect went seemingly quite well. The famous architect asked Frank if he could start on Monday. Why, yes, of course, Frank answered, excited at the success of the interview and that he would start the job right away.

Frank worked up the courage to ask what the starting salary would be. The famous architect looked at Frank and then calmly said that when Frank showed-up for work on Monday that he would be told then what the fee was. In other words, Frank would need to pay to be an apprentice architect there, rather than getting paid. This smacked Frank of being elitist and was the type of behavior that he abhorred and had seen time and again among several of the notable architects that he had come in contact with. He left the office and never returned to even turn down the job.

Frank then had various aspects occur including that he served in the US Army. After coming out of the service, he thought that he might enhance his capabilities as an architect by going to the Harvard Graduate School of Design. Turns out this was not what he had hoped it would be. The focus was mainly on city planning, and he also personally harbored a belief in socially responsible design that he thought was not being expressed there. He was considered an outcast, and he decided to come back to Los Angeles with his family.

He went to work as an architect for a firm that he had earlier been an apprentice while going to USC. He got his first break by being asked to design a home with the help of a friend and former classmate, doing so for a large cabin to be built in the mountains of Idyllwild in California. He soon began to question though that he might be embarking on a career of designing homes for wealthy people, which was not in keeping with his desires for doing something for society of a wider scope and impact.

He moved to Paris for a year to see what else he might do and worked at an architectural firm there. He then came back to Los Angeles, and in 1962 formed the partnership which he still runs today.

HIS OWN HOUSE AS HIS BRAND

His work as an architect was gradually becoming established but it was the design of his own home that ultimately helped spark interest in his style. Moving from Los Angeles to nearby Santa Monica, he bought a house in Santa Monica that had been built in the 1920's and had been relocated to the spot that it still resides at today. Nestled in a middle class neighborhood, most of the homes had a similar look-and-feel, offering a traditional and to Frank a bland sense of community and architecture.

He decided that he would re-design the house to be more of a standout. He wanted to keep most of the structure, and so would wrap around it an exterior exoskeleton, and still allow portions of the home to be seen. The house itself cost him $160,000 in 1977, which was a lot of money for him at the time, and he put down $40,000 which he had borrowed to even get the loan for the rest. Whatever he might want to do as a redesign would be severely limited because he had essentially no budget to work from.

He believed that architecture should not be diminished to simple and pure geometric forms (i.e., his rejection of minimalism), and the existing house blared minimalist. Taking various cheap and somewhat discarded materials that he was able to get from other work sites, he used corrugated aluminum, unpainted wood, and even chain-link fencing to create a façade surrounding his home.

In one sense, Frank was combining his love for art with his love for architecture. It was like some kind of Picasso painting but rendered as architecture on a limited budget. The home began to become the talk of the local architecture community. He then got coverage in the press and by a known architectural publication. Soon, people of all walks of life were driving over to Santa Monica to see his home.

What did his neighbors think? You might assume they were delighted to see such an expression of art and architecture.

Keep in mind that Frank was not well known at the time. And, at the time, his architectural approach was considered strange and unusual. Furthermore, the house which once blended into the block was now out of character with the neighborhood. Plus, strangers would drive up and down the street at all hours, wanting to see the house.

For some neighbors this was a complete nightmare. One neighbor across the street came to talk with Frank about the home. When complaining to Frank about how the re-designed house now looked, Frank pointed out that the man's own home had a car on blocks in the front yard and had two trailers sticking in the backyard that could be seen via the chain-link fence around the back of the property. To Frank, this was visually unappealing and a blight on the neighborhood. The man told Frank that is what the neighborhood consists of, and was normal there.

From Frank's viewpoint, his neighbors were living in an illusion. They were living in a messy world and refused to see it that way. His home sparked them to think about their own homes and he hoped would give them an opportunity to emerge from their illusion.

Some neighbors were worried that Frank's house would depress home values on the block. A neighbor said it looked like a Tijuana sausage factory. Some thought it looked unfinished and were concerned as to how long it was taking him to actually finish what he had started. There were complaints made to the mayor and the city.

In the end, Frank was able to hold his ground and keep the house as he had re-designed it, and it became a worldwide signature that helped propel him into the architectural world. To this day, many of his designed and built buildings are met with a similar reaction by those that don't know his style. The reaction is that his buildings seem to be more art than building, unfinished, and the shapes and look are considered bizarre for some.

ARCHITECTURE AS A BUSINESS

In his initial days, Frank tended to use everyday materials for his buildings. Some derided his style by calling it "Cheapskate Architecture." Once his style caught on, he then confronted a different concern, namely that if someone wanted to build say a large tower, the added cost to make it into a "Frank Gehry building" was actually very immense and did not particularly add to the structure of the building from a purely functional viewpoint. In other words, his art-like structure was an added cost that could not be justified as part of building a building for the sake of having a building.

For example, a museum that wants to attract patrons would see the value in the unusual design, since even though it increased the cost for building the museum it would then be noticeable and bring business to the museum. But if you were building a commercial tower, the builder and the banks loaning the money to make the building would have to ask whether the added cost of having the elaborate and wavy style of a Frank Gehry design was worth the added cost. Would businesses or consumers come to the building more so due to the design, or would the design not promote such an added value?

Frank still finds himself having to explain that the added cost is not as bad as one might think. He does this to avoid being so typified such that no business comes his direction, since potential builders might think that the likely cost of having an "original" Frank Gehry design would be astronomically expensive and don't even come to his firm for a quote.

Frank is also realistic too to know that what he can imagine must also ultimately be buildable. If he comes up with an incredibly creative design, but if it cannot be built in any practical sense, it does him no good to have come up with such an impractical design.

He often starts by taking a piece of paper and crumpling it up. From that starting point, he then begins to shape and reshape. There are some that call his approach "Action Architecture" since his structures suggest dynamic motion. This is a description that he enjoys and fits with his philosophy about architecture.

One accusation that is often made is that he has become repetitive, merely using the same style over and over again. Though he might have been original earlier, there are those that say he has become lazy and just repeats his prior success. To this criticism he becomes at times incensed and argues that such critics do not fully comprehend what he is doing. For Frank, his style is like a language, a new language, and each of his designs is a further utilization of that language.

Would you say that because one work of Shakespeare is written in a similar fashion as another that Shakespeare was lazy and merely copying himself? Frank would emphasize that the language he has created of this unfinished, wavy, action oriented style can be expressed in a multitude of ways in terms of being instantiated as a particular building, each being original in its own sake.

For those that don't see or comprehend the language, all of his buildings seem to blur together and are merely carbon copies. For those that grasp the nature and depth of the language, each design provides an intriguing new expression that shows the range and capability of the language. This kind of argument is difficult for some to come to grips with.

Many either just viscerally like the Frank Gehry style, or they don't. It is so evocative and immediately apparent that people react either with a love or hate kind of response, mixed in with a bit of curiosity as to why and what it all means.

THE FAME AND THE ACCOMPLISHMENTS

Frank has been able to dovetail art and architecture, and his contrarian views led him toward a style of architecture that gave him distinctiveness. This distinctness gradually brought fame and fortune. As a child, he was attracted to playing with wood scraps and exploring shapes and structures that would later become his signature approach. In college, he wandered somewhat aimlessly until happening upon a form of art that made him realize his potential.

He could have pursued an architectural career of a "me too" kind of style, adopting a popular style already in vogue. His personality and upbringing was part of the spark that drove him to seek something else, something more unique and noticeable.

His father had done many different jobs and tried many different businesses but had failed at them all. His father had repeatedly told Frank that Frank was an idealistic dreamer that would never amount to anything. In spite of his father's abuses, Frank to this day still wishes that his father could see what he has accomplished. Frank sincerely hopes that his style enriches people's lives and in some fashion will be to the betterment of society. This is what seems to continue to both haunt Frank and keep him vigorous even as he far exceeds any kind of retirement age.

CHAPTER 12

COLONEL SANDERS
(LUMINARY,
FOUNDER KFC)

CHAPTER 12

COLONEL SANDERS
(LUMINARY, FOUNDER KFC)

PREFACE

Colonel Sanders is more than a household name. His image and name have been likened to an icon, known worldwide, almost in the same way that Mickey Mouse represents Disney or the giant golden arches makes us think of McDonalds. Some are unsure whether there ever really was a Colonel Sanders (those perhaps of a younger generation). Some assume that the name Colonel Sanders is a made-up name, created just to push Kentucky Fried Chicken (KFC). I can say first-hand that he was a person, and that he was called the Colonel, as I was lucky enough to meet him, and then later on I did management consulting for KFC and got to know more about his history and the true story of his business accomplishments.

What makes his business path so interesting and useful is that it has numerous twists and turns. It shows that you need to be able to pivot. He kept pivoting his personal life and his business life. He pivoted his businesses. And most endearing, I would say, he opted to do a business pivot at a time of life when most people would have called it quits. His small chicken restaurant that had been sufficient to make a living was faced with a business hurdle at his retirement age. A new highway had been built that essentially bypassed his restaurant and so customers no longer came there. He decided to go on-the-road and sell his recipe and cooking innovation of chicken, doing so door-to-door of one restaurant after another. Via this means, he landed in a new business model, franchising his delicious chicken and launching the now behemoth of KFC.

CHAPTER 12: COLONEL SANDERS
(LUMINARY, FOUNDER KFC)

They called him the Colonel. I was lucky that when I was in my college days, I happened to meet Colonel Sanders, doing so at a community event where he came to promote his chicken restaurant chain called Kentucky Fried Chicken (ultimately to be renamed KFC, as will be discussed herein).

Years later, and after he had passed away, I did management consulting at KFC in Louisville, Kentucky at their corporate headquarters, and remembered back to when I had met the Colonel in-person. A KFC museum at the headquarters commemorates him and the history of the company (side note: make sure to go visit the KFC museum when you are in Louisville, it's worth a look see).

Today, his image continues to be used as the enduring brand symbol for KFC. In more recent times there have been attempts at having various actors portray him, of which some KFC diehards are exasperated and irked by these at times humorous or even denigrating portrayals. Either way you look at it, his image is known worldwide and is recognized by old and young alike.

Harland David Sanders had a lot of up's and down's in his life. Many might assume that he had early in his life launched and ran Kentucky Fried Chicken, and further assume that he was undoubtedly wealthy throughout his lifetime from the lucrative chain. The truth is actually quite afar of that common misconception.

Indeed, I often describe key aspects of his business career to highlight how sometimes you can strike out in life and yet come back, and furthermore that even when you get to a later age in life that you don't have to give up, encouraging us all to try and reboot our careers and still have room to accomplish great things.

That's in a nutshell the inspirational elements of Colonel Sanders and his business career path. In this chapter, I trace the details of his career and help illuminate the various business lessons and pivots that are tremendous lessons to be learned.

I know that some people might find his food to be "fast food" and decry the fatness it can imbue, but I suggest that you look beyond that dietary aspect and consider how he beat the odds to create a worldwide product and service that he started at an age when most people are retiring from their business careers.

As an aside, I am going to refer to him as "Colonel Sanders" throughout this blog, rather than using his actual name per se. I do this simply because we've all come to know him by that moniker and so it is a convenient way to refer to him. Take a look at Figure 1 to see an indication of some of the key business lessons revealed by the story of the Colonel.

BUSINESS LEADERSHIP LESSONS

- Cooking for the household at a young age (interest, passion)
- Raised in a strict fashion with intense sense of cleanliness
- Left home at young age, early drive of independence, spirit
- Various odd jobs, mercurial personality, demanding, determined
- Starts up a business, does well, starts another which flops but a worthy chance
- Ends-up running gas station and opts to prepare chicken meals on-the-side
- Economic conditions lead to focus on the restaurant aspects
- Late in life, his restaurant put out of business but he opts to try franchising
- Successfully leverages his skills and grows the franchisees, one at a time
- Ultimately sells KFC, remains as ambassador, new management spurs it further
- Management makes changes to lift KFC to next level of maturity and growth

LESSONS LEARNED

Figure 1: Eliot – Business leadership insights as gleaned from the career of Colonel Sanders

THE BEGINNING OF HARLAND SANDERS

Colonel Sanders was born in 1890, growing up in Indiana. His mother was a devout Christian and raised the Colonel in a very strict manner. This strictness included the avoidance of alcohol, tobacco, and gambling. This was significant for the Colonel and later on in life, during the KFC days, he continued to have a very strict view of what he expected of his chicken business. It seemed that the strictness of "cleanliness" that he learned as a child was a factor in his later success.

When he was just 5 years old, his father died. To make ends meet, his mother took a job at a cannery. His mother then decided he should take on duties at home to help care for his younger siblings. Among his duties was the chore of cooking for them. Some indications are that by the tender age of 7 that he was already pretty good at cooking. This early age exposure to cooking and the aspect that it became a passion for him was an instrumental factor in his later success with KFC.

At the age of 13, his mother had remarried and he did not get along with his new stepfather. He left the household and went to work at a nearby farm. He also quit school, doing so in seventh grade. Later in life, he explained that he hated algebra and that he decided going to school just wasn't something befitting his style and interests. This is somewhat notable too in that when he got KFC going, his focus was more on the food and the people side of the business, and much of the financial and accounting was not of particular interest to him. I am not saying that he wasn't eager to know how much money was being made, but just that the numbers side of the business was not his forte.

At the age of 16, he had left the farm and went to work as a conductor for a streetcar company. He then enlisted in the U.S. Army and served in Cuba, eventually getting an honorable discharge and then moving to Alabama where an uncle lived. He worked as a blacksmith helper. That only lasted two months and he then took a job cleaning ash pans of trains. He later progressed to become a steam engine stoker.

These a random collection of so-called odd jobs and are worthwhile to know about because they paint a picture about his business upbringing. For much of the early part of his life, he had nothing at all to do with chicken restaurants. He tried again and again to find a job, any job, and do what he could to make a living. He had no idea of what the future might hold. At the time, his future looked pretty bleak and he had no particular direction of what he might do.

Take heart for those of you that are equally in the doldrums, since as you know, KFC ultimately became big time, and yet as you can now see, during the early parts of his business career there was not a visible clue of what was to later emerge.

A TASTE OF BEING AN ENTREPRENEUR

Moving forward in time for brevity about the Colonel's business path, he eventually got a job for the Illinois Central Railroad in Tennessee. He meanwhile studied law by correspondence. He lost his job at the Illinois Central Railroad by having an ugly brawl with a fellow worker there. Finishing his law studies, he then practiced law in Little Rock for several years. Unfortunately, he had a courtroom outburst with his own client that led to the end of his legal career.

This part of his life illustrates that he had the capacity to learn and enough smarts to practice law, but it is also illustrative of his mercurial personality. He was known for having a short fuse and was insistent that his way was the right way. Though obviously this tends to be a disadvantage in business, in one sense it was later a positive in some ways because he became extremely dogged in his pursuit of KFC (especially when there were a lot of naysayers).

Colonel Sanders wandered again from job to job. He got a job to sell life insurance for Prudential and then got fired for insubordination. Having a hard time holding down any kind of conventional job, he at the age of 30 tried something quite different. He sought funding to start-up a ferry boat company.

The ferry boat company did pretty well. He then sold his shares and put the money toward a new company that he helped form. The new company manufactured acetylene lamps. At the time, it seemed like a good idea, but shortly thereafter an electric lamp was brought to the market by Delco and put his start-up out of business.

This part of his life was indicative of his entrepreneurial spirit. He launched one company that successful. He launched a second company that was not successful but that at the time seemed to have good potential. He was willing to take risks. He was eager to start companies. He had seen that sometimes you win, sometimes you lose. These were key factors later on regarding the starting of KFC.

INKLING OF A CHICKEN RESTAURANT

We are now getting to the first point of his career that one could say directly pertains to his KFC efforts. These prior years were illustrative of his approach overall and what he had learned prior to starting KFC. After the failure of the lamp company, he moved to Kentucky to take a sales job at Michelin Tire Company. In an unfortunate turn of events, Michelin opted to close a manufacturing plant and so laid him off. But, this turns out to be a blessing in disguise.

He had met a general manager of Standard Oil of Kentucky while working at Michelin. Upon getting laid off, the general manager offered that he could run a service station in Nicholasville. He did so. The station closed in 1930 due to the Great Depression, but he now had experience running a service station. The Shell Oil Company offered him another service station, this time in North Corbin, Kentucky.

The deal was that he would pay the Shell Oil Company a percentage of the sales of the service station, and would otherwise have the service station rent free. How does any of this relate to chicken restaurants, you might wonder?

Colonel Sanders opted to run that service station for the Shell Oil Company, and lived in the rent free quarters adjacent to it. When people came to the service station, he realized that they were often hungry for food. He began to make cooked chicken, along with other items such as hams and steaks, and served the customers in his living quarters.

Starting to sound familiar? To help though show how things are rarely a straight line in a business career, there are several twists yet to tell in this story.

A competing service station decided to put up a sign directing road traffic away from the Shell Oil Company service station and toward the competing station. This infuriated the Colonel. He and a Shell Oil Company official went to confront the other manager, and a shootout ensued. The other manager shot and killed the Shell Oil Company official, was arrested and convicted of murder and sent to jail.

Believe it or not, this wiped out his competition for the Colonel's service station. Now that's an unusual way to defeat your competition.

COLONEL NAME AND HOW IT CAME TO BE

Colonel Sanders was involved in various community activities during his time managing the Shell Oil Company service station. He was able to get the attention of local politicians. Using these connections, he in 1935 had the governor of Kentucky commission him as a Kentucky Colonel. You now know why he is called Colonel Sanders.

As the food side of the service station grew, he opted to open a restaurant adjacent to the service station, rather than continuing trying to serve customers from his own living quarters. Locals began to come to the restaurant, doing so not to get gasoline at the service station, but due to the good food he was serving.

A bit of a fortunate break happened when a notable food critic visited his restaurant. The food critic wrote that it was a good place to eat, including having sizzling steaks, fried chicken, country ham, and hot biscuits. Lunch was about fifty cents to a dollar in price, and dinners about the same. This was published in a guide to restaurants in the United States. At the age of 49, things seemed to finally be going relatively well. He had the service station and the restaurant. He even used some of his money to buy a motel. A bustling empire was being built.

MORE DETERMINATION

Everything was looking up. On the downside, a fire wiped out his restaurant and motel. Yes, that's right, a fire destroyed it all. Did he give up? Nope. He rebuilt the motel and made a new restaurant that was bigger than ever, seating 140 customers.

The next year, just as the United States entered into World War II, gasoline was rationed. This knocked out the service station. It knocked out the motel because there weren't many tourists anymore due to gas rationing and the war effort.

The restaurant was still doing relatively well. He credited this to his "Secret Recipe" for the chicken. He also opted to cook his chicken in a pressure fryer, which was unusual and at the time most restaurants used pan frying. Not only did he believe this use of the pressure fryer helped the taste, but it also sped up the cooking process.

He could serve customers more quickly. The customers were happier that they could more quickly get their meals. He could also then serve more customers per hour by reducing the cooking time and have a faster turnover per customer while eating at the restaurant.

SECRET RECIPE AND COOKING METHODS

Most people think of the Colonel's "Secret Recipe" as the trick that makes his chicken so "fingering licking good" (per the KFC advertising). It was also his innovative use of the newly emerging pressure fryer, along with lots of experimentation of variations among the factors of cooking time, the amount of fat, the fat filtration, and other factors that eventually got him to the end result of chicken that was just right, and in a short amount of cooking time (usually about 8 minutes, versus the conventional approach was often 20-30 minutes of cooking time).

He had been innovative in achieving a cooked chicken that was not overly greasy and was not overly dry. It had moisture and contained a pleasing finish. The point here is that he "invented" a better kind of chicken, at least in terms of how to prepare the chicken.

Plus, he reduced the time required to prepare the chicken. This was a factor not only in the success of his restaurant, but when you think forward in time and realize that the drive-thru and take-home craze was soon to arise, having the ability to quickly cook chicken was instrumental to the advent of consumers craving for reasonably decent and quickly provided fast food.

SHARING HIS INNOVATION WITH A PAL

After World War II ended, Colonel Sanders continued to do pretty well with his restaurant. He was now in his early 50s. A good friend of his lived in Salt Lake City. The Colonel had opted to show his friend the innovative chicken-frying that was doing so well for his own restaurant. His friend adopted the approach. Lo and behold, the restaurant in Salt Lake City began to sell chicken like hotcakes.

This is a crucial part of the business path because up until this point, the

Colonel alone was making his special chicken. He now knew that it could be achieved by someone else, as long as they were shown how to do so and knew the magic tricks involved.

Notice that at first it was only with someone that the Colonel believed in and trusted. Someone that was a confidant. Someone that would take as much care about the chicken cooking as he did. Someone that would honor the commitment to keep the chicken cooking process a secret.

The Colonel would carry that same concern for quality into the franchising of KFC. Consumers visit fast food chains because they come to know and expect a certain standard of quality. If the quality is low, or if the quality is haphazard, it becomes the death knell of that business.

AND THEN THE WORLD PIVOTED

In 1956, at the age of 66, something happened that was pivotal for Colonel Sanders. A new interstate highway was introduced in front of where his popular restaurant was. This new interstate road routed prospective customers away from his restaurant and they were inclined to drive right on past the restaurant.

Rather than going on the old highway that his restaurant faced, drivers jumped onto the speedy interstate. Customer traffic at his restaurant dried up. He decided to sell the restaurant. He took quite a loss on selling it. He was left with some savings and his now Social Security check.

I would guess that most of us would have tossed in the towel. Might as well just use the rest of your years while in retirement. Go fishing. Take it easy. Not so for Colonel Sanders. Leveraging his experience of showing his friend in Salt Lake City how to improve his chicken and his revenues from selling chicken, the Colonel decided he could try doing the same with others. His friend had been able to differentiate the chicken by claiming that it hailed from Kentucky. A clever sign painter for the restaurant even came up with a name for it, Kentucky Fried Chicken.

DOOR-TO-DOOR AND FRANCHISE EMERGES

The Colonel decided to go on-the-road and sell his chicken recipe and cooking approach. He would visit restaurants and offer to cook his chicken for them, and then show how fast it was and how much their customers loved it. He would often sleep in the back of his car, driving from town to town, restaurant to restaurant. He took along some pressure cookers and bags of spices so that he could do these selling like demonstrations at the restaurants that he visited.

He usually did a handshake deal with the owner of the restaurant that became convinced after the demonstrations that selling the Colonel's chicken would help their business. They were to pay him 4 cents per each chicken sold that used his recipe and approach. The restaurant owner could decide to use or not use the Colonel's approach, and would only pay when they did adopt it. This reduced any outlay by the owner and made using the Colonel's approach relatively low in risk.

Meanwhile, back in Kentucky, his now second wife would put together the spices and ship the secret money maker to the restaurants that did the handshake deal. It is somewhat hard to imagine in today's world doing a handshake deal like this. But, in the 1950s, the sense of integrity was a bit different than it is today.

Anyway, it was his having shown his friend how to prepare and cook the chicken, and its success for his friend, combined with the closing down of the restaurant in Kentucky that led the Colonel to thinking that he could franchise his approach.

He had the tenacity to do so. He had prior experience at doing start-ups. He believed completely in his chicken and was determined that it should become popular, in addition to hopefully making money. Notice how these many factors of his prior business path, and this adverse occurrence of wiping out his existing restaurant were all contributors to what occurred.

THE FRANCHISING BEGINS

At first, the Colonel drove from place to place. He would size up a restaurant. If it was dirty and an establishment that would be the wrong image for his chicken, he would opt to not try doing his demonstration there. In other words, rather than going anyplace at all, he was choosy and wanted to make sure that his chicken and the reputation of his chicken would be held high.

Imagine if he sold his chicken at restaurants that were crummy restaurants. Those restaurants could have messed-up making the chicken, and spread word that his chicken was terrible tasting and a worthless approach. Another aspect was that he realized pretty quickly that trying to sell one restaurant at a time was a very slow way to try and sell his approach. He desired to instead try and get an owner of a group of restaurants to be interested, rather than having to do them one at a time and all the exhausting traveling too.

He was routinely turned down for any such attempts to convince owners of multiple restaurants or restaurant chains. And, he even tried his buddies at the National Restaurant Association to help connect him into the big time operators, but that didn't work either.

The Colonel already had a pretty sour view of larger companies and this soured him even more. He recalled afterward that there weren't any big operators that would give him the time of day. In the end, he made a lot of smaller mom-and-pop restaurateurs very wealthy and was happy that he did so, if nothing else as a kind of revenge against the big operators.

So, from the humble start of his franchising in 1956, by 1960 he had about 200 restaurants using his chicken. By 1963, he had about 600 franchised outlets. Competitors such as Chicken Delight were not even close to his incredible growth.

SELLING OF KFC & NEXT GROWTH STAGE

Finally, at the age of 74, he got talked into selling the firm. A lawyer that he had gotten to know had teamed up with a wealthy businessman from Nashville. The young lawyer (age 29) was ambitious and had been a salesman with entrepreneurial qualities, having sold the Encyclopedia Britannica door-to-door while a freshman in college and becoming a top seller in his district. His father was a well-known Kentucky politician and lawyer.

While working as the lawyer for the Colonel, at first he tried to start a barbecue business. The millionaire businessman went in on it, but it fizzled very quickly. They decided that it made more sense to try and buy out KFC. At first, the Colonel was insistent that he would not sell KFC. It was his baby and how could he sell it? The young lawyer tried to convince him that they would never tamper with the chicken recipe and that quality would be the key consideration for the firm.

They then tried the old end-around. They approached the Colonel's family and friends, and his business acquaintances. They included talking to the franchisees. They spoke to the banks that KFC did banking with. After pretty much cornering the Colonel, he finally decided to sell KFC, and on January 6, 1964 he signed it away.

He was to get about $2 million, and he would keep Canada, England, Florida, Utah, and Montana. He also was to receive a life time salary of $40,000 per year. They were going to provide him with 10,000 shares of stock but he opted not to take it (some say due to tax reasons, others say it was not a genuine offer to him, and so there is some speculation about the shares aspects).

They agreed that the Colonel would remain involved as a spokesperson for the company. I know that some of you are thinking that he sold out too low. Probably so. Was he tricked into it? Did he not realize that the future value warranted more? These are facets we'll never really know, but anyway, he opted to proceed. It was his decision.

CRUCIAL PIVOT THAT LED TO BIG GROWTH

The young lawyer and the wealthy businessman proceeded to assemble a seasoned management team. They purposely included top franchisees to be involved in the firm and wanted to make sure that first and foremost that the franchisees would be pleased with whatever changes they might make.

This idea might seem obvious, but there are many franchises that fell apart because they were run by "professional" managers that could care less about the franchisees, or that had no understanding of what the franchisees wanted. So, that was smart of the new owners to take that approach.

Their first smart move after assembling a good team was to ensure that the Colonel remained as an ambassador of goodwill for KFC. The Colonel had grown his mustache and goatee, and used his white outfits, as a means to look the part of a southern colonel. The new KFC proceeded to get the Colonel booked for all of the popular TV talk shows of the era. They ran large advertising campaigns. They had him travel endlessly to towns and cities and make appearances. People would flock to his appearances and it would enhance the visibility of KFC in that locale. I know that meeting the Colonel in my city was very exciting and boosted my interest in eating KFC.

A second and simultaneous move was the beefing up of the advertising budget for KFC. The Colonel had been stingy about using money for advertising. This is often the case for many entrepreneurs. They tend to be reluctant to spend money on something that they cannot see per se, and also they tend to believe that their product or service should be good enough to carry its own weight and that word will naturally spread about it.

A third step they took was to overhaul the franchise agreements. Gone were the 4 cents or 5 cents per chicken of the handshake era. Now, a percentage of franchise sales would be owed to KFC. This helped immensely since the franchisees were making money off of selling other items and weren't having to pay anything to KFC for doing so. Furthermore, rather than a set flat fee, the percentage allowed KFC to benefit incrementally as the sales increased.

The fourth step involved halting the practice of franchising to restaurants of all sizes and shapes. Instead, they were going to standardize on a common look-and-feel of KFC. They wanted consumers to recognize a KFC while driving down the street. The franchised outlets were to be designed for take-home and be in freestanding structures, rather than storefronts. The menu of the outlets was to be standardized.

A basis for the take-home aspect was that Americans were eating at home now, rather than going out to eat. During this era, women were less likely to cook at home and were interested in and willing to have someone else do the cooking and just bring food home for major meals.

RECAP OF THE KEY BUSINESS LESSONS

The business career path of Colonel Sanders is very revealing when pieced together and looked at in a holistic fashion. He was essentially forced into cooking at a very early age, due to the death of his father and the focus of his mother on working outside the home. Turns out that he had a knack for cooking, and a passion for cooking. This might not have ever become known to him, had it not been that he was led there by unfortunate family conditions and household circumstances.

We have seen that when he was first getting his chicken recipe and cooking approach off-the-ground in the forerunner days of KFC that it required experimentation and innovation. It is reasonable to speculate that his prior grounding in cooking from an early age was a factor that led to his willingness to undertake these kind of innovative attempts at improving chicken and the cooking of chicken.

He was impatient in school, left school, took a multitude of odd jobs, all of which suggests that he was the type of person that was always on the look for the next thing, and not sure what it would be, but that continual exploration was needed. His mercurial personality, often a large disadvantage, seemed to be combined with a fierce determination, which is often an advantage, and he was fortunately able to channel the determination aspects into forging ahead with KFC when most might have not pursued something seemingly so unlikely.

He started up a new business (ferry boat), showcasing the kind of entrepreneurial spunk that later was instrumental in the launching of KFC. He also started a second new business (lamps), which though it flopped, it demonstrated that he was an earnest entrepreneur willing to continue the path of creating start-ups and make a business rather than work in a conventional business per se.

Eventually, the restaurant focus that ultimately proved his chicken to be highly successful might have been sufficient for the rest of his life. In other words, had the new interstate not been put in place, he presumably would have been content with the restaurant and not have felt compelled to venture much further. The interstate that forced the closure of the restaurant became a trigger to do something else.

PIVOT AT ANY AGE, BY CHOICE OR FORCE

Though already at an older age and near retirement, and an age when most would never think of trying to start a new business, he opted to try his hand at doing so. This seems befitting the nature of his determination and spirit. It was also driven by his passion for cooking and his belief in what he had done with chicken and the cooking of chicken. This was not a belief based only on his own enthusiasm, as he had seen how popular his chicken was by how well it worked at his restaurant. Some entrepreneurs believe in their own minds that their product or service is fantastic, but the marketplace has not yet equally verified it. For the Colonel, he knew his chicken was successful. This was a worthy factor in terms of taking risks to go further with it.

Equally vital was that he had already started down the path of an avenue towards franchising by having had his friend in Salt Lake City use his chicken recipe and cooking methods. Had this not have occurred, it would have been much more of a shot in the dark as to whether his approach could be replicated by others and elsewhere. He already knew that it could. Sometimes an entrepreneur has a great product or service, but only they can produce it. This becomes a limiting factor to growth. If no one else can produce the product or service, then the entrepreneur alone becomes the biggest bottleneck.

The Salt Lake City aspect revealed something else crucial too. The chicken being cooked in a southern style and by using the image of Kentucky style cooking was as much a factor in gaining traction for the chicken as was the chicken itself. In other words, yes, the chicken tasted good and was fast to cook, but that alone is not enough. People liked the imagery of eating this special, down south kind of cooking. It helped to further differentiate the chicken and be able to succinctly describe why it was so special.

That was an important catch that would make the chicken memorable and be able to spread word about it. If you have a fantastic product or service, but people do not know how to describe it, they cannot aid in the spreading of the word about the product or service. Having a truly marketable product or service means that you can actually market it, and do so in the simplest and most impressionable way.

The Colonel's efforts to get his franchise model going was an example of guts and determination that often is integral to being a successful entrepreneur and business person. The arduous aspects of driving from town to town, going to restaurants that he did not know, selling the restaurants on letting him do a demonstration, and then often sleeping in the back of his car to make ends meet, these are difficulties that might have stopped most from proceeding. His willpower and belief in himself and what he had were factors that kept him going.

Having grown up in an era where a handshake was a bond, he used that same approach with his franchisees. He even avoided potential franchisees that were not up to his high standards. This protected his brand and his image, which otherwise at the start could have been spoiled and then ruined any further growth. His inability to break into the big operators was perhaps another blessing in disguise. The odds are that the big operators would have been more demanding and forced the Colonel to change his approach. He might have had to compromise how the chicken was cooked or even his secret recipe, in an effort to appease the big operators.

As an entrepreneur and founder, his skill set was befitting the initial foundational building of KFC. Strict to keep to the brand, controlling of the product, pushing hard to get the business underway, and other such characteristics can be vital to a start-up like this. Eventually, though, if a start-up business is to reach higher levels of growth and maturity, the founder often holds back that growth. They won't let go of what worked before, not realizing that those same methods won't work for gaining the next level of growth.

When the Colonel finally agreed to sell the business, this was probably another moment of crucial pivot for him and for KFC. It is reasonable to speculate that KFC might not have become the behemoth that it is today, had the Colonel stayed firmly affixed in the company. The new management put in place a structure and model that was scalable in a manner that the Colonel might not have ever gotten to on his own.

HANDING OVER THE REINS SOMETIMES BEST

Speaking of which, the new management could have easily killed off KFC. This is not unusual that a new management team, taking over from the founder, often loses sight of what made the company great to start with. In their ambitious effort to want to take the company to the next level, often a new management team actually undermines the company. This undermining can then lead to the demise of the company.

Fortunately, the new management team for KFC was able to head in the right direction. By forcing for example standardization, this allowed customers to comfortably and reliably visit any KFC and know that they would get the same level of service and product that they were used to. Inconsistency in the product or service would have certainly led to consumers staying away from KFC.

The new management shifted the advertising into high gear, promoting KFC and getting the brand to become a household word. They were fortunate too that society was undergoing changes that welcomed the notion of getting cooked food from outside the home and bringing it home to eat. In the prior era, the classic model of cooking only at home and putting a home-cooked meal on the table would have not been as conducive to the growth of KFC. Timing of a business and the model of the business must coincide with the changes in societal culture. The new management team was able to exploit that aspect.

In the end, no matter what other trickery might be tried, if the basic product and service is not good then by a Darwinian process of the marketplace a given product or service will fall by the wayside. Colonel Sanders, Harland, managed to find a better way to cook chicken. The rest of the world might not have never known about it, but by luck, grit, and determination, the business of that better cooked chicken became big business and worldwide business, thanks to the Colonel.

.

CHAPTER 13
PIVOT TRANSPARENCY, SATURATIONS

CHAPTER 13

PIVOT TRANSPARENCY, SATURATIONS

PREFACE

The business pivots that a business leader and a business undertake can be highly visible. The market knows about it. The media knows about it. Your competitors know about it. Word spreads. There are some occasions though where the business pivot is not quite so visible. The business pivot might be intentionally hidden from view, which we'll discuss in this chapter. I refer to this as the amount of transparency of the pivot.

Another interesting and important aspect of pivots is the potential for reaching a saturation level of pivoting. Some businesses do a pivot, then another, and yet another, seemingly endlessly doing business pivots. This can have adverse consequences, even while presumably trying to steer the business in a better direction. We will look then at two vital topics about business pivots in this chapter, namely pivot transparency and then the second topic involving business pivot saturations. There is nothing that makes these two topics particularly intertwined, other than as you will see that sometimes when there are a multitude of pivots (which can tend toward saturation) the aspect of transparency also becomes more involved.

———

CHAPTER 13: PIVOT TRANSPARENCY, SATURATIONS

For some readers of this book, you might have completed reading the prior chapters and now have reached this chapter. This means that you will have trekked through the many mini-case studies of business leaders. We last discussed the business pivot framework in Chapter 2, prior to then taking a look at the numerous business leaders covered in the intervening chapters (Chapters 3 through 12).

We are now going to get back into the overall paradigm of business pivots. I mention this since it can be a bit of shocker to go from reading about the rather entertaining mini-cases and then switch back into the mental hat of more intense thinking about the overarching and underlying phenomena of business pivots and business leadership. Please prepare yourself accordingly.

Recall that in Chapter 2, we presented this below diagram. Let's revisit it, now that you've hopefully read the case studies (even if you didn't read the case studies, this all will nonetheless still make good sense).

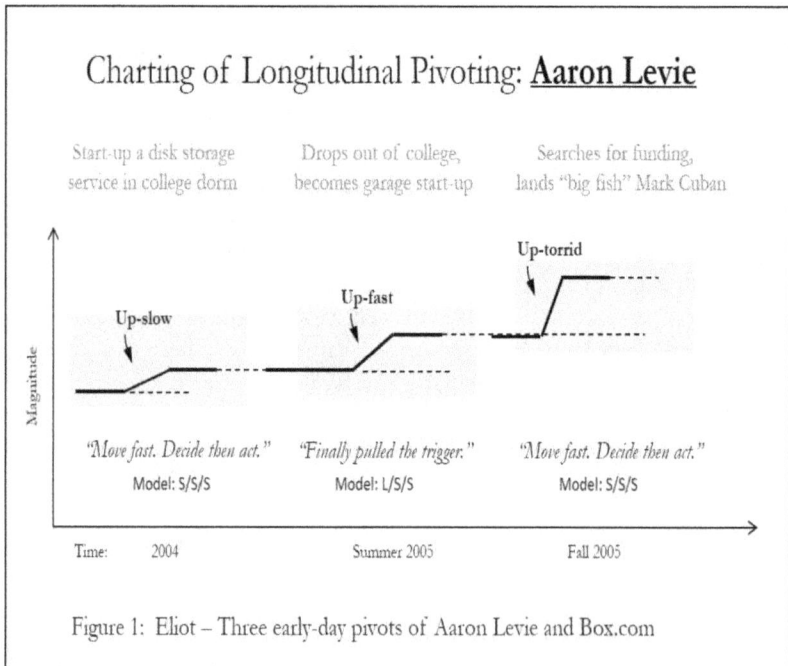

Charting of Longitudinal Pivoting: **Aaron Levie**

Figure 1: Eliot – Three early-day pivots of Aaron Levie and Box.com

The diagram of Aaron Levie and some of his pivots is instructive as a means to highlight what business pivots he undertook as a business leader, and those pivots that his business undertook with him. The visualization of the pivots makes it easy to quickly understand the nature of the pivots and then look at them overall, perhaps trying to discern patterns or at least as a minimum be able to grasp what pivots took place without having to read a thousand words to get there (i.e., a picture being worth a thousand words).

You'll note that in his case, we show that he started-up his disk storage business in his college dorm, he then did a pivot into dropping out of college and doing the classic garage-based start-up, and then he pivoted via his getting a "big fish" investor. Not shown are additional pivots further covered in the case study of Chapter 3, including that he next changed direction from consumers toward enterprises and his "big fish" dropped out due to that change of direction. There are other pivots that we could also list in his case. There are quite a number of them that he has undertaken over the course of his career and the life of Box.com.

If you research about Aaron, you might not see anything mentioned about his dropping out of college and going into a garage start-up mode. Sometimes this is mentioned, sometimes not. I show in Figure 2 an indication of suppose that it isn't mentioned, it would then look like he went from his college dorm start-up and then next was the funding miracle of getting Mark Cuban, the "big fish" to aid his firm.

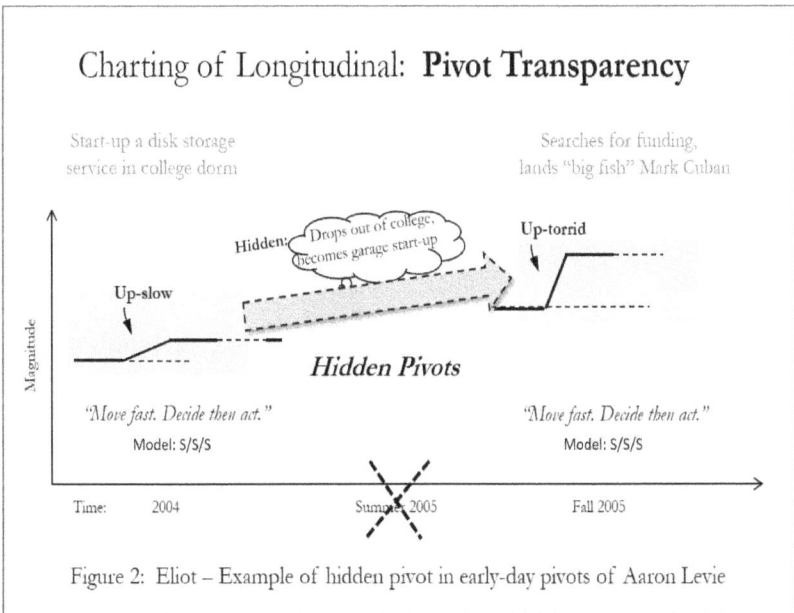

Charting of Longitudinal: **Pivot Transparency**

Start-up a disk storage service in college dorm

Searches for funding, lands "big fish" Mark Cuban

Hidden: Drops out of college, becomes garage start-up

Up-torrid

Up-slow

Hidden Pivots

"Move fast. Decide then act."
Model: S/S/S

"Move fast. Decide then act."
Model: S/S/S

Time: 2004   Summer 2005   Fall 2005

Figure 2: Eliot – Example of hidden pivot in early-day pivots of Aaron Levie

PIVOT TRANSPARENCY

I refer to whether we see a pivot or don't see a pivot as the amount of **Pivot Transparency**. Why would we not know about a pivot? In some cases, the pivot is not mentioned by the firm, or the business leader, or by researchers or reporters that describe the business leader and the business. So, by kind of happenstance of omission, the pivot is not revealed. This can be because others might think the pivot is not worthy of attention. It might seem like it is a minor pivot and not of enough consequence to bring up.

There are other aspects involved in the pivot transparency. A business leader might not want others to know about the pivot. For example, suppose that Aaron was personally dismayed that he dropped out of college and so he didn't want that aspect to be brought up. He might either not mention it or perhaps downplay it. He might also genuinely not see that as a material pivot, in that suppose he was not going to really pursue his college efforts anyway, and so he was on the verge of dropping out or wanted to do so. As a side note, none of that is the circumstances per se for Aaron, but I am just saying that those could be factors for other instances impacting pivot transparency.

For any business leader and business pivots, they should be consciously and explicitly considering how much transparency they want for their pivots. You can divided this into two aspects:

o   Internal Pivot Transparency = within the enterprise

o   External Pivot Transparency = outside the enterprise

We will next discuss these two aspects, first by covering the internal pivot transparency and then next we'll cover the external pivot transparency.

Internal Pivot Transparency

Internal pivot transparency refers to how far and deep do you inform your own firm about a potential business pivot, and at what juncture do you inform them, if at all. I was consulting to one firm that the top executives were secretly having discussions about a major business pivot. They opted to include me into the inner sanctum because they knew that there was aspects I could help with. Once told about it, I was sworn to utter secrecy about it, not being able to discuss it with anyone else in the company other than those on the short list of "in the know" of the firm.

This very narrow kind of awareness made sense at first, since they were not sure they were really going to carry out the pivot. They were concerned that if they let word out, it would either scare employees or get them on alert for something that might not ever materialize. The danger of employees knowing too early is that they might begin to change what they do and react as though the pivot is happening, when it might not happen at all and so they have jumped-the-gun (a pivot pitfall we'll revisit later on).

In today's world of the "politically correct" notion that business leaders are supposed to be fully transparent, it can be daunting to not tell the employees about the potential pivot. A business leader finds themselves in a quandary, do they let the cat out of the bag, or do they keep it close to their chest. Letting the cat out of the bag, at the wrong time, can create real havoc and possibly even undermine and prevent the pivot from happening. Keeping the pivot close to the chest can cause later resentment by the employees that they did not know what was coming and so they accuse the leader of failing to be transparent.

Balancing the transparency internally is something a business leader needs to judge for their particular firm and particular circumstance. A business leader that is already on thin ice with the employees and considered not very transparent can probably get away with not being transparent about an upcoming pivot, since it is already how they are viewed. It can add some damage as another nail in the coffin for that business leader, as far as the employees see it, but anyway it is in keeping with their style already. A business leader that is known for their absolute transparency will have a tougher time if they aren't transparent about the pivot, since the employees will be dazed and perhaps rethink their faith in the transparency of the leader.

One should also consider the timing of when to be transparent. At the Pre-Pivot, it might be premature to be widespread in transparency. The business leaders themselves are unsure of what the pivot will be, and this lack of clarity can cause the employees to be confused if the pivot is openly discussed – they will have a thousand questions about the pivot, of which few answers will be available. Toward the tail end of the Pre-Pivot, it might make sense to start to enlarge the circle of participants (we will discuss later on the team needed to carry out pivots). During the Pivot Point, it might make sense to be wider on the transparency since it likely now touches so many areas of the firm, and similarly during the Post-Pivot. Again, each pivot will have its own "best" way to consider how to do the transparency.

I'll also mention and caution that there is a chance that whatever kind of transparency approach a business leader desires might be set asunder during the pivot. Sure enough, at the firm that I just mentioned that invited me into the inner circle about the pivot, about a week later, and not due to anything I did, there were others not in the inner circle that brought up the pivot to me. They had heard about it through the grapevine. Worse still, the business leaders had a meeting in a conference room and forgot to wipe clean the whiteboard in the conference room.

The executives had left the conference room at the end of their discussions and neglected to think about wiping the board clean. The employees that had booked the conference room for the next time slot came in, and were stunned to see the whiteboard contents. They knew it was real and not faked, because they had seen the top executives come out of the conference room before they had entered into it.

In short, loose lips sink ships. A business leader that thinks they can keep a lid on something that might upend the company, which many major pivots do, will find it hard to keep it a secret. I am not saying it is impossible, but just that you'll need to really figure out how to plug all the leaks and be diligent during the pivot accordingly.

External Pivot Transparency

External pivot transparency refers to how much the world outside the firm is informed about or finds out about the pivot. This is just as tricky as the discussion we've just had about the internal pivot transparency. Do you think for a particular pivot that the outside world should know about it, or not know about it? What is the timing of their knowing about it? What amount of detail should they know?

For publicly traded companies, the regulations about notification will come to play and shape your decisions on the external transparency aspects. For privately held firms, there is a bit more leeway. No matter either aspect, the nature of who is informed, how they are informed, when they are informed, what they are informed of, where they are informed, and why they are informed are aspects that you need to nail down.

A business leader might use a potential business pivot as a feigned tactic to confuse a competitor. An early announcement that you are going to enter into another market might get those market competitors to take actions that will cause them to consumer resources, perhaps needlessly if you don't actually do the pivot. It might cause them to back away from the market, if they fear that your entry will make things worse for them. You might even "leak" a business pivot as a sleight of hand trick, whereby you are really thinking of doing business pivot X, but are communicating about a business pivot Y, and that your competitors will react in a way to the perceived pivot Y that plays into your more readily be able to do pivot X.

Those kinds of tricks can be hard to pull off. For example, if you have communicated about doing pivot Y but don't intend to do it, meanwhile your own employees will certainly hear about the upcoming pivot Y, and so they will react too. If at the same time you are pushing for pivot X in the firm, you can have quite a lot of chaos as the employees are overwhelmed as to two pivots taking place at the same time, when in fact you are really only trying to do the one pivot X.

These kinds of Sun Tzu art-of-war tactics are tough to enact in today's world, especially with the advent of social media and the ready sharing of information. There are aspects of Sun Tzu's advice that might not be so readily applicable now, if he had a smartphone, as do millions and millions of other people, along with the Internet and social media. Imagine Sun Tzu's Facebook page. But anyway, not to digress, the point is that being tricky about communicating externally can boomerang back into the internal transparency too. Also, keep in mind that no matter how secretive you are internally, somehow the word might get to the outside world. This often creates a hornets nest within the firm, since if the outside world knows about the pivot, but the inside the firm employees don't, they will be likely irked to first know of it by an outsider.

PIVOT SATURATIONS

Let's move to our next topic in this chapter, **Pivot Saturations**. This refers to the notion that a business leader and a business might have a series of pivots, one after another.

Why would you do a series of pivots? One approach to pivoting involves doing smaller, incremental pivots. Suppose you are trying to ultimately turn yourself 90 degrees, but don't want to do it all at once. Sometimes the "big bang" approach to making one humongous pivot is overly risky and not readily tackled. So, you make a series of 10 degree turns, nine of them in all, in order to make that 90 degree pivot.

The problem with doing this incremental approach is that after a while there is the chance of pivot saturation. The firm will say to themselves, oh my gosh not another pivot (insert four-letter words in that commentary). They might think that the pivoting will never end. They might not also understand the rationale for the pivots and believe that the firm is pivoting simply for the sake of pivoting. None of this is going to help you and the firm as it tries to successfully carry out these pivots.

Knowing how many pivots to undertake and the timing is going to be up to you and your firm, gauging its capacity and willingness to undertake pivots. Maybe the "big bang" makes most sense for your firm and your leadership style. Get it done, all at once. Like pulling off the Band-Aid with one swift yank. Also, your firm might not have the time available to do a series of pivots and so by expediency you are forced into the one big pivot or maybe two. Or, maybe the series of pivots is better. It could even be that the pivots are arising by happenstance and thus you did not and were not able to plan them out beforehand into a "big bang" and they just came along as they did.

Take a look at Figure 3. This shows a firm that has done six pivots. Some of them worked out well, others did not. Is this a sign of pivot saturation overall, i.e., is the number of pivots here sufficient to say it is a saturation? I don't think we can put an absolute number on it.

Suppose that these were pivots done over a 20 year time period, and let's say it was one pivot per every 3 years on the average. That might not be so bad. On the other hand, suppose these were pivots all squeezed into 18 months, and also assume they were major pivots that really impacted the business. That could be a circumstance of pivot saturation.

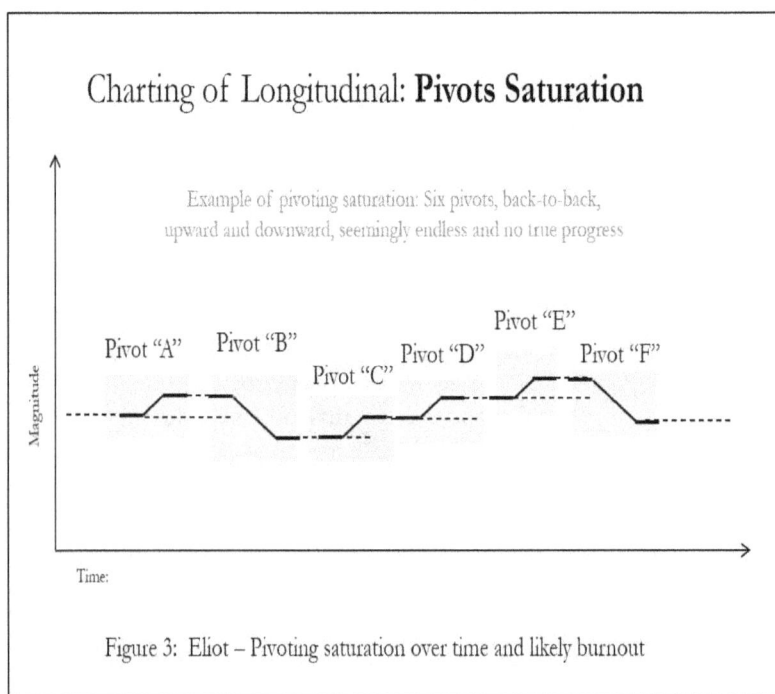

Charting of Longitudinal: **Pivots Saturation**

Example of pivoting saturation: Six pivots, back-to-back, upward and downward, seemingly endless and no true progress

Pivot "A"   Pivot "B"   Pivot "C"   Pivot "D"   Pivot "E"   Pivot "F"

Magnitude

Time:

Figure 3: Eliot – Pivoting saturation over time and likely burnout

This diagram happens to also imply that the pivots seemed to come equally spaced. Don't interpret this diagram overly literally. It could be that a pivot happened one year, then three years occur, then the next pivot happens, and then perhaps five years occur, and so on. The saturation will depend upon how many there are, the size of each, the length of each, the time in-between them, etc.

Mainly, I want you to be thinking about how many pivots you are doing and planning to do. Be watchful of *pivot saturation*. And, with a series of pivots, also consider the amount of *pivot transparency* that you want for each pivot. Some of the pivots might be higher in transparency than others.

CHAPTER 14

PIVOT

GRAVITATIONAL FORCE, PIVOT-FLOP, PIVOT-NOT

CHAPTER 14

PIVOT GRAVITATIONAL FORCE, PIVOT-FLOP, PIVOT-NOT

PREFACE

A business pivot is subject to forces that will try to keep it from occurring. Sometimes this is simply due to inertia. It can be hard to get a business to pivot, and the status quo often is the prevailing way of doing things and resists the pivot. The business leader will need to explicitly drive the pivot upward and forward, and overcome the organizational inertia that works against the pivot. Whether you see them around you with your own eyes, the pivot gravitational forces surrounding the pivot will be pushing your pivot back towards the normal state of affairs that were in place prior to the pivot getting underway. Simply stated, when you try to walk uphill, you don't see gravity draining upon you, but you can certainly feel its impacts.

There is a chance that a business pivot won't achieve what the business leader hoped would occur. We will be looking at how gravitational forces prevent or inhibit a pivot. There are lots of other ways in which the pivot can get waylaid (we'll cover that later on when we discuss pivot pitfalls). In the end, a pivot might arrive back at the same place that the business was before the pivot (I call this a pivot-not situation), or it might even be worse off due to the pivot (I call this the pivot-flop situation).

CHAPTER 14: PIVOT GRAVITATIONAL FORCE, PIVOT-FLOP, PIVOT-NOT

A business leader has in mind a pivot for the business. It's a big one. The business will become better, stronger, more revenue, more clout, and otherwise hit the big time; if it can pull off the pivot successfully. The business leader is very enthused about the pivot. They light up when asked about it. They give speeches throughout the company, showing incredible passion that this pivot is the life saver of the firm. It is bold. It is inspiring. Their fellow business leaders are all on-board and equally excited about how this pivot will make a difference to them and the firm.

They do the right thing and carefully do a Pre-Pivot, making sure to plan out the pivot. Seemingly covering all needed details, they know when the Pivot Point will get underway and they have a fifty page long playbook for the pivot that covers the essentials.

Yet, once they get into the Pivot Point and the pivot is underway, it stalls. Dates that were on the plan are now outdated, and delays keep happening on every facet of the pivot. The pivot is costing more than they had thought. Employees are grumbling about the pivot. Enthusiasm has waned. What's happening to the pivot? It could be that the dreaded and at times invisible **Pivot Gravitational Force** is at work. Take a look at Figure 1 as illustration.

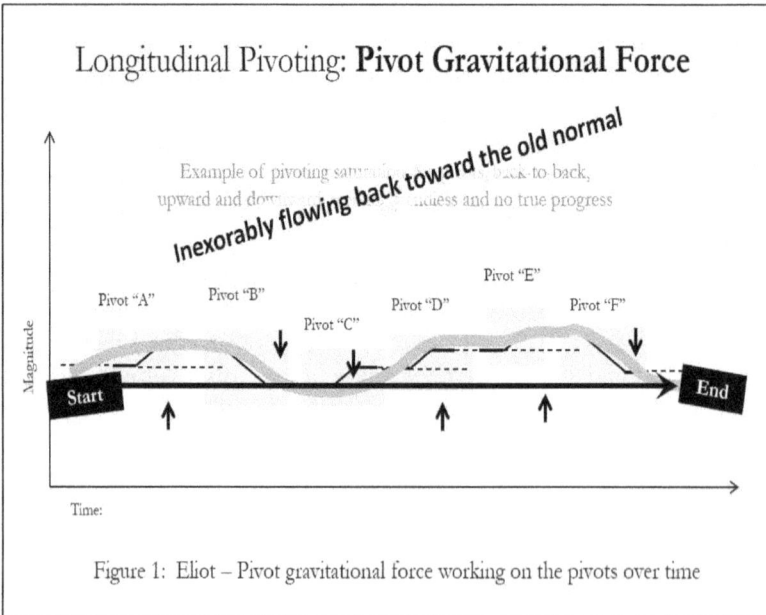

Figure 1: Eliot – Pivot gravitational force working on the pivots over time

Nearly all research and studies of business change will tell you that making a change to a business is hard work and that there are lots of forces that will resist. Sometimes this resistance is by innocence, namely that the resisters don't even realize they are resisting. Perhaps they are doing their job, as they had been taught and as they have done it for ten years. They might not understand how they are to pivot and don't know how to change to whatever new way that the business pivot is headed. Fearful of doing the wrong thing, they dutifully continue what they have always been doing.

There are some resisters that are aware of their own resistance and are resisting by their intentional personal preference. Maybe they are clever enough to resist without even getting caught per se, and can appear like the innocence resisters when in fact they are doing the resistance by purposeful design. Of course you can even have resisters that are outright dissenters. They might not believe in the pivot. They might think that the pivot is wrong. From their perspective, even if the business leader is saying it will save the company, for them they might view it as being disastrous and destroy the company. They are willing to speak-up and urge others to resist the pivot. This can be infectious and spread throughout the firm.

I have seen these kinds of resistances time and again. Especially in firms where the nature of the pivot is departing from the core business model or vision of the firm. A start-up that has been around long enough to become stable and has hired lots of talent into the firm, will likely have a hard time making a pivot that radically changes the vision and direction of the firm. This is partially due to the fact that the talent brought on-board probably came to the firm because they fervently believed in that business model and vision. They were hired because they vowed the vision was what sparked them and got them to work each day. It has become their daily mantra. And now, that is going to be pivoted away from. That's a hard pill for anyone to swallow.

The founder of a firm can sometimes be either the greatest cheerleader for a pivot, or the biggest doomsayer for a pivot. In some cases, the founder realizes that a pivot is needed and uses their company goodwill to get others to go along. Others in the firm that believe in the founder, even if they are unsure about the pivot, will tend to do as the founder urges. There is the other side of the coin, circumstances involving a founder that won't accept the notion of the pivot and clings to the way things have been. In some cases, they might be right, in others maybe not. One of the biggest fights between a founder and the investors or a Board of Directors can occur over the efficacy of doing a business pivot. You see from time-to-time founders that are forced out of their firm, because they won't go along with a pivot that the funders and the Board believe is necessary.

Overall, these various forces will be yanking at the business pivot and trying to keep it from going to its destination. I like to refer to this as gravitation forces because it helps to invoke a sense that the forces can be powerful, they can be unseen, and they are tending to drive the pivot back to earth, rather than allowing it to go upward and forward.

PIVOT-SLIM, PIVOT-NOT, PIVOT-FLOP

A pivot can be undermined by the Pivot Gravitational Forces. It can also be undermined by its own hand, as we will see when we discuss in later chapters the pitfalls of pivots. However it happens to occur, there is a substantial chance that the pivot will not occur as planned and will end-up less than hoped.

We will introduce some additional catchy language for these circumstances. Take a look at Figure 2. I show the **Pivot-Slim**, the **Pivot-Not**, and the **Pivot-Flop**. We use our diagrammatic technique earlier covered to show that there is desired pivot (left side of the diagram) which had hoped to be an Up-Torrid (suggesting a radical pivot), but let's assume it did not achieve its aim.

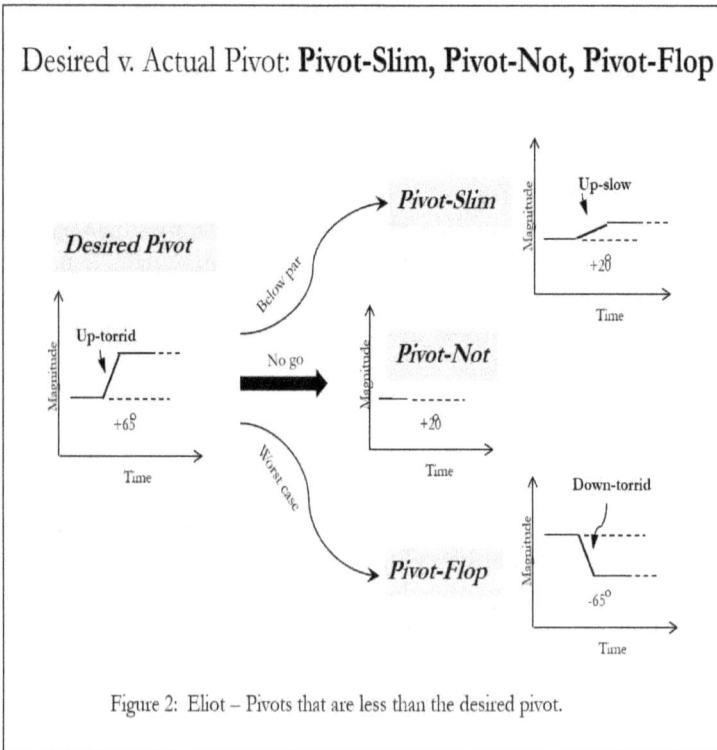

Figure 2: Eliot – Pivots that are less than the desired pivot.

Instead of ending up with an Up-Torrid, suppose the result was an Up-Slow, meaning that rather than pivoting perhaps the entire business model that we settled instead with some more less radical action and only got a piece of the business model to be pivoted. I call this the Pivot-Slim because we did not get as much as we wanted and so the result is slimmer than hoped, but at least it was still progressive and upward, presumably aiding the firm.

Another possibility is that the pivot tried to happen and in the end it did not happen. We are back where started. I call this the Pivot-Not, since we did not achieve the pivot. Even though we are still operating with say the same business model as before and so it might seem like the firm has been unharmed by the attempted pivot, there are potential harms involved.

This can be something that is harmful to the firm since the firm likely expended resources and attention to the pivot. It might be a let-down to the morale of the firm. The employees might see this as a defeat or failure, and perhaps lose faith in the company's business leaders because of it. The old adage of nothing ventured, nothing gained, might seem inspiring to a business leader that led the pivot, but to others it might be that they lost sleep and sacrificed their personal lives believing that the pivot had to happen. For them, the amount ventured is real and hurtful.

There is the even worse possibility of the pivot actually causing harm to the firm and leading to an outcome that is worse than anticipated. This is shown on the diagram as a swing from an upward trajectory to a downward trajectory. The "worst of the worst" would be the case of the Up-Torrid turning out to be the Down-Torrid. It is one thing to end-up back to where you started, and another thing entirely to have usurped the business and now it is in a worse state than before.

I will use this added terminology henceforth in this book and provide insights about how to try and avoid ending up in the Pivot-Slim, Pivot-Not, and Pivot-Flop categories, along with ways to overcome the Pivot Gravitational Forces that can contribute towards landing into one of those less-than-stellar positions.

CHAPTER 15
PIVOT RETREATMENT

CHAPTER 15

PIVOT RETREATMENT

PREFACE

The best laid plans of mice and men sometimes go awry. At some juncture of the pivot, it might be timely to pull the plug. I refer to this as retreating from the pivot. Some business leaders will realize it is time to curtail the pivot, and yet not know how to properly stop it. Like a conductor on a train that is barreling along, they might simply pull the stopping cord and bring the train to an immediate halt. This can be nearly as disastrous or even more so than allowing the pivot to continue for a bit and slowly stop the pivot.

One other aspect is the realization that the pivot is not going well and needs to be retreated. Many times, a business leader is so personally committed to the pivot that they will ignore any telltale sign of it going sour. They want to see the pivot to the end. Come heck or high water, as they say. Any dissension in the ranks is considered as mutiny. The business leader will at times downplay the mutiny as merely whining by those that don't get the big picture, or that they are evil doers out to prevent the company from succeeding. Anyway, for that business leader, retreatment is probably not in their mind and not going to be in their mind, but at least you can be ready with some aspects of how to do a retreatment if a sanity returns and the pivot really should be curtailed.

————

CHAPTER 15: PIVOT RETREATMENT

Not all pivots will succeed. Maybe the pivot was not crafted well. Maybe the timing is off, and it should be tried at a different future time. Perhaps the pivot was the "big bang" and it needs to be recast into smaller chewable pivots. There are lots of ways in which the pivot is not going to succeed.

As we saw in the prior chapter, there are Pivot Gravitational Forces fighting against the pivot. The pivot, if left on its own accord to get to the end, might become a Pivot-Slim (only gaining a fraction of what was hoped), a Pivot-Not (making no gain and being back to where we started), or it might be a Pivot-Flop (putting the firm into a worse situation than before the pivot began).

You can either let the pivot play out entirely, or you might at some juncture realize "hey, got to pull the plug on this" and want to get out of the pivot, earlier than anticipated. I call this the **Pivot Retreatment**.

I am using the word "retreatment" because I found that when I said "pivot retreat" that some business leaders thought I was saying that we should have a meeting or a business retreat to talk about the pivot. The word "retreatment" seems to avoid that confusion. Just wanted to let you know, since you might have thought that the word "retreatment" seems kind of unusual and why didn't I pick the simpler word "retreat" (now you know why).

So, let's suppose you want to do a Pivot Retreatment. What should you do? The answer partially depends upon how far along on the pivot you are. This takes us back to our handy 3-stages framework for thinking about pivots. As you might recall, we have the Pre-Pivot as the first stage, the Pivot Point as the second stage, and the Post-Pivot as the third stage.

Your retreatment will differ depending upon which of the three stages the pivot is in. That being said, I am an advocate of beforehand anticipating that a pivot retreatment will be needed. Thus, during the Pre-Pivot, you should be planning for a pivot retreatment, and that the pivot retreatment could occur while in the Pre-Pivot, or while in the Pivot Point, or while in the Post-Pivot. This is proper contingency planning.

I have found that business leaders often object to doing this kind of contingency planning. They frequently say that if we at the start are already trying to figure out how to get out of the pivot, it sends a message that we obviously don't believe in the pivot. It is a sign of half-heartedness that the pivot will actually happen.

This is definitely a valid concern that by discussing the ways in which the pivot can fail, it maybe gets people thinking it will fail. On the other hand, if you stick your head in the sand, and if you have no contingencies ready, this is not going to look very good when the proverbial you-know-what hits the fan.

When the pivot veers afoul, there are going to be a lot of stakeholders asking what kind of contingency you prepared. Apparently your answer is going to be, well, none. That's not going to look very good. You can at that time try the spin that you didn't want to alarm people about the possibility of a retreatment. That's going to pretty much fall on deaf ears. Imagine you are in a hotel that did not put up fire extinguishers and they tell you during a fire that they opted to not put up the extinguishers because it would just make you fearful that a fire might someday hit the hotel. That's fine, you say, while the hotel burns down around you. I don't think so.

Let's take a look at the pivot retreatment per each stage. Take a look at Figure 1. We are in the Pre-Pivot, and something has caused us to realize that it is best to not proceed, so we will do a **Pivot Early Exit**.

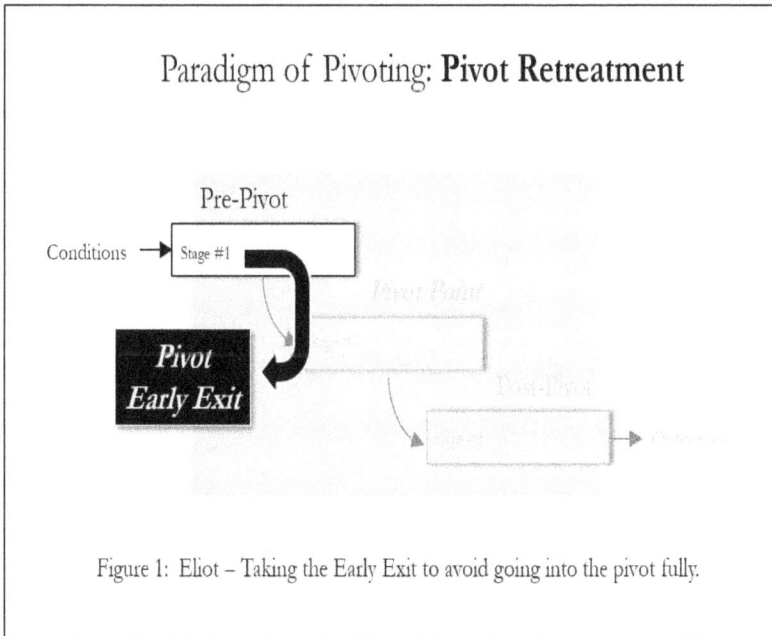

Figure 1: Eliot – Taking the Early Exit to avoid going into the pivot fully.

The good news is that usually doing a pivot retreatment in the Pre-Pivot is the easier of the three stages to pull the plug. The commitment to the pivot is lower than it will likely be during the Pivot Point and the Post-Pivot. The costs and reputational damage will likely be less by pulling the plug now, versus once you get into the Pivot Point or the Post-Pivot.

You can frequently back away from the pivot in the Pre-Pivot by simply pointing to an analysis that shows the pivot was not right or ripe. By ripe, I mean that you can say that yes, a pivot is needed, but now's not the right time for it. This bolsters that doing the Pre-Pivot was not a waste of effort.

Sometimes it will be important to not only curtail the pivot, but also show that the pivot had value even if not completed. You could say that the pivot planning did what it was supposed to do, namely, identify whether or not the pivot was sensible and the right thing to do. Furthermore, it hopefully can be claimed that by doing the Pre-Pivot work that you learned something useful about the company and that you are better prepared for when the next pivot opportunity comes along. Maybe you are next time able to do the Pre-Pivot in half the time, because you now have established a means of figuring out at the firm how to do pivots.

Next, take a look at Figure 2. Here we depict the pivot retreatment happening during the Pivot Point (this is considered a **Pivot Costly Exit**). This will almost definitely be harder to do than retreating during the Pre-Pivot. The rule-of-thumb is basically pull the plug as early as possible, and hopefully before you get into the Pivot Point. Do not sway overly in that direction, in that during the Pre-Pivot you do not want to be so skittish that you drop out of the race before it has really begun.

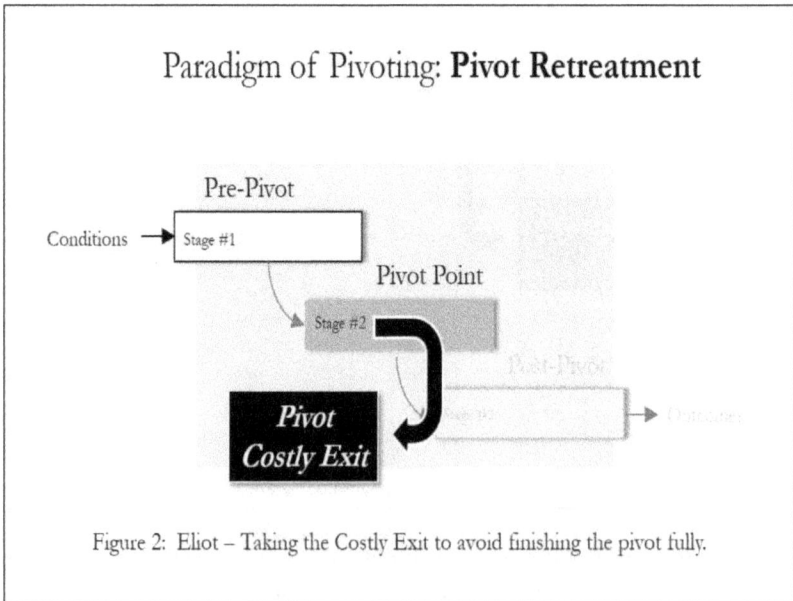

Figure 2: Eliot – Taking the Costly Exit to avoid finishing the pivot fully.

The odds are that retreatment during the Pivot Point is going to be painful in many ways. You will probably incur costs to stop the pivot, and will need to figure out what those costs are. Are there licenses that maybe need to be undone? Are there contracts that had clauses about early exit?

Will the employees understand why the pivot was stopped, now that it is underway? You will want to use your Pivot Team (which we'll discuss later on), and leverage all areas of the firm in curtailing the pivot, including finance, accounting, legal, marketing, talent management, and so on.

The contingency plan that you had put together during the Pre-Pivot, which should have looked ahead at what to do when a retreatment has to occur during the Post-Pivot, opt to cover all of the essentials of backing out of the pivot. This includes the very important aspect of how to properly communicate that the pivot is being curtailed.

I use the word "curtailed" which is a bit softer on the eyes and ears, while I have seen some firms say that the pivot is being "abandoned" – I suggest trying to avoid the abandonment word. Most people think of abandoning something as a sign that you goofed-up and also that you are leaving things in a lurch. Orphans are abandoned. Sinking ships are abandoned. Ending a pivot early does not necessarily mean it is a sinking ship, and nor an orphan.

Ending a pivot can be a good sign. It can mean that the firm anticipated there might be reasons, sound reasons, why the pivot could not achieve its aims, and the pivot plan involved gauging the pivot progress throughout the pivot. This would then allow for the retreatment to occur at an appropriate time.

I am not saying that it will be easy to do a retreatment once you are in the Pivot Point. In spite of your strenuous efforts to assure people that you had anticipated the pivot might need to be curtailed, it still is going to be ugly when you pull the plug.

There is also a "politically correct" aspect to retreatment that can be used these days, namely, the now "failure is a good thing" movement. Lots of businesses, business leaders, and the media are touting that failure is good, it shows that you are trying new things, it shows that you are daring, it shows that you are willing to take chances. You can try to sugar coat a pivot retreatment with that message.

This does bring us to a related tangent. What does it mean to fail at something? In the case of the pivot, if the failure is based on not finishing the pivot, then you are admittedly trapped into the aspect that a retreatment was presumably a failure. On the other hand, if the pivot was about taking chances, and you did take a chance, you were successful in taking a chance. You did not "fail" at taking a chance, you took a chance.

Don't want to split hairs on this, and probably it is best to avoid trying to argue with someone about whether the pivot was a failure or not. You can try the other angle, saying that it was a "fast failure" which is the notion of trying to fail quickly so that it does not do as much harm and that you can learn from it and move on.

The other timing of doing a pivot retreatment is at the third stage, when in the Post-Pivot. If you thought retreating at the Pivot Point second stage was tough, the Post-Pivot can be even worse. The odds are that there has been a lot of resources, energy, time, attention, devoted to the Pre-Pivot and the Pivot Point. It now will seem like it was all tossed down the drain.

For these reasons, I refer to this as the **Pivot Gaffe Exit**.

See Figure 3.

Try to avoid waiting this long to exit from the pivot. If you really think it needs to be undone, so be it, and use the same suggestions made about the Pivot Costly Exit in planning for and carrying out the exit at this third stage.

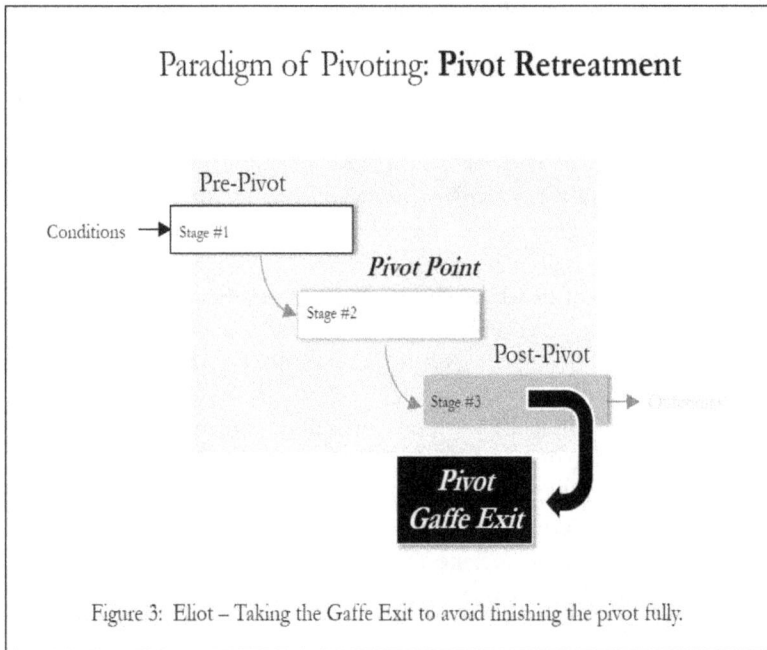

Figure 3: Eliot – Taking the Gaffe Exit to avoid finishing the pivot fully.

Another kind of trick is to tee up another pivot that rectifies whatever was wrong about the pivot that you are thinking of exiting during stage three. I call it a trick, which I suppose suggests it is somehow a marginal ploy, but I don't intend it to seem that way. This is a legitimate strategy that can be used.

Rather than focusing on backing down from the pivot that is now being completed, you instead put attention towards the next pivot, which wraps into whatever might be needed to boost the prior pivot to where you were trying to go.

That's the "world will be a better place" optimistic way to handle things, if possible, and hopefully takes attention away from the prior pivot that some might see as a disaster and instead put focus on the next pivot which will be the savior. You can do a lessons learned while in the Post-Pivot, which are supposed to be doing anyway, and then put together and get started the Pre-Pivot for the next pivot. The next pivot is going to fix whatever was supposed to happen and possibly even take you a bit further along.

Lance B. Eliot

CHAPTER 16

INGREDIENT CO-INFLUENCES, MVPP, SRRS, BRRS

CHAPTER 16

INGREDIENT CO-INFLUENCES, MVPP, SRRS, BRRS

PREFACE

The ingredients of business leadership were discussed in the opening chapter of this book. Each of the ingredients influences the others. They are each like distinct superpowers, which can then help or hinder the other superpowers. We will revisit the ingredients and be exploring especially how the added ingredient, being Pivot-Wise, is impacted by and also impacts the other ingredients.

In this chapter, I assert that there is a minimum level of capability that a business leader needs to exhibit in the ingredients for purposes of undertaking a business pivot successfully. I also provide a means to gauge whether the business leader themselves might be on the verge of a pivot, stoked by a life event that has happened in their personal life. This retains my earlier contention that we cannot separate out the business leader as a person and the business entity, in terms of considering when and whether business pivots will occur. I then also provide a similar means to gauge what kind of business concern is in need of readjustment and thus presumably the candidate for seeking a business pivot.

———

CHAPTER 16: INGREDIENT CO-INFLUENCES, MVPP, SRRS, BRRS

We have a lot of new ground to cover in this chapter. First, let's reminisce about the opening chapter of the book. In the beginning, the ingredients of business leadership were identified and discussed. Those ingredients consisted of the now-classic tried-and-true set, consisting of a Guiding Vision, Passion, Integrity, Trust, Curiosity, and Daring. I then proposed that we add a further ingredient, which I have named as being Pivot-Wise.

The notion is that with the rise of business pivoting and the importance to the survival and thriving of a business on achieving timely and apt business pivots, along with the need for the subsistence and success of the business leader as hinged on pivots and even instigating pivots, the capability of being business savvy or Pivot-Wise as a business leader about business pivots is now on the same playing field as the other ingredients. That's a mouthful, for sure, but nonetheless seems sensible and contemporary.

It is akin to adding a new superpower to business leaders. Business leaders so far had let's imagine a superpower of X-ray vision, a superpower of being able to generate lasers beam from their eyes, and so on, and now they have an added superpower to undertake and enact pivots (doing so in a more powerful way than a locomotive and even faster than a speeding bullet, if you will).

This brings us to one of the main topics in this chapter. If you have a superpower, it does not mean that it is necessarily strong enough and mighty enough for the task at hand. Maybe you can lift tall buildings with one hand, but does your super strength also allow you to lift an entire city of buildings? Maybe not. But suppose you are faced with the task of lifting an entire city? Also, sometimes to save the day you need to use your superpowers in conjunction with each other. Perhaps you need to look into those buildings with your X-ray eyes, before or during you effort to lift the buildings.

I think that's probably enough for the moment on the analogy to superpowers. Here, what we are interested in involves the strength of a business leader in each of the ingredients. How strong are you in terms of being able to create, communicate, and otherwise sustain a Guiding Vision for the company and your followers? How strong is your Trust, in terms of how much trust do others have in you? Maybe they have enough trust to follow your lead when trying to add a new product to the product mix of the firm, but if you try to completely alter the core business model of the firm, they are queasy because they don't quite trust you that much.

As shown in Figure 1, we can identify for any given business leader their strength level on each of the stated ingredients. We will use an easy scale of 1 to 10, whereby the business leader is rated as either not having much strength on the ingredient, which is the lowly score of 1, or they are extremely strong on the ingredient, which gets a top score of 10.

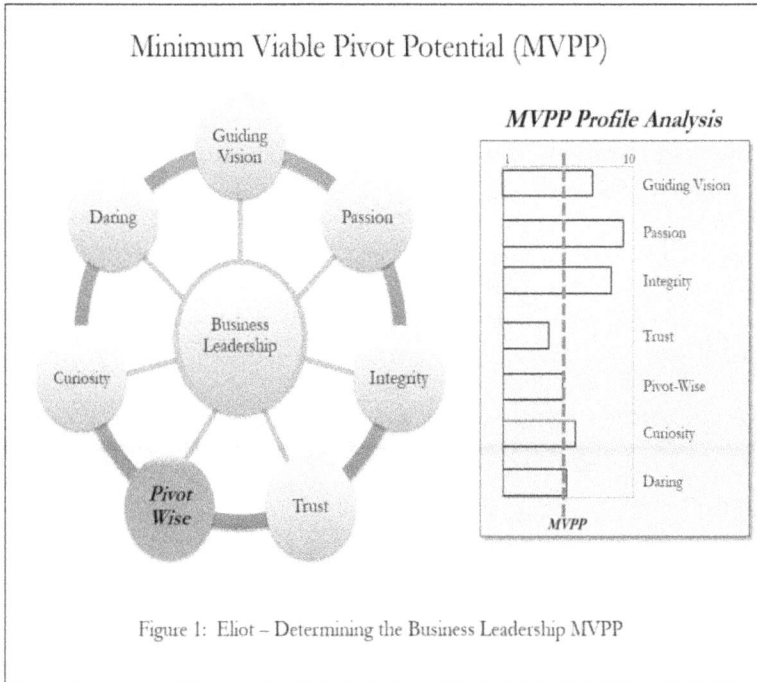

Figure 1: Eliot – Determining the Business Leadership MVPP

If you like, we could start the scoring at zero, but in my view it seems unlikely that any business leader would score an absolute zero on any of the ingredients. A zero implies they have no capability at all in that ingredient, but this goes against our definition that a business leader must have these ingredients. Anyway, let's not fuss with that aspect and if you want to imagine the scale starting zero, I'm fine with that. I am sure that you are quietly chortling to yourself that you know some business leaders that have a zero on several of the ingredients.

In order to achieve a true business pivot, meaning a pivot of a major nature, I assert that the business leader needs to score a minimum threshold on each of the ingredients. I call this the **Minimum Viable Pivot Potential (MVPP).**

The threshold does not necessarily need to be the same minimum score across the board, per each of the ingredients, and can vary by ingredient. For sake of simplicity, right now let's assume that they need to score a 5 or more, on each of the ingredients, in order to be considered property ready for and able to carry out successfully a business pivot.

In looking at the example shown in Figure 1, we have a business leader that has been rated on each of the ingredients, including their Pivot-Wise capability. A dashed line is shown at the mark of 5 on the scale.

Overall, this business leader has pretty good scores, especially on the ingredient of Passion and on the ingredient of Integrity. This will certainly help during the business pivot. Their high-level of passion will help others to see the importance of the pivot and get them enthused about it too. Their high-level integrity will cause the business and stakeholders to closely pay attention to the business leader and do so because they believe the leader to be a person of high integrity, since they do what they say and what they promise.

The business leader just squeaks in with enough of a score on the new ingredient, Pivot-Wise. Alas, where they seem deficient is on their Trust score. The trust of the organization for this business leader is below where it needs to be.

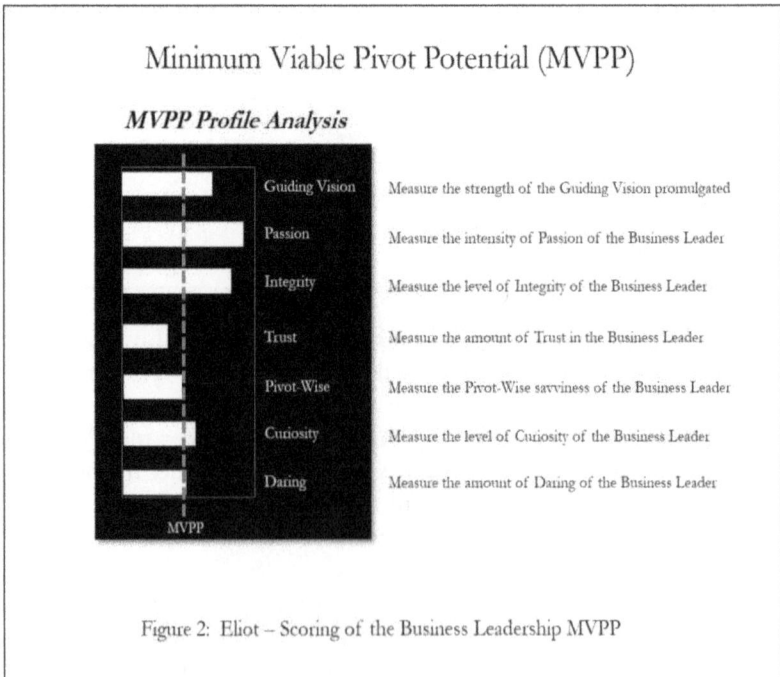

Figure 2: Eliot – Scoring of the Business Leadership MVPP

Figure 2 shows the MVPP scoring and includes a brief description for each of the ingredients and measuring the business leader accordingly.

Since this specific business leader is low on Trust, does this mean that we cannot envision this business leader being able to pull off a true business pivot? That's not quite how to interpret it. In this case, the business leader is low on just one ingredient, and low but not severely so. We would certainly want to be cautious and mindful about why the trust level is seemingly lower than it should be.

There are a number of other pointed questions to be asked. Could this be a sign that the business leader is not trustworthy enough for the type of business pivot being considered? And, what impact will this have as they pursue the business pivot? Can the business leader do something to further build trust, perhaps doing so before the pivot occurs? Does the risk of the business pivot rise because of this less than preferred level of trust?

Overall, the MVPP is a handy way to assess a business leader and try to get a sense of the chances of being able to achieve a true business pivot.

This MVPP can be used as a self-diagnostic too. A business leader having self-awareness would want to gauge how they are doing on each of the business leadership ingredients. Wherever they are scoring low, they should consider taking action to increase their capability in that ingredient. Wherever scoring high, make sure to leverage that ingredient.

SRRS: SOCIAL READJUSTMENT RATING SCALE

We have another means to take a look at the business leader. Besides their scores on the business leadership ingredients, we might also want to gauge their life events activities and how that might impact a business pivot. This might seem intrusive, and so let's carefully step into this part of the framework.

You have undoubtedly at some point seen a chart about life stresses. These charts try to indicate the most common kinds of life events and weight them as to which are the most impactful in your life. For example, death of a spouse is usually ranked as a very high stress inducer. Another is divorce. Another is personal injury. And so on.

One of the most famous such charts was developed by researchers Holmes and Rahe, back in the 1960s. It still is used today and there are also many variants of it. Some refer to it as the Holmes & Rahe Stress Scale. Another name for it is the Social Readjustment Rating Scale (SRRS). In this book, we'll will use the SRRS name to refer to it. I will also sometimes say "variant SRRS" or "SRRSv" to indicate that we are going to vary it a bit from the original. If you want to see the original version, you can readily find it online.

Shown in Figure 3 is the variant SRRS. The scaling uses numeric scores that are intended to add-up to a grand total of 600. There are more than 40 or so ranked events on the original SRRS. Here, we only show the top 10, thus, it is a variant. To give you a sense of the magnitude of the raw scoring, I have indicted how much the score represents as a percentage of the total of 600.

The top ranked and most stressful is the death of a spouse, which garners a score of 100. The original scale of the SRRS offers levels of stress as indicated by the score you would have. You of course can be undergoing more than one of the life events at the same time, and so you would add together those scores. The stress inducers are often referred to as Life Change Units (LCU).

What does this have to do with business pivots? Often, a business leader that has experienced one or more of these SRSS's will be contemplating a pivot, likely a personal pivot, and for which that personal pivot can carry over into their business life. Recall that William Wang, described in Chapter 6, had a near-death experience that led him to pivot his business. This goes back to the notion that there is an intertwining between the business leader as a person and business pivots in the business entity.

Business Leaders: Social Readjustment Rating Scale (SRRS)

Rank	Stress Inducer (LCU = Life Change Unit)	Score	Scale of 600
1	Death of spouse	100	17%
2	Divorce	73	12%
3	Martial separation	65	11%
4	Jail term	63	11%
5	Death of close family member	63	11%
6	Personal injury or illness	53	9%
7	Marriage	50	8%
8	Fired at work	47	8%
9	Marital reconciliation	45	8%
10	Other Major Life Event	45	8%

Figure 3: Eliot – Business Personal persona and Holmes & Rahe Stress Scale (variant)

BRRS: BUSINESS READJUSTMENT RATING SCALE

Let's next then consider a similar kind of Readjustment Scale, but now we'll look at the other member of our pair, the business entity. We have been looking at the business leader, considering the MVPP and their SRRS. Now, we should do the same with their dance partner, the business itself.

Look at Figure 4. Here, I have put some of the most significant kinds of business pivots and rated them accordingly. A pivot of the core business model of the firm is a doozy. It will likely utterly alter just about everything that the company does. It gets a score of 100.

Business Pivots: Business Readjustment Rating Scale (BRRS)

Rank	Business Pivot Inducer (BCU = Business Change Unit)	Score	Scale of 200
1	Pivot of Core Business Model	100	50%
2	Pivot of Company Vision/Mission	90	45%
3	Pivot of Primary Product/Service	80	40%
4	Pivot of Market Focus	70	35%
5	Pivot of Financing/Funding	70	35%
6	Pivot of Target Customer	60	30%
7	Pivot of Key Competencies	50	25%
8	Pivot of Partners/Suppliers	40	20%
9	Pivot of Operations/Production	40	20%
10	Pivot of Other Major Element	30	15%

Figure 4: Eliot – Business Pivot inducers on a rating scale referred to as BRRS.

A pivot of the company vision and mission is big too. It gets a score of 90 and appears second on the list. You might want to argue that a pivot of the vision and mission should be ranked higher than a pivot of the core business model. Yes, we could carry on that argument. Some might say that the vision and the mission alter everything else and so it should be the highest. Some say that a vision and mission are not especially earthshattering in comparison to making a core business model pivot in the organization. Others would say that if you pivot the core business model, the odds are that you are going to pivot the mission and vision too. Each of these ranked items are considered a Business Change Unit (BCU), using similar terminology as the LCU on the SRRS. We can have an endless debate about the ranking and scores of the BCU elements on the BRRS, which we could also do about the LCU's of the SRRS.

Note that just as the SRRS allowed for more than one LCU at a time, you can indeed have more than one BCU going on at the same time. You would add-up each of the pivot aspects and see what the total score is. The purpose of doing the scoring would be to gauge how massive a pivot you are trying to achieve. The larger the score, the higher the risk of the pivot, the likely higher cost, etc.

In terms of the scores shown on the BRRS sheet, you can certainly tailor this to your particular organization. The point of the template or chart is that it provides a means to examine and assess the business entity, in the same manner that we are assessing the business leader. In fact, let's take a look at both of the charts at the same time. Take a look at Figure 5.

As shown on Figure 5, we would consider the stresses of the business leader via the SRRS, which might lead to a business pivot, and we would consider the stresses of the business entity via the BRRS, in terms of what aspects of the business entity appear to need a pivot. Those two aspects, the SRRS and the BRRS can be explored and considered conjunctively.

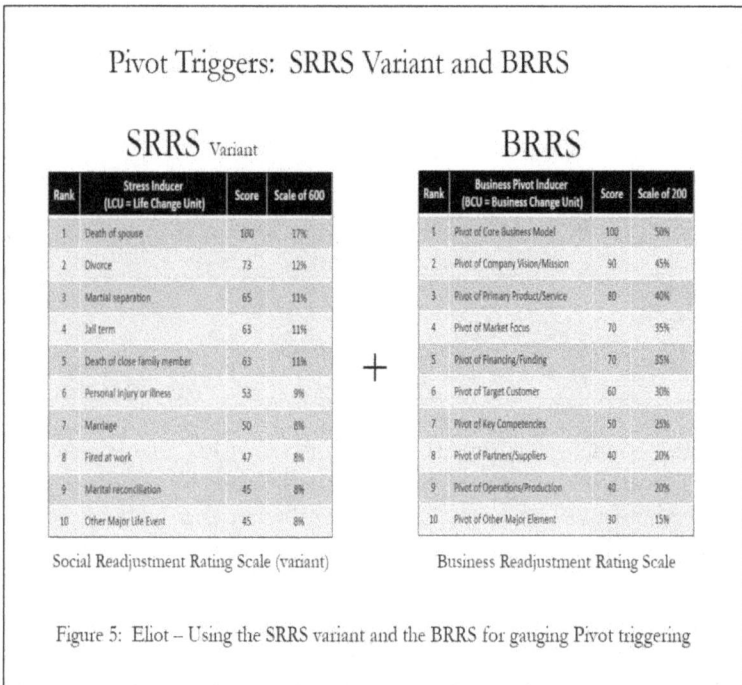

Pivot Triggers: SRRS Variant and BRRS

SRRS Variant

Rank	Stress Inducer (LCU = Life Change Unit)	Score	Scale of 600
1	Death of spouse	100	17%
2	Divorce	73	12%
3	Marital separation	65	11%
4	Jail term	63	11%
5	Death of close family member	63	11%
6	Personal injury or illness	53	9%
7	Marriage	50	8%
8	Fired at work	47	8%
9	Marital reconciliation	45	8%
10	Other Major Life Event	45	8%

BRRS

Rank	Business Pivot Inducer (BCU = Business Change Unit)	Score	Scale of 200
1	Pivot of Core Business Model	100	50%
2	Pivot of Company Vision/Mission	90	45%
3	Pivot of Primary Product/Service	80	40%
4	Pivot of Market Focus	70	35%
5	Pivot of Financing/Funding	70	35%
6	Pivot of Target Customer	60	30%
7	Pivot of Key Competencies	50	25%
8	Pivot of Partners/Suppliers	40	20%
9	Pivot of Operations/Production	40	20%
10	Pivot of Other Major Element	30	15%

Social Readjustment Rating Scale (variant)   Business Readjustment Rating Scale

Figure 5: Eliot – Using the SRRS variant and the BRRS for gauging Pivot triggering

This then leads us to Figure 6. Follow the arrows. The business leader can be a pivot driver for the business entity to undertake a pivot. The business entity can be a pivot driver on the business leader to undertake a pivot. I say that because I've stated earlier that business entities do not just miraculously by themselves do a pivot, they are not sentient. A business leader makes business pivots happen.

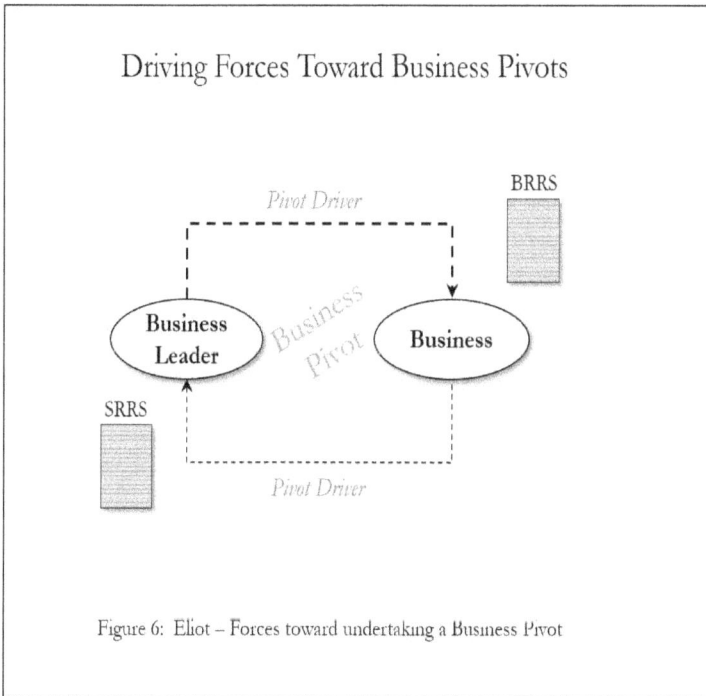

Figure 6: Eliot – Forces toward undertaking a Business Pivot

We now have added some handy tools to the Pivot-Wise toolkit. A quick recap might be helpful:

- ✓ The MVPP tells us whether the business leader has the "right stuff" to carry out a true business pivot,

- ✓ The SRRS tells us whether the business leader has stresses in their life that might lead them toward wanting to do a personal and business pivot,

- ✓ The BRRS tells us what the business is experiencing as "stress" and where it possibly needs readjustment, and the *readjustment* would be a business pivot in this context.

CHAPTER 17

PIVOT TRIGGERS, SUPPRESANTS, STAKEHHOLDERS

CHAPTER 17

PIVOT TRIGGERS, SUPPRESANTS, STAKEHOLDERS

PREFACE

The pivot stages' model that was introduced in Chapter 2 indicated that there are *Conditions* that feed into the pivoting process. Those conditions are the impetus to the business leader and the business entity that a pivot might be warranted. The other side of that coin is that the conditions can also act to dissuade the business leader and the business entity from undertaking a pivot. Here, we define those conditions that push toward the pivot as *Triggers*, and the opposite conditions that try to suppress the pivot as *Suppressants*. We will explore those aspects in this chapter.

A business leader must be cognizant of all the other "actors" that will come to play when considering and undertaking a pivot. These participants are usually referred to in business parlance as the business *Stakeholders*. We will identify and review the nature of the various stakeholders involved in the pivot process. The Pivot-Wise business leader had best make sure that they do not neglect, forget, or omit stakeholder positioning when forging a pivot, lest the odds are increased that a vital stakeholder might arise at an inopportune moment and possibly quash the pivot.

───────

221

CHAPTER 17: PIVOT TRIGGERS, SUPPRESANTS, STAKEHOLDERS

Recall that in Chapter 2, a model was introduced that indicated there are three stages to a pivot, consisting of the Pre-Pivot, the Pivot Point, and the Post-Pivot. The three stages can each vary in length of duration. There are Conditions that feed into the Pre-Pivot stage and also continue throughout the other remaining two stages.

Conditions can be shifting and changing throughout the pivot. This is important because putting your finger up in the air to see which way the wind is blowing would only give you the wind direction at that moment in time; the wind is going to be varying over time. The Pivot-Wise business leader will be periodically rechecking the wind conditions, so to speak, throughout the pivot process.

Take a look at Figure 1. You can see that we have added some additional aspects to the pivot model. On the left side of the diagram, the Conditions are shown as being fed into by **Pivot Triggers** and by **Pivot Suppressants**.

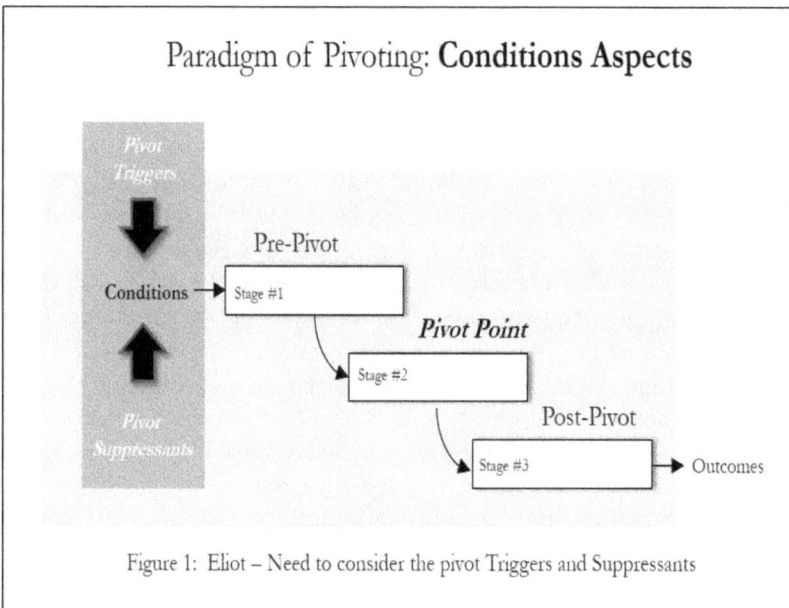

Figure 1: Eliot – Need to consider the pivot Triggers and Suppressants

Pivot Triggers are those conditions that are pushing toward the pivot. They will often be aspects that the business leader keeps hearing about, and that they themselves might be helping to identify and even induce. Sometimes the triggers are subtle and not so easily recognized as a precursor toward needing or warranting a pivot. Like the ball of snow that rolls down the snowy hill and grows in size as it does, the triggers can begin with not much weight and grow stronger and stronger over time.

What kinds of triggers might there be? We can use our prior groundwork to help on answer this question. If the business leader has a high SRRSv, which is the Social Readjustment Rating Score variant introduced in Chapter 16, then we might be steering toward a pivot. For example, suppose the business leader has had a near-death incident, a high score on the SRRSv, akin to what we saw with William Wang (Chapter 6), this might trigger the impetus for a pivot. The BRRS is another indicator of a potential trigger. If the Core Business Model rates high as an issue in the organization and needs to be readjusted, it is a trigger to the business entity that a pivot might be needed. Supposing that the SRRSv is high, or the BRRS is high, we also likely need the MVPP to be of a sufficient level to get us to a pivot. Recall that the Minimum Viable Pivot Potential (MVPP) indicates whether the business leader has the needed level of business leadership ingredients to pull of the pivot. See Figure 2.

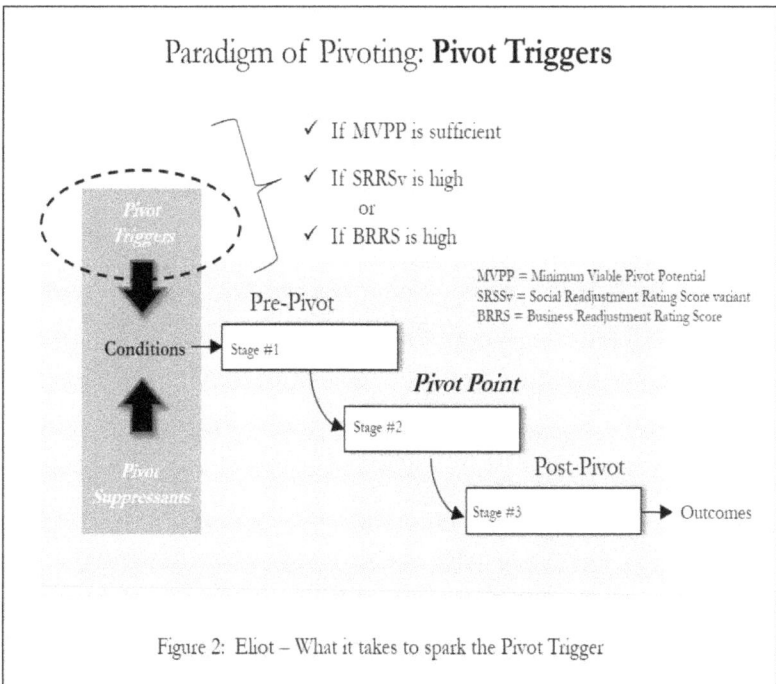

Paradigm of Pivoting: **Pivot Triggers**

✓ If MVPP is sufficient
✓ If SRRSv is high
or
✓ If BRRS is high

MVPP = Minimum Viable Pivot Potential
SRRSv = Social Readjustment Rating Score variant
BRRS = Business Readjustment Rating Score

Figure 2: Eliot – What it takes to spark the Pivot Trigger

Triggers will push toward a pivot. There are forces of an opposite or opposing nature that are likely going to be trying to suppress the pivot. Those Pivot Suppressants can be explored by using the same tools we used with the Pivot Triggers. Take a look at Figure 3.

If the SRRSv is low, meaning that business leader has no personal stresses that might be driving a pivot, this can be an indicator that the pivot might not be likely since the business leader is less motivated to be considering a pivot.

Don't take that notion in isolation. Simultaneously, there is the BRRS, and so if the organization is bleeding and wailing about aspects such as that revenue is weak, products are not selling, and so on, it can be equally alerting and awakening for the business leader to the need for the pivot. This also then partially depends on the MVPP of the business leader. Are they in a posture within the organization to be able to conceive of and carry out a pivot? This was explored when we introduced the MVPP.

As shown in Figure 3, if the MVPP is low, and if the SRRSv or BRRS are low, these are likely suppressants of the pivot.

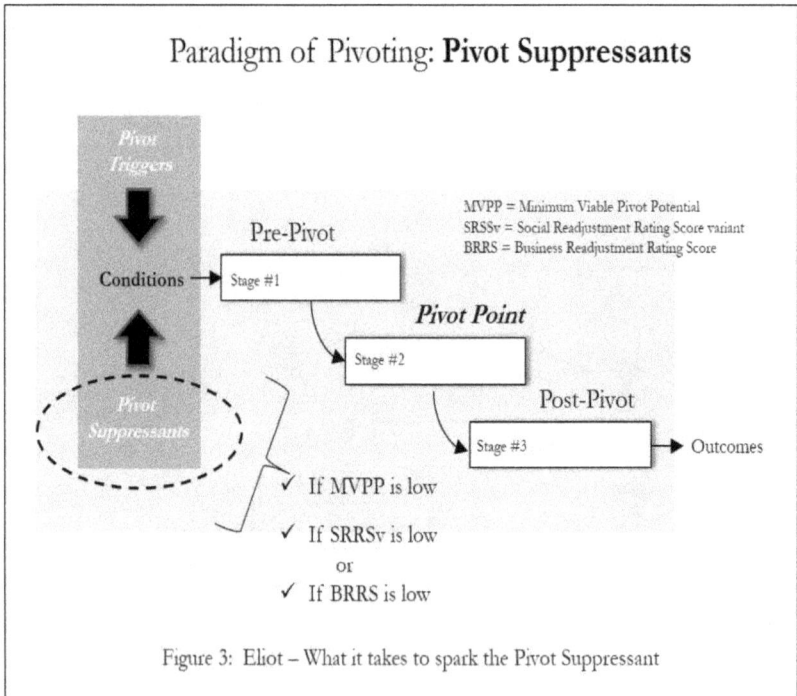

Paradigm of Pivoting: **Pivot Suppressants**

Pivot Triggers

Conditions → Pre-Pivot

Stage #1

MVPP = Minimum Viable Pivot Potential
SRSSv = Social Readjustment Rating Score variant
BRRS = Business Readjustment Rating Score

Pivot Point

Stage #2

Pivot Suppressants

Post-Pivot

Stage #3 → Outcomes

✓ If MVPP is low
✓ If SRRSv is low
or
✓ If BRRS is low

Figure 3: Eliot – What it takes to spark the Pivot Suppressant

STAKEHOLDERS AND PIVOTS

There will be a slew of stakeholders that will care one way or another about the business pivot. The odds are that the stakeholders will not be bashful about their opinions. Usually, one or more stakeholders is yelling to the rafters that a business pivot is needed. They might not know what way the pivot should go, but they want one anyway, since they figure anything is better than where the firm is now. There will be some stakeholders that have carefully considered the matter and might have a very directed kind of pivot in mind.

Take a look at Figure 4. Stakeholders consist of the Board of Directors, fellow executives of the business leader that is the focal point of the potential pivot, regulators such as congressional members or other local lawmakers or others, the shareholders, the funders of the firm, the media, and anyone else that perceives themselves as having a stake in the business.

Any and all of these stakeholders can be potential triggers toward the pivot. The Pivot-Wise business leader needs to undertake a continuous Stakeholder analysis, gauging which way the wind is blowing. These winds sometimes gust by themselves. In other cases, the business leader can help the winds to gust, by urging the appropriate stakeholders towards the pivot.

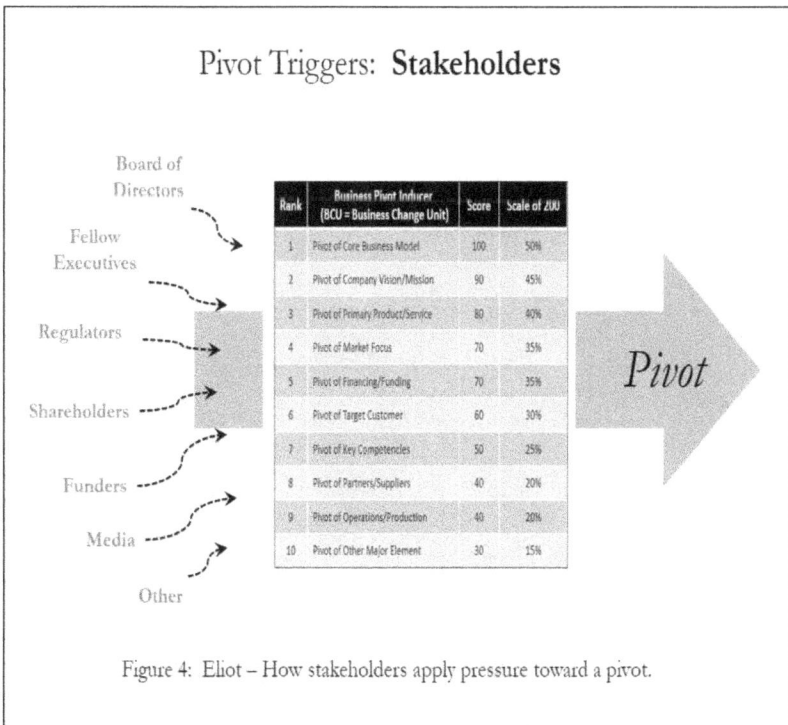

Pivot Triggers: **Stakeholders**

Board of Directors

Fellow Executives

Regulators

Shareholders

Funders

Media

Other

Rank	Business Pivot Inducer (BCU = Business Change Unit)	Score	Scale of 200
1	Pivot of Core Business Model	100	50%
2	Pivot of Company Vision/Mission	90	45%
3	Pivot of Primary Product/Service	80	40%
4	Pivot of Market Focus	70	35%
5	Pivot of Financing/Funding	70	35%
6	Pivot of Target Customer	60	30%
7	Pivot of Key Competencies	50	25%
8	Pivot of Partners/Suppliers	40	20%
9	Pivot of Operations/Production	40	20%
10	Pivot of Other Major Element	30	15%

Pivot

Figure 4: Eliot – How stakeholders apply pressure toward a pivot.

There will be stakeholders on the opposite side of the pivot push, and will be pivot suppressants. Take a look at Figure 5.

Stakeholders again consist of the Board of Directors, fellow executives of the business leader that is the focal point of the potential pivot, regulators such as congressional members or other local lawmakers or others, the shareholders, the funders of the firm, the media, and anyone else that perceives themselves as having a stake in the business.

Any and all of these stakeholders can be potential suppressants of the pivot. I shall repeat my earlier comment, namely that the Pivot-Wise business leader needs to undertake a continuous Stakeholder analysis, gauging which way the wind is blowing. As stated, these winds sometimes gust by themselves. In other cases, the business leader can help the winds to gust, by urging the appropriate stakeholders *against* the pivot.

You might have noticed that I just said that the business leader might be urging to go against the pivot. I think that's worthy of a moment of attention. Do not assume that I am advocating business pivots for the sake of glorification of pivoting. I am not. I have been trying to emphasize that the business pivot needs to be used wisely. The wise use of a hammer does not mean that you always use the hammer. You use a hammer when the right time, place, and need for it arises.

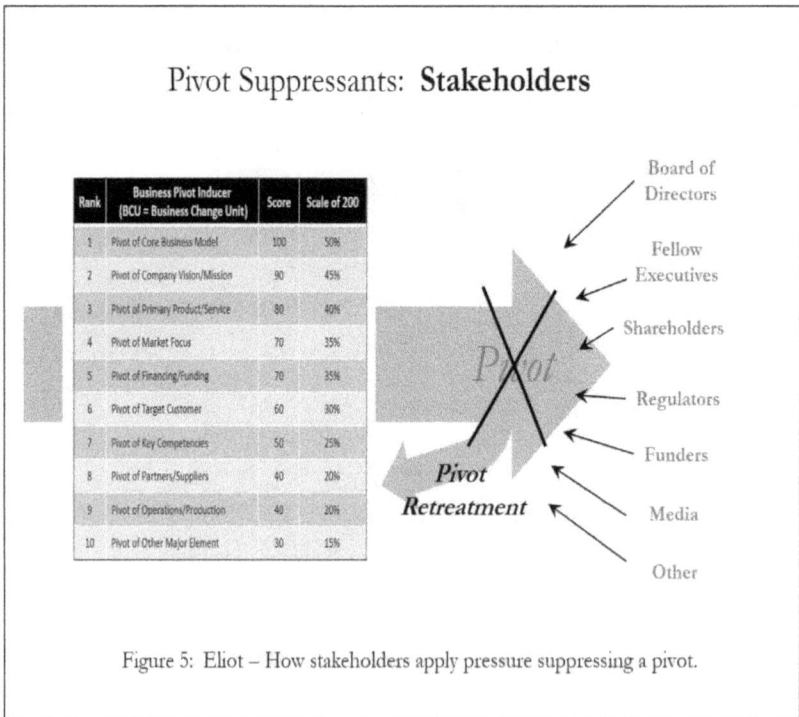

Pivot Suppressants: **Stakeholders**

Rank	Business Pivot Inducer (BCU = Business Change Unit)	Score	Scale of 200
1	Pivot of Core Business Model	100	50%
2	Pivot of Company Vision/Mission	90	45%
3	Pivot of Primary Product/Service	80	40%
4	Pivot of Market Focus	70	35%
5	Pivot of Financing/Funding	70	35%
6	Pivot of Target Customer	60	30%
7	Pivot of Key Competencies	50	25%
8	Pivot of Partners/Suppliers	40	20%
9	Pivot of Operations/Production	40	20%
10	Pivot of Other Major Element	30	15%

Board of Directors
Fellow Executives
Shareholders
Regulators
Funders
Media
Other

Pivot
Pivot Retreatment

Figure 5: Eliot – How stakeholders apply pressure suppressing a pivot.

It is my hope and contention that a Pivot-Wise business leader will use the tools of this book to ascertain when to go toward a pivot <u>and</u> when to go away from a pivot. There will be circumstances wherein a key stakeholder will be pushing mightily towards a pivot. The business leader, a Pivot-Wise one, if they have determined that a pivot at that time would be unwise, would be expected to try and oppose the pivot, if they can, and do so in a manner that would somehow appease the stakeholder or otherwise try to find some way to defuse the situation.

Conducting a stakeholder push/pull analysis is a handy approach to figuring out which stakeholders are supporting a pivot versus which ones are opposing the pivot. I provide in Figure 6 a diagram depicting this approach.

You likely might recognize this type of diagram; if you've seen other similar diagrammatic techniques, often referred to as a Force Field analysis, generally attributed to being popularized by Lewin.

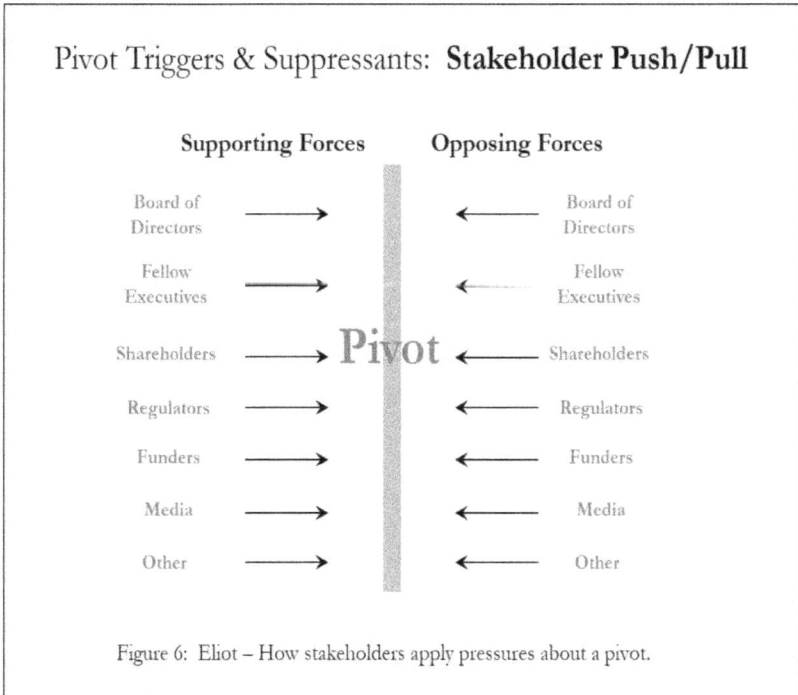

Pivot Triggers & Suppressants: **Stakeholder Push/Pull**

Supporting Forces   **Opposing Forces**

| Board of Directors → | ← Board of Directors |
| Fellow Executives → | ← Fellow Executives |
| Shareholders → **Pivot** ← Shareholders |
Regulators →	← Regulators
Funders →	← Funders
Media →	← Media
Other →	← Other

Figure 6: Eliot – How stakeholders apply pressures about a pivot.

In Figure 7, the same diagram is shown, except now I have indicated that in a particular circumstance there are particular stakeholders supporting the pivot and particular stakeholders opposing the pivot.

For example, suppose the Board of Directors is in favor of the pivot, as are fellow executives, the funders, and some other stakeholders. But, opposing the pivot are the shareholders, the regulators, the media, and some other stakeholders too.

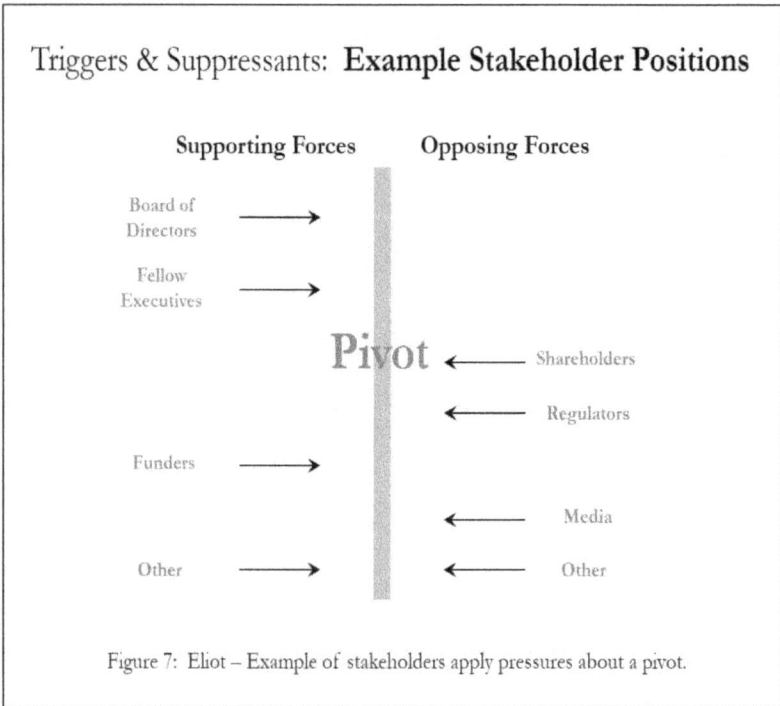

Figure 7: Eliot – Example of stakeholders apply pressures about a pivot.

This is going to be an uphill battle for the pivot. Pivots often are uphill battles, but the array of opposing forces looks especially daunting in this case.

The business leader will need to do their own calculus as to the strength of the opposing forces, and figure out ways to overcome their opposition, assuming that the business leader wants to proceed with the pivot. Of course, if the business leader believes the pivot to be unwarranted, they would presumably try to bolster the opposing forces and simultaneously try to find ways to placate the pivot desiring forces.

One approach of trying to woo a stakeholder to your side of whether or not to do a pivot can be by directly negotiating with them about the matter, while another approach is leveraging other stakeholders to do so. These can both be used.

In short, here's a quick indication of using the stakeholder analysis:

- Business leader in favor of doing the pivot
  - Identify supporting stakeholders, enlist their support
  - Identify opposing stakeholders, try to shift them to in favor

- Business leader opposes doing the pivot
  - Identify opposing stakeholders, enlist their aid in opposing
  - Identify supporting stakeholders, try to shift to be opposing

The delicate dance of dealing with a situation where there are powerful stakeholders on either side of the pivot is a sizable challenge for the likelihood of a pivot occurring and being successful.

If the business leader favors the pivot, and gets it to happen, doing so in say spite of the opposing forces, you can bet that those opposing forces are going to be eyeing every moment of the pivot and hopeful of finding a chance to dash it. If the business leader opposes the pivot, and prevents it from happening, doing so in spite of the forces in favor of it, you can bet those favoring forces are going to be eyeing the business leader and every little bump will be a sign that the pivot should have been undertaken.

As much as feasible, the business leader needs to try and align as many stakeholders toward whichever direction seems most appropriate. Of course, in the messy real-world, you cannot satisfy all of the people all of the time. There will be some that will always remain in-favor or in-opposition to whichever posture you take.

CHAPTER 18

THE PIVOT-W SEGMENT MODEL

CHAPTER 18

THE PIVOT-W SEGMENT MODEL

PREFACE

The stories of the founders and CEO's that were covered in this book provides some insight into the nature of pivots and business leaders, including the aspect of when pivots tend to occur.

Nearly all of the stories involve a pivot that happens prior to the advent of the working career per se of the business leader. This usually is a pivot during college days or otherwise somewhat earlier in life. There is then a pivot during the working career, often towards the first part of the working career. A kind of enlightenment or opportunity arises that leads to the pivot. Finally, there is usually a mid-career pivot that occurs. We take a closer look at this pattern of pivots in this chapter.

———

CHAPTER 18: THE PIVOT-W SEGMENT MODEL

The stories of Aaron Levie, William Wang, Jon Kraft, and the other founders and CEO's depicted in this book are quite inspiring. We can read their stories and look for clues about what it takes to do business pivots. We can also look for clues that provide an indication of when pivots take place. Maybe by examining their stories, we can relate to how our own careers and pivots might or even should take place.

It is probably helpful to keep in mind that these business leaders are the 1%, in a sense, meaning that not all business leaders will have the kind of career that they have had, presumably 99% won't. So, if we look only at them to find patterns, it is not clear how well this translates to the other 99%. But, in spite of that now gloomily pointed out qualm, let's take a look anyway.

At a macroscopic perspective, there seems to be a general pattern of approximately three major pivots in their careers. I say major pivots because there are lots of minor pivots going on too. Don't want to quibble over this major versus minor aspect, and so just go along for the moment. In Figure 1, I show a graph that has the pivot magnitude along the vertical axis, and the career timeline along the horizontal axis. There are three circles depicting shown at certain points in time and at certain levels of pivot magnitude.

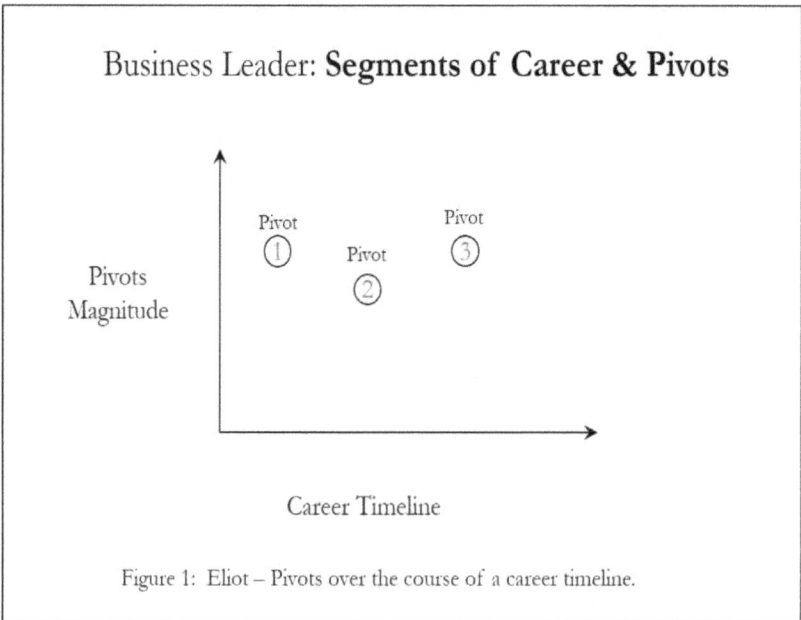

Figure 1: Eliot – Pivots over the course of a career timeline.

Next, let's layer into the diagram a pattern that seems to emerge about the business leaders. It seems that by-and-large they had a major pivot while in their pre-career portion of life. Usually, this takes place in college or in that same age range as a typical college student.

Then, there is another major pivot when they are early in their working career. There often seems to be a catalyst that after they've worked for a while, they seek to find something else or bigger to do. This can occur by their own volition and realization, or might be sparked by others around them telling them so, or by an opportunity that arises in front of them.

Finally, there is a mid-career or in rarer circumstances late-career major pivot. In Figure 2, the diagram has been augmented to show the three portions of the career timeline. A dashed line indicates the dividing line between the three portions. The three portions have been labeled.

Does this always happen this way? No. This is a generalized pattern. Does this mean that if you did not have a pre-career major pivot that you are somehow doomed to not having other major pivots in your life? No. You might not have any major pivots, you might have 5 major pivots, and any other combination or permutation. On the other hand, I am betting that on-the-average for those that fall into the 1% that they will have a pattern like this. Imagine that we have a coin, and we flip the coin. If we flip it say twice, will we for sure get one time a heads and one time a tails? No. It is only on-the-average over a large number of flips that we would expect to see the coin landing as we expect it to via probability of chance.

Business Leader: **Segments of Career & Pivots**

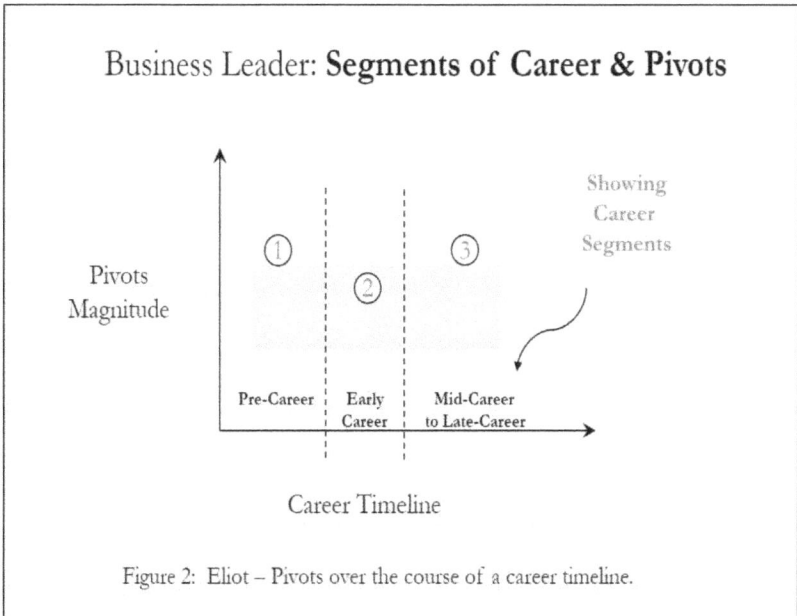

Figure 2: Eliot – Pivots over the course of a career timeline.

I have also now augmented the diagram further, shown in Figure 3, and linked together the three pivots. There is a line going from the first pivot to the second pivot, and from the second pivot to the third pivot.

Again, as a general pattern, the first pivot seemed to be of the most magnitude, the second pivot often of a greatly significant pivot but maybe not as high as the first pivot. Then the third pivot is nearly as high as the first pivot, and more so than the second pivot.

One interpretation is that the first pivot causes a re-direction that is career guiding thereafter and so of a very high magnitude for the business leader. The second pivot is somewhat more cautious, though still a major pivot. Then, at mid-career the business leader has reached a sense of confidence and desire that they seek to undertake another major pivot, perhaps this time with more aplomb than the prior two.

We will refer to this as the Pivot-W Segment model. The "W" is because the shape of the pattern looks like a big W. The word "segment" is used because it is a segmentation into three parts.

Review this model in light of your own career.

If you are just getting started in your career, this might be a pattern that you will experience, and so be expecting it to potentially happen. If you are further along in your career, reflect upon your experiences to-date and see if this fits.

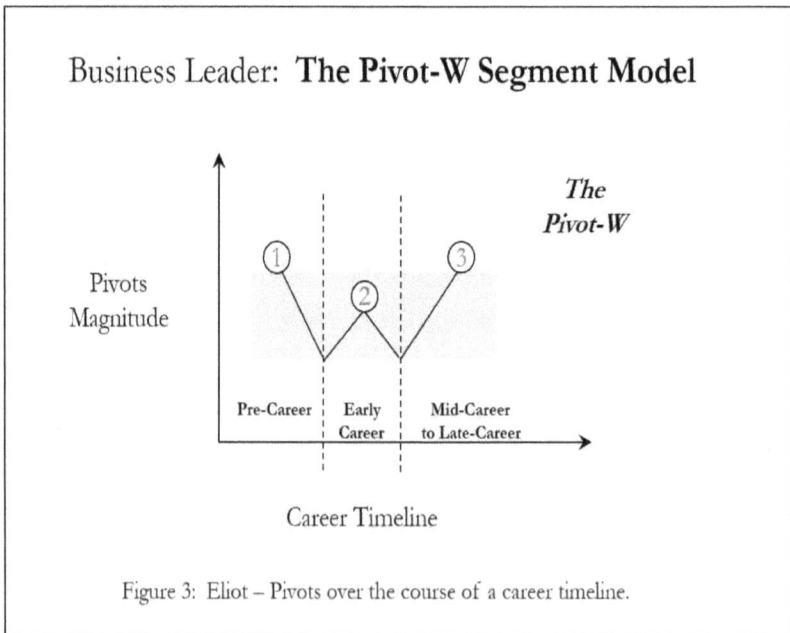

Figure 3: Eliot – Pivots over the course of a career timeline.

. When I was a professor, many students came to me and were worried that they did not like the major that they had declared upon entering into the university as a freshman. They were worried because they wanted to change their major, but thought it safer to stick with their first declared major, rather than changing it. I pointed out to them that on-the-average most college students change their major about two to three times over the course of getting their bachelor's degree.

It used to be that the initial year or two of college was intended to be a time of exploring courses and majors. You would purposely wait to select a major until after having a better and broader sense of what interested you. Unfortunately, nowadays many college degree programs are so packed with courses required for a major that if you don't start it as a freshman, your chances of finishing in four years is low. This forces students to make a life-long choice when they likely least know what they want to do.

The impact also of changing the major is that they then might fall behind in finishing the degree on-time. This potential penalty of switching a major is rightfully one that cause students to think twice before changing their major. Anyway, I tried to point out to students that if they stick with a major that they decidedly don't like, and if they are assuming that they will ultimately work in that same field, they are looking at doing something 8 a.m. to 5 p.m. (or longer) each day for the rest of their working career. They had better be choosing something that they have an interest and passion for. Otherwise, it is going to be a dreary work life ahead.

I will offer in a later chapter some similar stories about the early-career pivots and the mid-career pivots. Before ending this chapter, I'd like to point out that for you film buffs reading this book, if any doing so, you might recognize the shape of Pivot-W Segment model in terms of the famous "Big W" that was featured in the movie classic "It's a Mad, Mad, Mad, Mad World" (starring greats of the era such as Jonathan Winters, Mickey Rooney, Spencer Tracy, Sid Caesar, Milton Berle, Ethel Merman, Buddy Hackett, Phil Silvers).

.

CHAPTER 19

YOUR PIVOT TEAM

CHAPTER 19

YOUR PIVOT TEAM

PREFACE

It takes a village to properly achieve a business pivot. With that bit of tongue-in-cheek, let's focus in this chapter on the team that will be needed to undertake a pivot. I have been concentrating on the business leader throughout most of the material in this book. The business leader is not alone in the business. As a leader, they are charged with leading others. For undertaking a pivot, a properly composed team will be needed. The team will be involved in the three stages of the pivot process.

Assembling a team is not as easy as it sounds. For a business pivot, you might be tempted to just grab a few trusted allies and declare that you have a team. The odds are that the team you've assembled does not cover all the needed bases. We will explore the nature of the team participants that are needed for undertaking the business pivot.

———

CHAPTER 19: YOUR PIVOT TEAM

Now it's time to start thinking about the team you will need to assemble and guide in order to undertake a business pivot. The team might be small at the beginning of the process. During the Pre-Pivot stage, you might have a tightly woven team of just key participants, each there to help determine whether the pivot is viable or not. Once you've turned the corner on the pivot moving forward, the team will likely need to be expanded. At the end of the Pre-Pivot, you should have a clear picture of what kind of skills are needed for the team. You will also need to wrestle with how to get the team members to be on the team.

Allow me to explain that last remark. Getting team members onto a pivot team might be difficult. The odds are that they are some of the most valued members of the company. The odds too are that they are doing other tasks for the firm that are essential. Drawing them away from their other essential work is going to create a hole or gap in what the firm is doing.

These holes or gaps need to be shored up. Shoring up a hole or gap is not easy. Some business leaders falsely fall into the mental trap that they can just hire someone that has the same skills and use that person to back-fill for someone that's on the pivot team. Usually, a back-fill has no idea of what the specifics of the firm are, and cannot just be parachuted into doing the same work as someone that has shifted onto the pivot team. There is a learning curve involved that will take time. There is also usually a drain on the incumbent as they show the newbie the job. You will need to carefully and with distinct attention figure out how to cope with pulling key people away from "their day job" and ask them to serve on the pivot team.

Another mental trap of a business leader is that they think that the amount of time on the pivot team won't be very much. In other words, why not take someone that's working a full work week and just ask them to put a few more hours here or there toward the pivot team. The odds are that it will be a lot more than a few hours here or there. Many pivot teams begin with a trickle, but it eventually becomes a torrent of time once the Pivot Point is reached. Likewise, the Post-Pivot is often neglected when estimating the true amount of time that will be needed the pivot team members. It all adds up.

Let's contemplate for a moment what kinds of skills might be needed when considering a pivot. There is likely the need to figure out the financial aspects of the pivot. What are the potential benefits and potentials costs? What is the ROI? Where will the funds come from to undertake the pivot? So, you'll need some good financial wizardry on the pivot team.

The pivot might impact the accounting of the firm. There might need to be adjustments to the accounting structure and account codes. The company books might need to be changed. Overall, you are looking at having accounting wizardry on the pivot team.

From a marketing perspective, you'll likely be altering how you go to market and the markets that you are wanting to now target. You'll need a hotshot marketing person on the pivot team. The pivot is likely to impact people's jobs at the company. An organizational hierarchical restructuring might be needed. You'll need a topnotch talent management or HR person on the team. New systems might be needed or legacy systems might need to be altered, so get an Information Technology (IT) person on the team.

You will want to communicate internally and externally about the pivot. Grab the corporate communications guru. Operations and production are bound to be part of the pivot. Get key participants from Ops onto the pivot team. Whether you like it or not, there are sure to be legal issues, perhaps contracts need to be renegotiated or there might be potential legal landmines from the pivot. Put some legal counsel on the pivot team. And think about any other roles needed.

As shown in Figure 1, you will need to seed the pivot team with the appropriate talent from each of the functional areas.

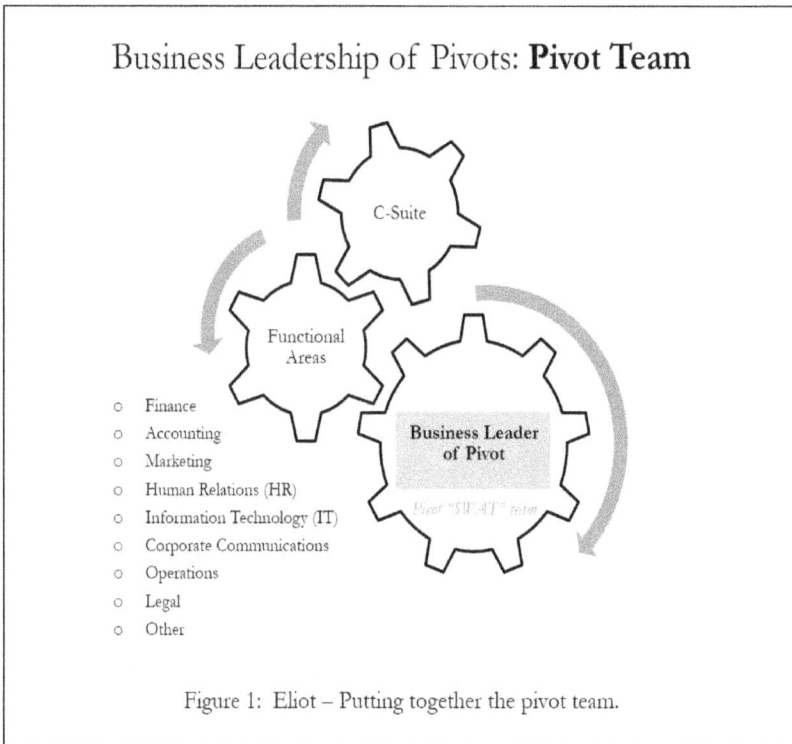

Figure 1: Eliot – Putting together the pivot team.

If you are a multi-divisional firm, you will likely need representation from the divisions too. Do not wait until it is too late to involve the cross-functional and cross-divisional representatives. Aim to get them involved as early as you can, preferably during the Pre-Pivot.

The logic is that if you wait, and if you add them at the Pivot Point once you have already committed to the pivot, the late-added participants might know of some Achilles' heel that the rest of the team did not think of. Better to know beforehand than to get caught once you are already into the middle of things.

Shown in Figure 2 is a list of the functional areas and what they will each likely bring to the table as part of the pivot team. Your role as business leader will be to get them to coalesce together. This can be hard. They all have different specialties and differing views of the firm. They will likely have differing views about the nature of the pivot, ranging from believing that one is needed to disbelieving that one is needed. This is where your MVPP comes to play, since you need to lead them. If you can't get the pivot team to play together, the odds of getting the pivot to work is seemingly slim odds.

Business Leadership of Pivots: **Pivot Team**

Functional Area of the Firm	Explanation of Role on Team
Finance	Estimate value of pivot, ROI, obtain funding, handle financial aspects
Accounting	Identify impacts to the books, restructuring of accounts, procedures
Marketing	Ascertain market impacts, rebranding and refocus, channels assessment and adjust
Human Relations (HR)	Talent impacts, job roles and reporting relationships, people backlashes coping
Information Technology (IT)	Systems impacts, upgrades to legacy systems, put in place new systems
Corporate Communications	Internal and external communications aspects, ascertain per stakeholder
Operations	Operational impacts, changes in practices, new procedures, production
Legal	Legal impacts, new licenses or contracts, potential for lawsuits and protection
Other	Other areas of the business as needed

Figure 2: Eliot – Team across all functional areas and representations needed.

I realize that a start-up venture is not necessarily going to have much vastness of resources to utilize for the pivot team. Most start-ups are barely hanging together in terms of everyone serving in many ways and wearing a multitude of hats. Your finance person is also your accountant which is also your IT person. That kind of thing.

Whether a small firm or big firm, you do need the specialties that I have mentioned. If you don't have them in-house, then get them from the outside. Consider using consultants, but be careful in your selections. Preferably, get ones that are not only versed in their particular profession, but have also been through a pivot before, successfully. Also, make sure that any such added team members are really part of the team. Sometimes, the outside consultant irks the internal team members, or the internal team members are upset about someone coming from the outside, and thus as the business leader you'll need to deal with those team dynamics.

I find it useful to estimate how much effort from each functional area you will need for the pivot. This allows you to then work within the firm if you are "borrowing" from the functional areas, since you can provide an indication of the anticipated duration and effort. Take a look at Figure 3.

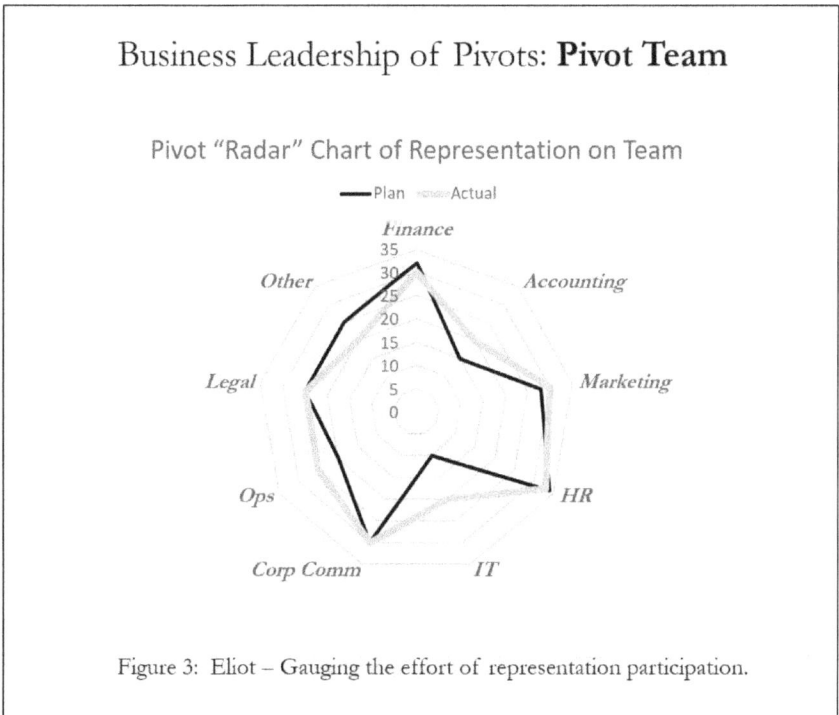

Business Leadership of Pivots: **Pivot Team**

Pivot "Radar" Chart of Representation on Team

Figure 3: Eliot – Gauging the effort of representation participation.

Figure 3 shows a "radar" style diagram in which I have estimated the total effort for the pivot team over the duration. I scaled it to a total of 35 which was based on an estimate of 350 person hours for the worst-case scenario of the maximum time needed for any single functional area (using 35 instead of 350 for ease of creating and showing the scale) for this particular pivot in a specific company.

The darker line shows the planned amount, while the shadowed line next to it shows the actual. You can see that the biggest gap between the estimated and the actual was for IT. Turns out that the number of systems that needed to pivot for the pivot was more than originally anticipated. Watch out for that.

Overall, the point of this chapter was to get you thinking about the composition of your pivot team. Think widely. Consider carefully the membership. A wrongly composed pivot team will be as much a detriment to the pivot as anything else that you do. A poorly constructed pivot team will end-up with the pitfalls that we'll be covering Chapter 21.

Having a good pivot team is more than just tossing together a bunch of people into a conference room. Some business leaders treat the putting together of the pivot team as a kind of checkmark exercise. Need a pivot team, assign some people, and voila, checkmark, it's done. That could be the writing on the gravestone for that pivot.

CHAPTER 20

LBE BUSINESS PIVOT METHODOLOGY

CHAPTER 20

LBE BUSINESS PIVOT METHODOLOGY

PREFACE

We have covered the fundamentals of the pivot process. There are three stages, the Pre-Pivot, the Pivot Point, and the Post-Pivot. There has been much discussion in this book about those stages. As a business leader, you probably would find it handy to have some further details underlying each of those stages. You need a methodology.

I present the key elements of the LBE Business Pivot Methodology. It describes the tasks that will need to be undertaken during each of the three stages. In this chapter, we describe the Methodology and give a sense of how to go about using it. There are other methodologies you can use. You can even create your own. Whichever you decide to use, at least make sure that you are using some methodology. I say that because if you don't have a set of tasks to be performed, you will be whistling in the dark in terms of bringing together your pivot team and having them do something useful towards the business pivot.

———

CHAPTER 20: LBE BUSINESS PIVOT METHODOLOGY

Undertaking a business pivot is essentially like a project. In fact, it is indeed a project. A special kind of project, but nonetheless a project. Many projects fail because they lack a proper set of steps or tasks to undertake. Without such a set of tasks, the project skips around and fails to do things that need to be done. The result is that the effort falters.

Presented in Figure 1 is the LBE Business Pivot Methodology. This provides the series of steps that should be undertaken when doing a business pivot. It is shaped around the three stages that we have already discussed at some length. There are tasks for the Pre-Pivot, tasks for the Pivot Point, and tasks for the Post-Pivot.

You can use this Methodology, or you can choose a different one, or you can make one of your own.

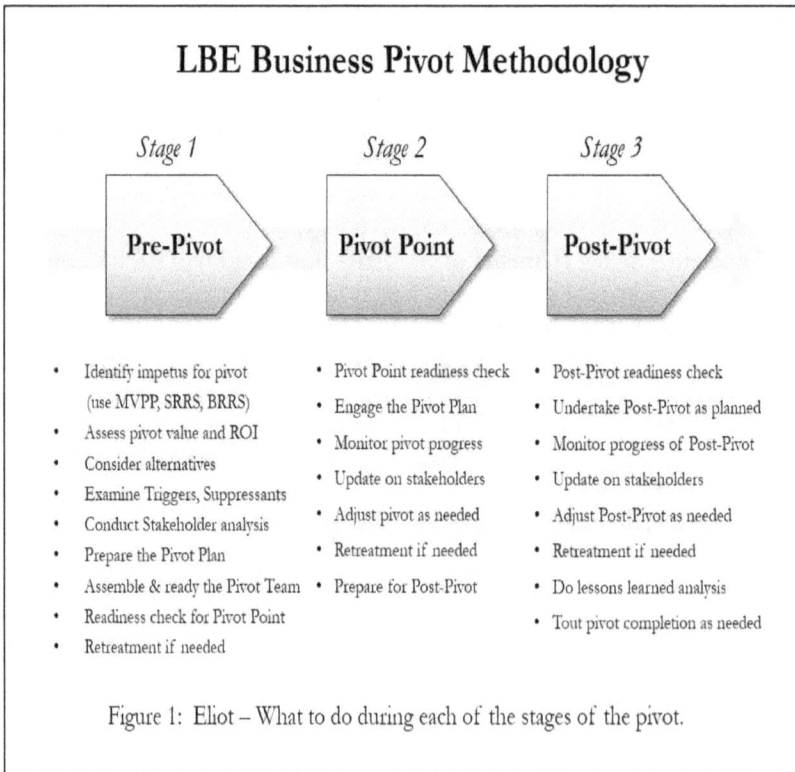

LBE Business Pivot Methodology

Stage 1 *Stage 2* *Stage 3*

Pre-Pivot **Pivot Point** **Post-Pivot**

* Identify impetus for pivot (use MVPP, SRRS, BRRS)
* Assess pivot value and ROI
* Consider alternatives
* Examine Triggers, Suppressants
* Conduct Stakeholder analysis
* Prepare the Pivot Plan
* Assemble & ready the Pivot Team
* Readiness check for Pivot Point
* Retreatment if needed

* Pivot Point readiness check
* Engage the Pivot Plan
* Monitor pivot progress
* Update on stakeholders
* Adjust pivot as needed
* Retreatment if needed
* Prepare for Post-Pivot

* Post-Pivot readiness check
* Undertake Post-Pivot as planned
* Monitor progress of Post-Pivot
* Update on stakeholders
* Adjust Post-Pivot as needed
* Retreatment if needed
* Do lessons learned analysis
* Tout pivot completion as needed

Figure 1: Eliot – What to do during each of the stages of the pivot.

Make sure to use a methodology. Some business leaders assemble the pivot team and seem to think that by some miracle they will figure out what needs to be done. Probably better to just go ahead and use a methodology to provide structure and an approach.

Plus, choose a methodology that makes sense to you. I say that because there are some methodologies that seem overly complex and arcane. If you, as the business leader, are faced with a methodology that seems top-heavy, you'd probably want to think twice about using it. Others on the pivot team will likely find it hard to follow too, and ultimately you might find yourself contending more with the methodology than actually doing the pivot.

Let's next do a walk-through of each stage. Shown in Figure 2 is a highlight of the Pre-Pivot stage.

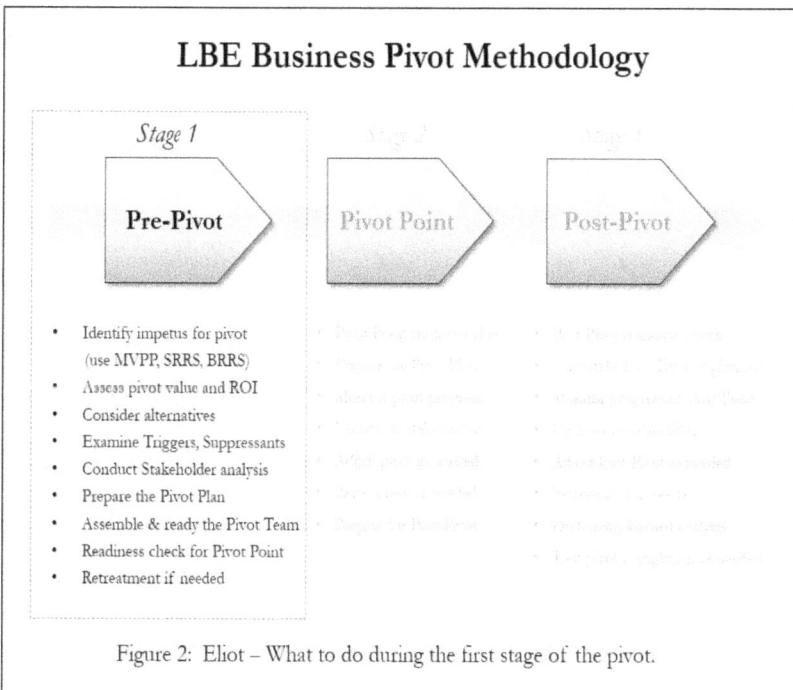

LBE Business Pivot Methodology

Stage 1

Pre-Pivot

Pivot Point

Post-Pivot

- Identify impetus for pivot (use MVPP, SRRS, BRRS)
- Assess pivot value and ROI
- Consider alternatives
- Examine Triggers, Suppressants
- Conduct Stakeholder analysis
- Prepare the Pivot Plan
- Assemble & ready the Pivot Team
- Readiness check for Pivot Point
- Retreatment if needed

Figure 2: Eliot – What to do during the first stage of the pivot.

For the Pre-Pivot, you'll want to identify the impetus for the pivot. Use the MVPP, SRRS, and BRRS tools to help. You will want to assess the pivot value and ROI (refer to the prior chapter about the Pivot Team, since you'll likely need some finance expertise for this aspect).

Examine the triggers and suppressants that have been discussed generically and see whether they apply to your circumstance. Conduct a stakeholder analysis, using the diagrammatic Push/Pull technique covered earlier. Prepare the Pivot Plan. Assemble and make ready the Pivot Team, as based on the advice and insights of Chapter 19. Do a readiness check that you are really ready for the Pivot Point.

If at the end of the Pre-Pivot things are not looking good, then go ahead and do a Pivot Retreatment (covered in Chapter 15). Let's hope that it does come to that aspect, but at least if it does, pulling the plug at the Pre-Pivot is bound to be better than doing so at the Pivot Point.

Shown in Figure 3 is the Pivot Point stage with the key steps highlighted. At the start of the Pivot Point, make sure that you are truly ready for the Pivot Point to get underway.

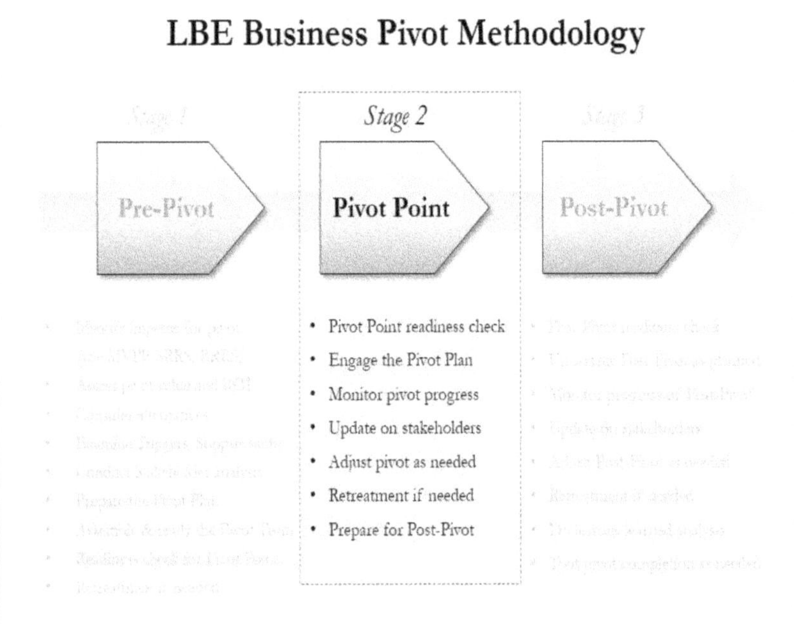

LBE Business Pivot Methodology

Stage 1

Stage 2

Stage 3

Pre-Pivot

Pivot Point

Post-Pivot

* Pivot Point readiness check
* Engage the Pivot Plan
* Monitor pivot progress
* Update on stakeholders
* Adjust pivot as needed
* Retreatment if needed
* Prepare for Post-Pivot

Figure 3: Eliot – What to do during the second stage of the pivot.

You should have prepared the Pivot Plan while in the Pre-Pivot. Dust it off, update as needed, and engage the Pivot Plan. Next, as the pivot takes place, monitor the progress of the pivot. Keep updating your stakeholders throughout. A stakeholder that gets blindsided and believes that they should have been kept informed, especially if things get dicey in the pivot, the stakeholder might switch from being an advocate of the pivot to being in opposition. This swing can occur not because they don't believe in the pivot, but simply because they are irked that they weren't being kept in-the-loop.

Shown in Figure 4 is the detailed list for the Post-Pivot. Assuming you have made it through the Pre-Pivot and the Pivot Point, you need to continue carrying forward with the pivot and get the Post-Pivot undertaken too.

You would do a Post-Pivot readiness check, and then undertake the Post-Pivot that should have been in the Pivot Plan that you did at the Pre-Pivot. When I say this, I do not mean that you had to be perfectly clairvoyant and have laid out the entire Post-Pivot during the Pre-Pivot, which might have been weeks or months before. You are certainly able and expected to be updating the Pivot Plan as you go along.

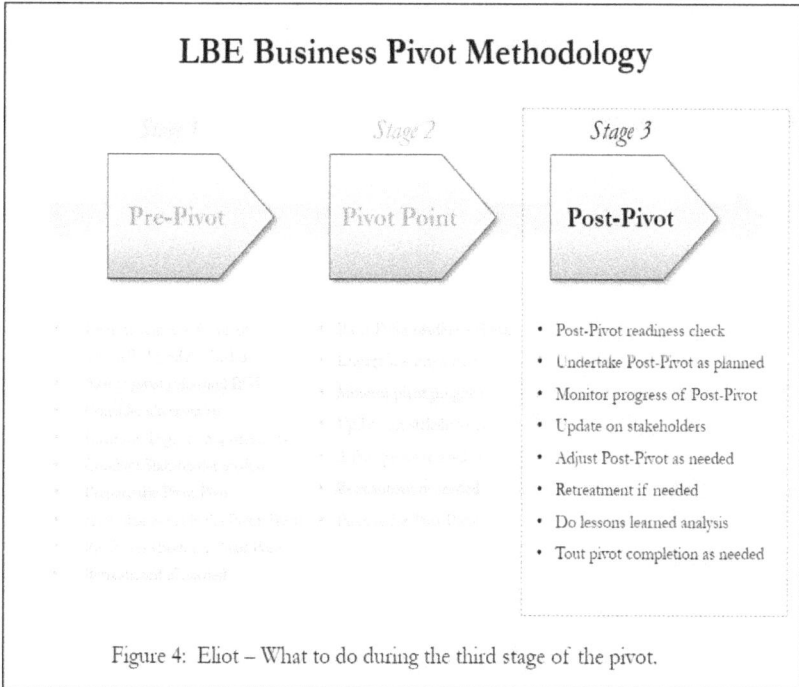

LBE Business Pivot Methodology

Stage 1 — Pre-Pivot

Stage 2 — Pivot Point

Stage 3 — Post-Pivot

- Post-Pivot readiness check
- Undertake Post-Pivot as planned
- Monitor progress of Post-Pivot
- Update on stakeholders
- Adjust Post-Pivot as needed
- Retreatment if needed
- Do lessons learned analysis
- Tout pivot completion as needed

Figure 4: Eliot – What to do during the third stage of the pivot.

Adjust the Post-Pivot based on the circumstances as they reveal themselves. Continue to keep the stakeholders updated. If you need to do a Pivot Retreatment, you can try to do so, but as we've discussed it is one of the worst things to do when waiting until the Post-Pivot. As suggested, you might consider instead the ploy of getting a next pivot established that hopefully can overcome whatever causes you to believe a retreatment is needed at the end of this pivot.

Do a lessons learned analysis. As previously advised, don't use this to do a witch hunt. For whatever rough spots the pivot has had, a witch hunt is likely to undermine the completion of the pivot and also cause hesitation and concern for any future proposed pivots. Focus instead on lessons learned and what can be improved or enhanced for future pivots.

FAULTY OMISSIONS

When using this particular Methodology, there are some common omissions that some business leaders make, producing a faulty pivot. Take a look at Figure 5.

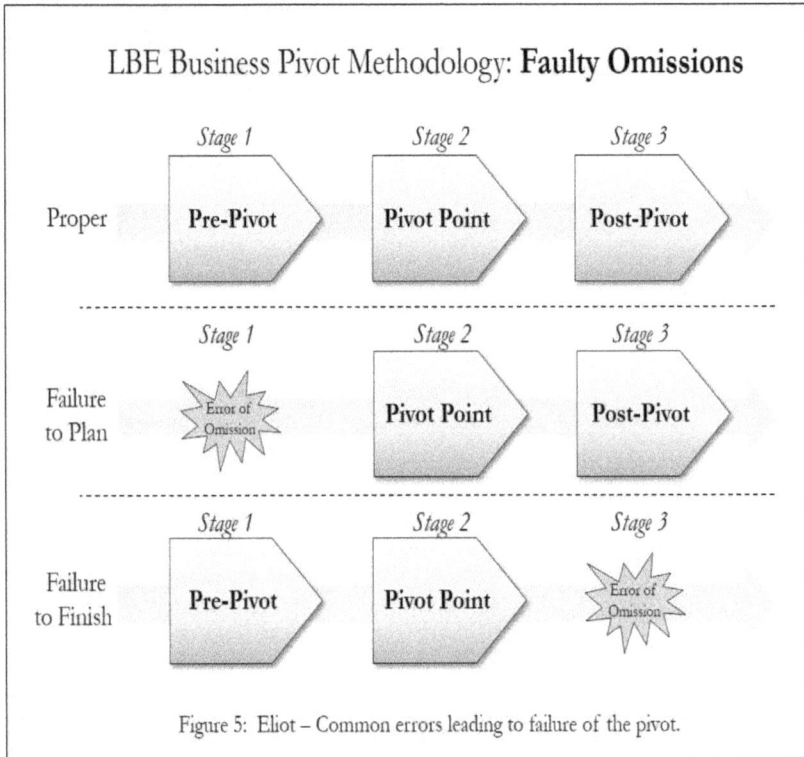

Figure 5: Eliot – Common errors leading to failure of the pivot.

The top sequence of stages is the proper set. These are the three stages as advocated. Do each stage. Don't skip any. Do not pass go. Do not collect $200. Sorry, got carried away there.

The second sequence below the top sequence is shown to indicate that one big omission is skipping past the Pre-Pivot and jumping straight into the Pivot Point.

As they say, if you fail to plan, you plan to fail.

The third sequence shows an omission of the Post-Pivot. I would bet that the Pivot Gravitational Force will undermine the pivot if you don't do a Post-Pivot, plus other maladies will surface. You'll see more about various pitfalls in the next chapter.

CHAPTER 21

KEY PITFALLS

THAT WRECK PIVOTS

CHAPTER 21

KEY PITFALLS THAT WRECK PIVOTS

PREFACE

Any seasoned business leader knows that what happens inside companies can be messy, ugly, convoluted, confused, and be like watching sausage being made. What happens in Vegas, stays in Vegas, they say. You do need to be wary of the pitfalls that can befall pivoting. There are about a thousand ways to mess-up a pivot. Even if I listed the thousand, I'm sure you could come up with one more and we'd have ourselves one thousand and one ways to mess it up.

In this chapter, I provide a list of some of the major ways to create a pivot wreck. Any of these aspects can readily have your pivot become a Pivot-Flop (as covered earlier in Chapter 14). You should also be ready with your Pivot Retreatment approach (see Chapter 15), if you begin to see that any of these pitfalls is confronting you. I also would then wish you best of luck if you are in the midst of one of these pivot wrecks. You might try some Jack Daniels to take the edge off things.

———

CHAPTER 21:
KEY PITFALLS THAT WRECK PIVOTS

Things that go bump in the night. Spooky ghosts floating around. You have just entered into the pivot House of Horrors. That's right, there are lots of ways to mess-up a pivot. I purposely waited until this latter part of the book to bring this up. Didn't want to discourage you at an earlier time in the book.

As a business leader and being Pivot-Wise, you need to know these pitfalls. You should strive mightily to not fall into one. Falling into one or more would mean that I would have to ask you to turn-in your Pivot-Wise certification and badge. Seriously, I really hope you don't encounter these pitfalls, and so do what you can to avoid them. If you do get into one, I provide some overall advice about how to try and get out of it.

As shown in Figure 1, these are some of the most common pivot pitfalls.

Business Leadership Pivots: **Pivot Pitfalls**

Ref	Pivot pitfall	Explanation of problem
1	The pivot "one man band"	Business leader tries to go solo
2	Emperor has no clothes pivoting	Failure to recognize pivot concerns
3	Jumped the gun on the pivot	Lack of Pre-Pivot preparation
4	Train wreck ahead of the pivot	Lousy direction and Post-Pivot nightmare
5	Pivot stakeholder rebellion	Stakeholders lose faith in the pivot
6	The Pivot "scatter gun"	Wild shot pivot with no solid aim
7	Pivot bites off more than it can chew	Jam packed pivot is bulging at the seams
8	Mega-pivot is mega-disaster situation	"Big bang" pivot unsuitable in this case
9	Gravitational force wins over pivot	Status quo overpowers the pivot
10	Pivot is needed, but no leadership	Headless floundering and void of pivot

Figure 1: Eliot – Common ways in which pivots go awry.

The pivot "one man band"

A business leader might be tempted to try and do a business pivot by themselves. They don't assemble a Pivot Team. They don't try to involve and interact with Stakeholders. They take the "one man band" approach (I should say the "one person band" approach).

This solo notion is especially common among founders of firms. They are used to running the show. They figure that they will do the pivot and just magically everyone will follow along. Rarely does that work out.

Advice, dump the solo approach, and go for the team approach. I know that some solo "strong ego" business leaders might complain that a team will just slow things down and make things more complicated. Maybe so, but in the end, you'll be more likely to have everyone on-board to the pivot, versus left in the dust and trying to figure out what happened.

Emperor has no clothes pivoting

The business leader is usually gung ho about the pivot. They have to be, in order to gain support and inspire others. At the same time, the business leader can be so focused that whenever someone says that there is something wrong about the pivot, the business leaders tries to chop off their head. People figure this out and stop offering feedback. The business leader then assumes that since no. one is complaining, it must be coming along swimmingly.

This aspect of unwillingness to tell the emperor that they have no clothes can lead the business leader into a dark alley of horrors. Inch by inch, things are going to go awry. The business leader won't know until the inches have become the length of a football field. Key to this is being a business leader that welcomes and encourages feedback. Of course, you need to filter it, since you are for sure going to get a lot of complaints that are either not true or that are true but not especially important.

Jumped the gun on the pivot

This pitfall equates to the Chapter 20 on the LBE Business Pivot Methodology. You might recall that at the end of the Chapter 20, we pointed out that you should not skip the Pre-Pivot. Doing so is jumping the gun. There are penalties for jumping the gun, including possibly being knocked out of the game.

Train wreck ahead of the pivot

You need to be looking ahead to the Post-Pivot, doing so during the Pivot Point especially. If your Pivot Plan that you did in the Pre-Pivot was any good, you hopefully aren't headed to a train wreck.

I realize that circumstances might have changed during the Pivot Point, and so what you planned has now become obsolete. You should have been adjusting and updating the Pivot Plan, as advocated in the Methodology. Now, if the train wreck is really bad and there seems to be no means to avoid it and do pivot, you might need to consider your Pivot Retreatment options.

Pivot stakeholder rebellion

A business leader should be watching for the potential of some or maybe even all of the stakeholders ganging up to fight and stop the pivot. These rebellions do happen. The stakeholders might have been silently opposed, or waiting to see whether the pivot was going to be real.

However it occurs, the stakeholders will sometimes confer among each other and then hit the business leader like a ton of bricks. You probably want to avoid getting hit by a ton of bricks, since, well, it hurts. You need to keep in-touch with the stakeholders throughout, as advocated in the Methodology. Do not let them gang up on you. Or, at least if they do, you should be aware of it before they reach a critical mass.

The Pivot "scatter gun"

A pivot that is all things to all people is a scatter gun. It aims everywhere. The pivot should be well specified in terms of what the scope is. I am betting that a scatter gun pivot will be utterly confusing to most of the stakeholders as they won't know which way the firm is going.

You are probably familiar with the story of the wise men that were blindfolded and brought up to touch an elephant (this is my version, just to say). One touched a leg and thought they were in front of a tall study pillar. Another touched the tail and thought they had a harsh rope in their hands. And so on. None of them knew what was really there. A scatter gun pivot is like that, with no one understanding what it is and why or how it should go.

Pivot bites off more than it can chew

Try to keep the pivot to whatever it needs to do, and not more, and not less. On the more side, you might be tempted to put some extra zing into the pivot. This might make sense, given the old line that once you already have the patient open for heart surgery, might as well take care of other organs in there at the same time.

The only problem with that mindset is that by distracting from the heart surgery and keeping the patient open too long, you might doom the patient. Sometimes, it is better to do what you need to do, and come around a second time to do other aspects.

Mega-pivot is mega-disaster situation

The "big bang" pivot is a rough road. These mega-pivots are sometimes the only way to get things done. The risk of a mega-disaster comes along with it. Make sure that if you are doing a mega-pivot, you really do a tremendous job of preparations and planning during the Pre-Pivot.

Gravitational force wins over pivot

We've discussed previously that there are gravitational forces trying to drive the pivot back to the status quo that existed before the pivot. Keep this in mind while planning the pivot. The Post-Pivot is the place that will especially help deal with the earthly gravitational pull.

Pivot is needed, but no leadership

This is the circumstance where a firm sorely needs a pivot, but no business leader either realizes it, or maybe is not willing to risk it.

If you are a business leader that realizes a pivot is needed, you can either remain silent and watch as the business goes along without the pivot that you think is needed, and maybe that's the way to handle things, or, you can test the waters as to becoming the pivot business leader, which might do wonders for you and your career (or, of course, could knock you out of the firm). Grabbing a bull by the horns, or not doing so, will be a matter that you will need to resolve.

BULLSEYE AND DANGER ZONES

The last item to cover in this discussion of pitfalls is the Figure 2. Take a look. You want to aim for the bulls-eye, meaning that you encounter no pitfalls at all. That's maybe going to happen, once in a million pivots.

More realistically, aim for the area around the inner circle, this is the Tolerable pitfalls zone. It places you in the danger zone, but there is a chance you can get out of that zone and resolve the pitfalls.

Then there is the Catastrophic pitfalls zone. It is the worst of the danger zone. This means that a Pivot Retreatment is going to be very costly. The pivot will likely fail in such a fashion and flair that there is no escaping its explosive results.

Aim for the bulls-eye, be prepared for the Tolerable pitfalls, and avoid like the plague the Catastrophic pitfalls. Which are which, you might ask? I'd say that if you look at the pitfalls list of Figure 1, any of those can be a tolerable or a catastrophic, depending upon the situation and context of a particular business pivot. As a business leader involved in a particular pivot, you'll need to assess which zone fits.

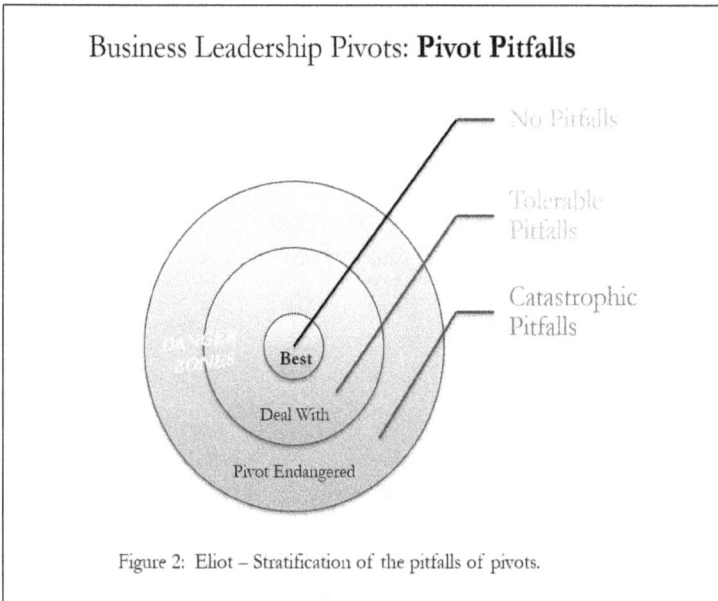

Figure 2: Eliot – Stratification of the pitfalls of pivots.

.

264

CHAPTER 22

BUSINESS LEADERSHIP'S PIVOT PRINCIPLES

CHAPTER 22

BUSINESS LEADERSHIP'S PIVOT PRINCIPLES

PREFACE

In this final chapter of the book, I'd like to cover some business leadership pivot principles. Then, the conclusion coming after this chapter will offer some final comments and summary points.

By pivot principles, I am suggesting that these are aspects about business leaders and what they are likely to encounter in terms of business pivoting over their working career. The principles are based on the various mini-case studies and stores of founders and CEO's. It is admittedly more speculative than pure research based, so take it in that manner and think of it as merely thought provoking rather than some kinds of "laws" or scientifically based principles.

CHAPTER 22: BUSINESS LEADERSHIP'S PIVOT PRINCIPLES

There are ten pivot principles that I have derived from the various stories of founders and CEO's while considering the role of business pivots and pivoting.

There are likely to be more than ten principles out there, and I opted to just confine myself to stopping at ten, for now. Ten seemed like a good number and covers much of what I think is vital to consider. We will walk through each one of ten, doing so briefly. The principles are probably relatively self-explanatory and so not much is needed to further elaborate about them.

Take a look at Figure 1 to see the ten key principles.

Business Leadership Pivots: **Key Principles**

Ref	Some Key Principles about Business Pivots
i	Any Business Leader will have 1 or more business pivots in their career
ii	Likely to be 3 pivots: *Pre-Career, Early Career, Mid-Career to Late*
iii	At least 1 business pivot will arise unexpectedly or unawares
iv	1 or more business pivots will go negative during the business career
v	The first-time pivot by a Business Leader will be least well-handed
vi	1 or more business pivots will involve a Pivot Retreatment (backing off)
vii	So-called "Dumb Luck" will be involved in at least 1 business pivot
viii	Opportunistic luck ("Made Luck") will be involved in 1 or more pivots
ix	Being Pivot-Wise will positively impact the business pivot success
x	Most Business Leaders are not yet Pivot-Wise

Figure 1: Eliot – Some guiding principles about business pivots.

i. Any Business Leader will have 1 or more business pivots in their career

Years ago, you would go to work for a company and stay there for the rest of your career. During that time, you would be a good corporate citizen and try to rise gradually through the hierarchy of the firm. The company was doing whatever it did, pretty much the same way, throughout much of your working career there. At the end, you got a handy gold watch and retired.

Flash forward. Most businesses today are being rocked by disruption. They are needing to transform to survive and thrive. The start-up craze has brought us zillions more new businesses. All businesses are trying to figure out how to best pivot to keep up with the Jones's. Business leaders are like football coaches, if they are winning they get to stay around, if they aren't winning they are out the door.

Contemporary business leaders are going to experience pivots. At least one or more during their career. Probably best to be prepared, and be Pivot-Wise.

ii. Likely to be 3 pivots: Pre-Career, Early-Career, Mid-Career

As per the Pivot-W Segment model, it is a reasonable bet that a Business Leader will have at least three pivots, taking place at their Pre-Career, Early-Career, and Mid-Career times. Be on the look. Be thinking about a pivot. Do not though do a pivot for the sake of having a pivot. The pivot should make sense to do.

If you are in a smaller firm, the pivot will likely be co-joined with your personal aspects, as discussed when going over the SRRSv. In larger firms, even if there is not a spark along the SRRSv, there should be something in the BRRS that provides a spark for the pivot. You, then as a business leader, are effectively pivoting in addition to getting the business entity to do so.

iii. At least 1 business pivot will arise unexpectedly or unawares

The stories of founders and CEO's provided in this book are replete with situations whereby the business leader did not realize that a pivot was going to arise. They were caught unawares. Same is true of the business entity.

Be on the look and keep your eyes and ears open. As a Pivot-Wise business leader, the odds are that a pivot is coming down the pike.

iv. 1 or more pivots will go negative during the business career

The "failures" of pivots are not covered as much as the successes, nonetheless they exist. In today's world, we seem to be tolerant of business pivots that are "failures" as long as they are quick and as long as they don't break the bank.

That being said, those that keep saying that they are Okay with failures because it shows that you are daring and willing to take a chance, many of those same statements are not fully backed when the failure actually hits the fan. Having tolerance for failures can be more talk than walk.

v. The first-time pivot by a Business Leader will be least well-handled

There is little or no training taking place about how to do business pivots. Thus, a business leader thrust into a business pivot is likely to be ill-equipped to handle it. The first-time pivot will likely be the most awkward and poorly undertaken.

This seat-of-the-pants way of learning about pivots is hopefully being overcome by aspects such as the Pivot-Wise approach covered in this book. You have taken a great step toward being ready for a business pivot by wanting to learn about them and doing so via digging into the details of the topic. Congrats.

vi. 1 or more business pivots will involve a Pivot Retreatment (backing off)

There is no guarantee that a business pivot is going to go as hoped. The odds are that at some point, you will be involved in a business pivot that is going sour. You will need to use some of the Pivot Retreatment techniques we described earlier.

Having contingencies is a sound approach. Those that say that contingency planning is simply "planning to fail" are clever in using that saying but utterly false in believing that the statement is true. Those that don't do contingency planning are more than likely aiming to fail because once things go awry they will be completely at a loss of what do. Boom.

vii. So-called "Dumb Luck" will be involved in at least 1 business pivot

There is one kind of luck that sometimes is referred to as "dumb luck" and it is the kind of luck that just happens by pure chance. There is no underlying aspect that can be readily seen as to why the particular event or occasion occurred. I realize this is a deeper philosophical point about whether our lives are controlled by something or someone else and whether fate or destiny exist. That's not this book, sorry.

Anyway, it seems like there is the likelihood that at least one business pivot will involve this dumb luck. There is not much you can presumably do to force it to occur, but at least if the dumb luck happens you opt to exploit it as best you can. I realize sometimes it is hard to do that, since you wonder whether it is a trap or maybe that if you use the dumb luck now that it uses it up for you entirely, like a capped amount of fuel and you don't want the tank to run dry. Best to use it, if it falls into your lap, I say.

viii. Opportunistic luck ("Made Luck") will be involved in 1 or more pivots

There is another kind of luck, contrasting to the preceding principle, called opportunistic luck or "made luck" and this is something I urge you to help happen. By putting yourself or your business into circumstances wherein good things might happen, you are creating opportunities where luck might just make it so. Don't bet the farm on it. Try to have a portfolio of opportunistic luck going at any point in time, so that one of them will strike oil. Be in the right place at the right time, and be ready.

ix. Being Pivot-Wise will positively impact the business pivot success

I firmly believe that by your becoming or being Pivot-Wise it will make a positive impact in whether you are successful with business pivots. I suppose that I should create a controlled experimental study to examine those that are Pivot-Wise versus those that are not, and then see what happens over a suitable multi-year time frame of business pivoting. I leave that to researchers interested in trying that out.

x. Most Business Leaders are not yet Pivot-Wise

It is my contention that most business leaders are not Pivot-Wise. I say this because I see pivots taking place all the time and the business leaders involved are often unaware of what they need to do. I don't fault them for this, since it is a topic that seems to have just snuck up and few have realized it is a specialty in its own right. Let's get the word out – urge business leaders to become more pivot savvy.

PIVOT-WISE AND CO-INFLUENCES

To end this chapter, I thought we'd take another look at the ingredients of a business leader, as covered initially in Chapter 1.

As shown in Figure 2, we have added the Pivot-Wise ingredient to the set of business leadership ingredients. I remind you that the ingredients co-influence each other.

We have focused specifically on the Pivot-Wise ingredient, and asserted that the business leader and their strength of Guiding Vision, Passion, Integrity, Trust, Curiosity, and Daring all play a significant role in being Pivot-Wise and being able to carry out business pivots.

The business pivots that you carry out will influence the other ingredients too. If you mess-up a major pivot, the odds are that your Guiding Vision and strength will be lessened in it, your Integrity might take a hit, and so on. Keep in mind the ingredients as you do your daily work as a business leader. In the throes of the daily business battles and crises, it is hard to keep a big picture in mind of what it takes to be a successful business leader.

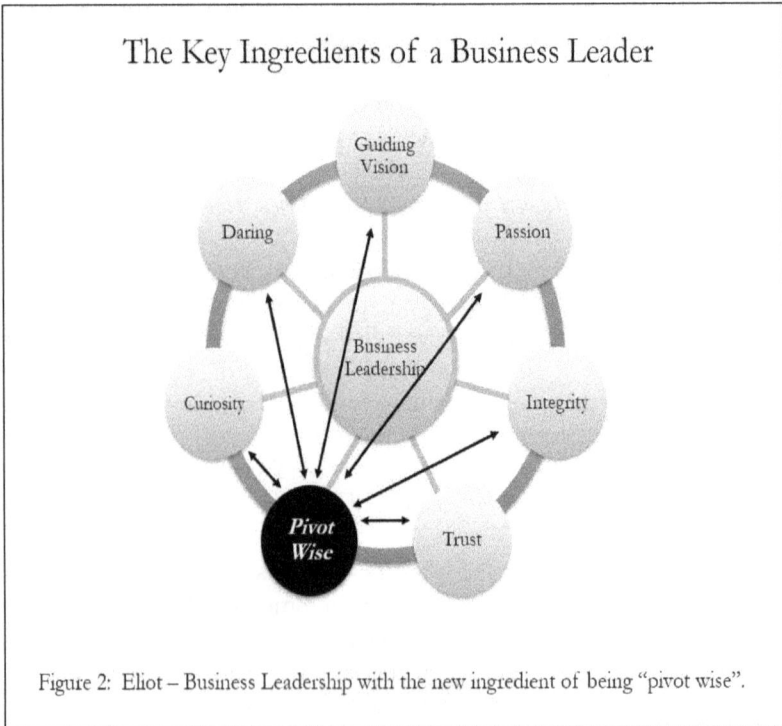

Figure 2: Eliot – Business Leadership with the new ingredient of being "pivot wise".

Being Pivot-Wise has other qualities beyond just knowing about how and when to do pivots. You have likely noticed that there are a variety of other crucial business skills wrapped into being savvy about pivots.

You need to be a strategic thinker and doer, acting in a macroscopic way to guide the firm. The true business pivot usually tinkers with the most important aspects of what the firm does and is. Pivoting a core business model and the vision of the firm is about as big time as you can get when doing something in a firm.

You need to be introspective and be aware of your own circumstances and approach as a business leader and of your own personal persona. Are you personally facing a pivot? How does that impact your business also facing a pivot? If your business is facing a pivot, how will that impact you, assuming that you weren't anticipating a pivot? These are all the kinds of questions that a business leader needs to be asking themselves.

My goal was to get you up-to-speed on business pivots, on the ins and outs of pivoting, and also provide some inspiring true stories of founders and CEO's that have experienced and achieved great success due to their pivots. Good luck, of all kinds of manner and luck, as a business leader.

CONCLUSION

We have covered a variety of interrelated topics in this book and it hopefully has been a useful journey for you. Business pivoting is the primary focus, but so is the role of *Business Leadership*. I prefer to look at the two topics as co-joined. They need to be examined hand-in-hand. There is also an undercurrent of start-ups and entrepreneurship involved in this book. This makes sense because, as asserted earlier, smaller firms are more likely to be able to undertake a major pivot than are more established firms. In fact, as mentioned, there is heightened expectations that start-ups and smaller firms will indeed pivot.

We covered various fascinating and insightful stories of some quite notable founders and CEO's in terms of their business careers, their business entities, and their business pivots. The stories are inspiring. They are also useful as a means to look underneath the hood and see how pivoting takes place.

I have tried to assemble a toolkit for Pivot-Wise business leaders that will aid them in considering pivots. The Pivot-Wise toolkit has been presented during the various chapters, and explanations of the tools provided too. You now have a new vocabulary, structures, diagrams, templates, and the like, which can be used to help either push toward a pivot or help you to try and prevent a pivot that seems unwarranted.

I introduced a career segment model, called the Pivot-W, and mentioned that it seemed to be a common pattern. If I may, I might offer next a short story about my own career as further illustration (I have otherwise refrained from talking about myself in most of the book, and focused on the other founders and CEO's covered in the business stories).

As a corporate officer and senior executive, and as a management consultant, I would often have managers and staff that would come to me with questions about potentially pivoting in their business careers. I would often tell them the story of what occurred during the first part of my working career.

EARLY CAREER PIVOT

I went to work for a large company after graduating with my bachelor's degree. I was lucky to be placed upon entry into their fast-track to management via their management rotational program. They only had about ten such participants each year, in a company employing thousands and thousands. Furthermore, most participants had worked at the firm for several years, and had applied only after putting in their time in a junior capacity and proven themselves as exceptional. My admittance and participation was a combination of dumb-luck and made-luck (I'll tell you about that aspect some other time).

In any case, after completing the management rotational program, I was supposed to pick a particular division of the company, whichever ones wanted me and that I wanted to join, and then go into the division for the next chunk of my working life there at the firm. The company wanted to have uprising managers that would know the entire breadth of the firm. I had worked directly with every division head during the rotations. The thinking by the firm was that these chosen upcoming managers would avoid viewing the firm in silo's, even once in a particular division, since they had seen the company across all divisions in an intimate way.

During the time that I had been in one of the divisions during my rotation, the firm did business with a small company that we provided services to. I had gotten to know the founder of the firm. He knew that my rotations were done and I was making a choice. He offered to bring me into his firm as a top executive. I had to make choice between staying with a big firm as a low to mid-level manager, or going with a small firm as the big cheese, if you will. The classic of being a small fish in a big pond, or a big fish in a small pond.

I thought that if I did not stay at the big firm, the business leader that was the top executive, whom had hired me and fought for me to be in the rotational program, would be livid and I'd be on his banned list the rest of my career. Also, the firm had kindly invested in me, allowing me to participate in the rotational program. The whole concept was to make an investment for the long-term. Would I be an ingrate for now leaving the firm? On the other hand, I had invested my time toward them, and they toward me, in presumably an equal arrangement. They could have let me go at any time.

After soul searching, I decided to "pivot" into the small business, and went to tell the business leader at the firm I was with. I thought for sure that I would barely make it out of his office alive. You can imagine the many sleepless nights I had beforehand, trying to decide how to explain the circumstances and readying myself for the backlash yet to come.

Believe it or not, he listened calmly to me, and then after a moment, he offered this sage advice.

Lance, he said, if he hung onto me and tried to insist that I should stay, I would forever believe that I had made the wrong decision by staying. I would constantly think the grass was greener on the other side of the fence. He would have someone in his midst that always harbored the notion that he had let the better fish get away (i.e., the opportunity at the small business).

He said that it was my decision to make, and he would support me in it. He pointed out that I would gain experiences that he could not readily replicate at his large firm. And, I would be a more seasoned business leader after my experiences at the small firm. He suggested that we keep in touch, because who knows what I might do later on, and he would welcome that we might work together again. With this, we did a handshake, and I walked out of his office in a daze. Had I dreamed this happened in this way? I had not considered at all that he would react in such a positive and uplifting manner.

I went to the small business, and then later on started my own business, in fact several other businesses. Going to a smaller firm got my sea legs in small businesses and helped me immensely when I opted to go out on my own. I doubt that the same would have been true if I had stayed at the large firm. The large firm was a great experience, and when I did management consulting I was comfortable working in big firms because of the experience. Later too, I eventually became a corporate executive in a large business.

This story is more so about the pivot that I undertook and how it matches to the Pivot-W segment model. It was an Early-Career pivot for me, as a business leader. It also shaped my business leadership philosophy and outlook. I realized that business leaders will come and go, and that one should look at a longer time horizon when interacting with fellow business leaders. The head of the large firm and I did keep in touch, and remained colleagues throughout our careers, often helping each other along the way.

MONTAGE AND PIVOT BY FOUNDER

Alan Fuerstman, founder of the fantastic Montage Hotels & Resorts luxury resorts, tells a somewhat similar story, though on a much grander scale. In my next book, I am aiming to include his story, but for now, since I opened the door to the topic, he had been with the Marriott for many years, then switched to the Sheraton. He was then recruited by Steve Wynn, billionaire and casino/hotel magnate, in order to open the Bellagio in Las Vegas. It was a huge pivot for Alan. He left the relative safety of the Sheraton chain to take a chance with the Bellagio.

After completing the Bellagio, he went to Steve Wynn and said he wanted to leave and start his own luxury resort chain. Expecting that Steve would be irked, and of course concerned since Steve would not be the type of person you'd like to have coming after you, Alan indicates that Steve wished him well, understood what he was trying to accomplish, and said that they should get together each quarter for lunch, and see how things are coming along.

CONCLUDING COMMENT

I hope that this book will prepare businesses for undertaking pivots, and prepare business leaders for undertaking pivots. The material should provide guidance to whether or not to do a pivot, and the intertwining of the pivoting of the business and the business leader. I will conclude the book with this famous Latin quote with my own variant of the translation:

Aut viam inveniam aut faciam (as always; find a way, or make one).

APPENDIX

APPENDIX A:
SELECTED PIVOT DIAGRAMS
AND CHARTS

This Appendix A contains selected pivot diagrams and charts that were used in the chapters of this book. They are shown here too, in addition to being shown in their respective chapters, in order to enlarge them for ease of reading and also to collect them into one contiguous section to readily peruse. The backside of the pages are left open for you to take notes, if you wish to do so, about a particular diagram or chart.

Lance B. Eliot

What Leaders Say About Business Pivots

This Book

	Leaders About Business Pivots	"Business Leadership Pivots"
i	Wasn't thinking about pivoting	
ii	Don't know how to do a business pivot	
iii	Caught off-guard by pivot clamor	Solutions · Examples · Mini-cases · Heuristics · Insights · Paradigm · Checklists
iv	Fouled-up a business pivot	
v	Why and when do others pivot	

Figure 1: Eliot – What business leaders say about pivots and pivoting.

INTRODUCTION – FIGURE 1

Firm Size & Maturity: **Four-Square on Business Pivots**

	Start-up	Insufficient	"Required"
Business Size & Maturity	Mature	Assured	Shocking
		Minor Pivot	Major Pivot

Magnitude of the Pivot

Figure 2: Eliot – Examining the business pivot by firm size and maturity.

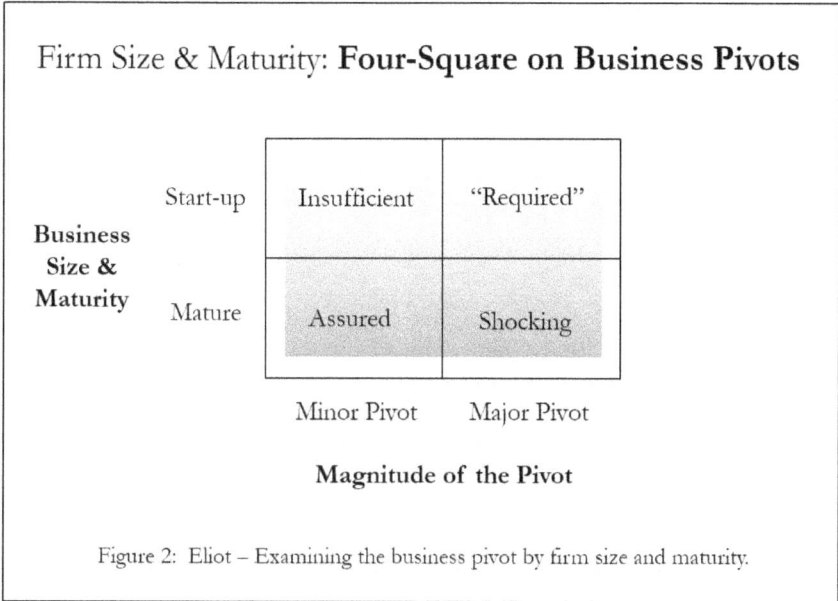

INTRODUCTION – FIGURE 2

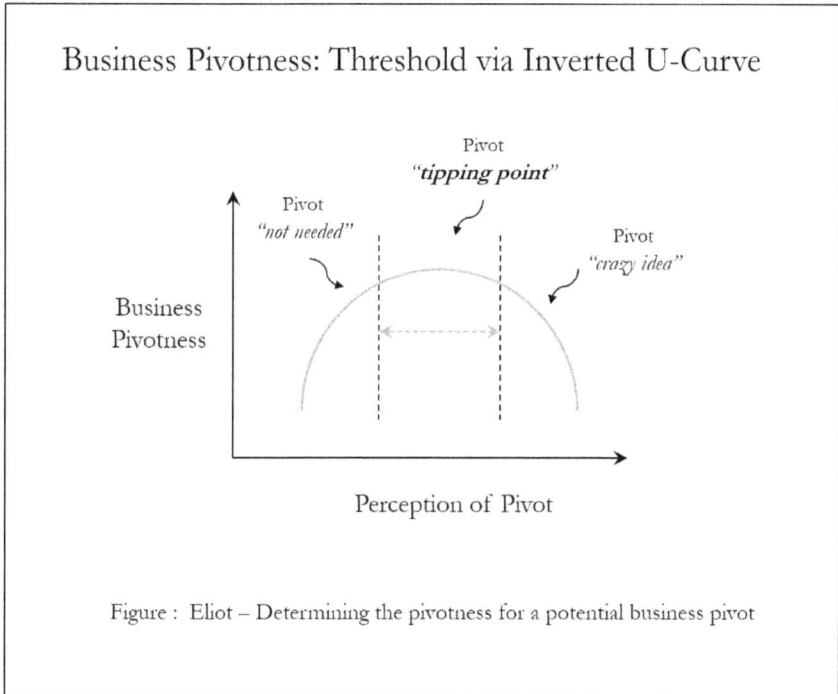

Business Pivotness: Threshold via Inverted U-Curve

Pivot
"tipping point"

Pivot
"not needed"

Pivot
"crazy idea"

Business
Pivotness

Perception of Pivot

Figure : Eliot – Determining the pivotness for a potential business pivot

INTRODUCTION – FIGURE 3

On Being or Becoming a Business Leader

What is Business Leadership	On Becoming a Business Leader	Key Points
Intertwining of Personal persona and Business Leadership persona	"The process of becoming a leader is, if not identical, certainly similar to the process of becoming a fully integrated human being."	• Warren Bennis cornerstone • Business Leaders in a business context and their persona • Personal persona • Integrating together of the two into one cohesive whole
Relative meaning over time and culture of Business Leadership	"To an extent, leadership is like beauty: It's hard to define, but you know it when you see it."	• Business leadership is both art and science • Beauty in eye-of-the-beholder • Ever present facets
Nature versus nurture in role of gaining Business Leadership	"Leaders are made, not born"	• Business Leadership in DNA • Or Business Leadership made • Classic of nature vs. nurture
The ingredients of being a good Business Leader	"Guiding vision, passion, integrity, trust, curiosity, daring"	• Ingredients and not traits • Each ingredient is needed • Can be wielded wrongly too
The willingness and adroitness of knowing when and how to pivot and do pivoting as a Business Leader	"The manager does things right, the leader does the right thing."	• Pivots & pivoting in business • Add pivoting as ingredient • Popular today for start-ups • Becomes standard fare

Figure 1: Eliot – Business Leadership defined and the added ingredient of pivoting.

CHAPTER 1 – FIGURE 1

Pivoting Alignment of Business Leader & Business

		No Pivot	**Pivot**
Business Leader	**Pivot**	Mismatch *Pivot Misaligned "Type 1"*	Aligned ★
	No Pivot	Match	Mismatch *Pivot Misaligned "Type 2"*

The Business Entity

Figure 2: Eliot – Pivots in Business Leadership and the Business

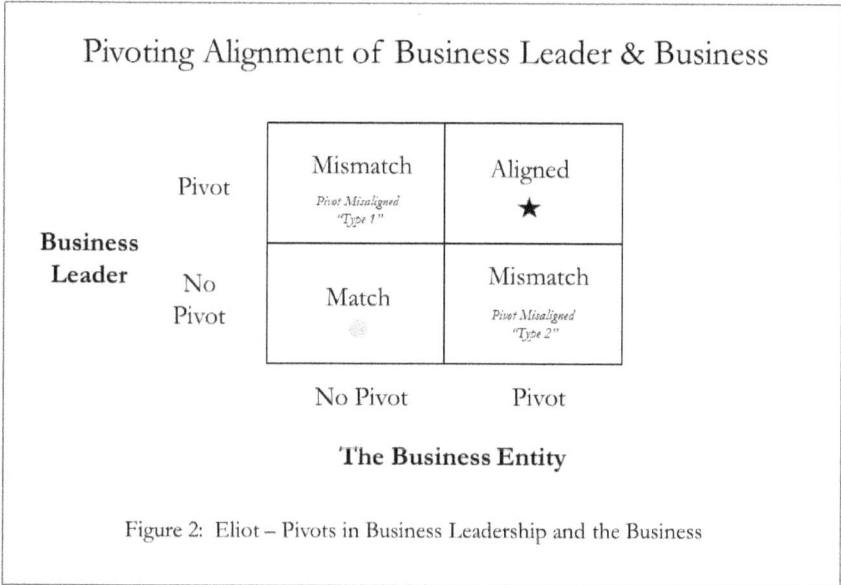

CHAPTER 1 – FIGURE 2

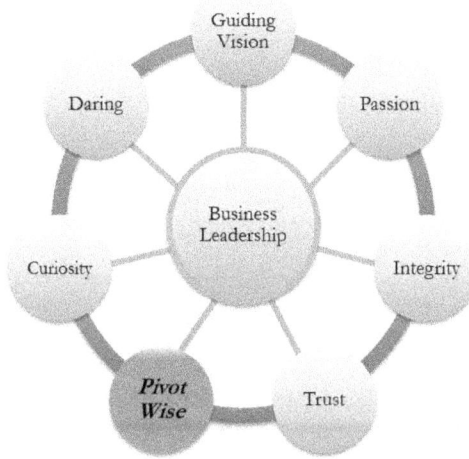

The Key Ingredients of a Business Leader

Figure 3: Eliot – Business Leadership with the new ingredient of being "pivot wise".

CHAPTER 1 – FIGURE 3

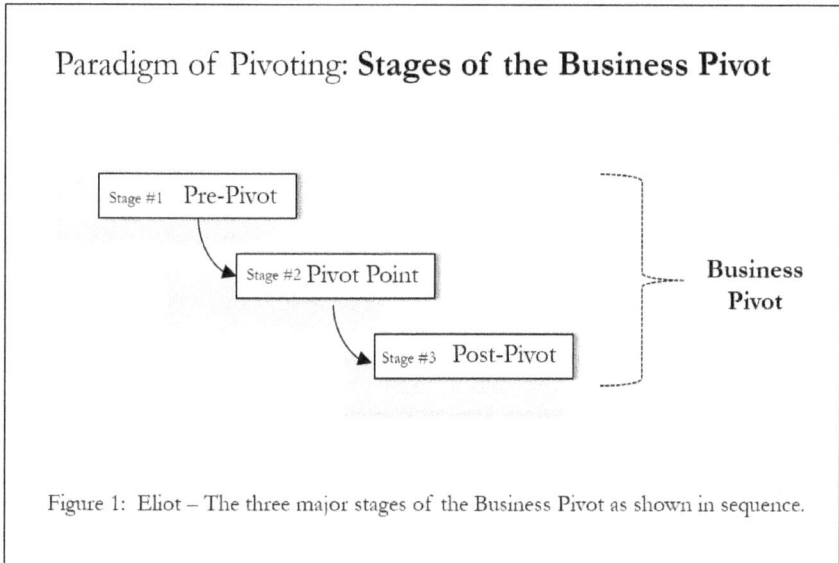

Paradigm of Pivoting: **Stages of the Business Pivot**

Stage #1   Pre-Pivot

Stage #2 Pivot Point

Stage #3   Post-Pivot

Business Pivot

Figure 1: Eliot – The three major stages of the Business Pivot as shown in sequence.

CHAPTER 2 – FIGURE 1

Paradigm of Pivoting: **Stages of the Business Pivot**

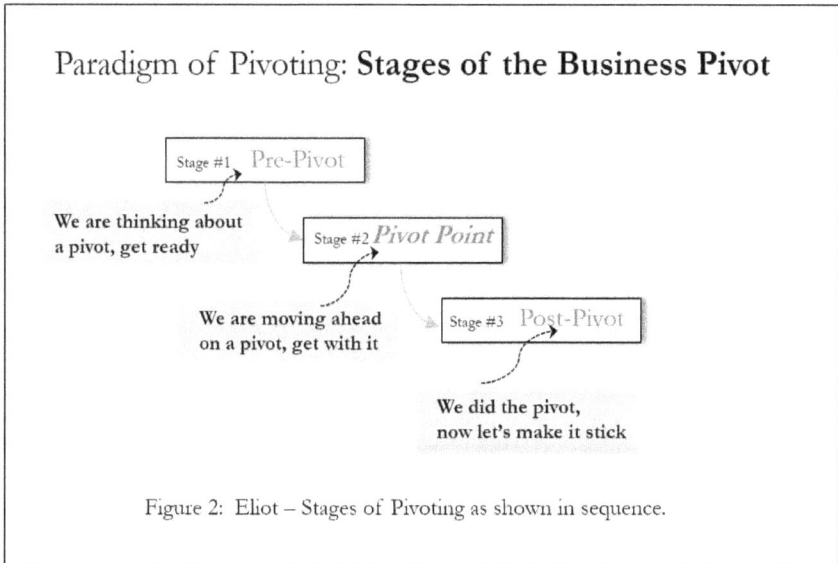

Figure 2: Eliot – Stages of Pivoting as shown in sequence.

CHAPTER 2 – FIGURE 2

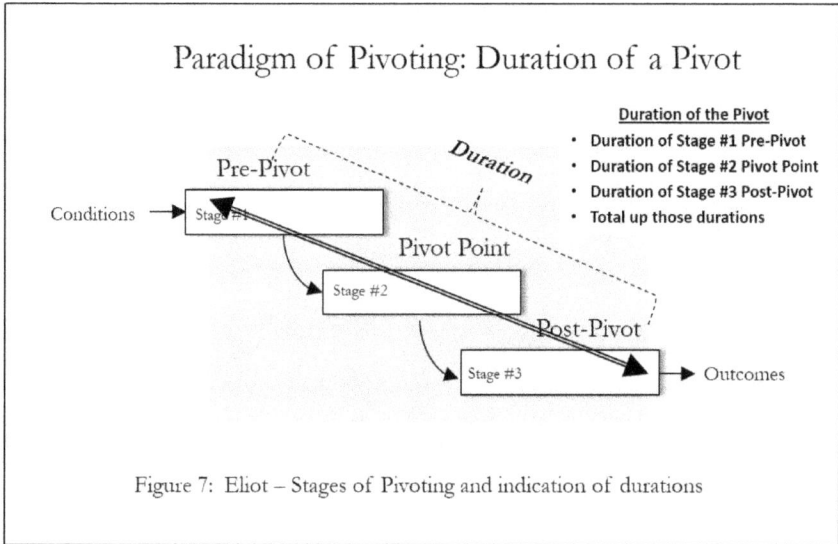

Figure 7: Eliot – Stages of Pivoting and indication of durations

CHAPTER 2 – FIGURE 7

Paradigm of Pivoting: Stages Process

Ref	Pre-Pivot	Pivot Point	Post-Pivot	Description	Phrase
i	Long	Long	Long	Long pivot	"I took my time"
ii	Long	Long	Short	Pivot lengthy with short end	"Did it and moved on"
iii	Long	Short	Long	Quick at Pivot Point with tails	"Mulled it, before & after"
iv	Long	Short	Short	Gestation, then quick to pivot	"Finally pulled the trigger"
v	Short	Long	Long	Fast into pivot, long pivoting	"Wanted to see it play out"
vi	Short	Long	Short	Long pivot with short tails	"Nearly stuck in the middle"
vii	Short	Short	Long	Upfront fast, follow-on long	"The end of it was key"
viii	Short	Short	Short	Fast pivot	"Move fast. Decide then act."

Figure 10: Eliot – Stages of Pivoting as chart of varying durations of the stages

CHAPTER 2 – FIGURE 10

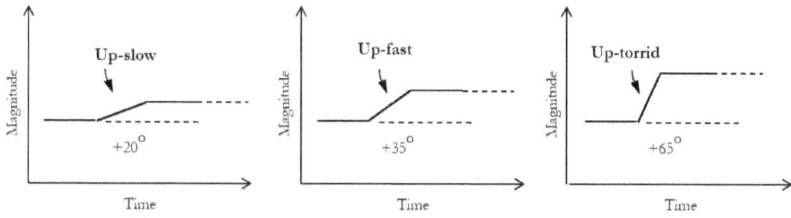

Figure 12: Eliot – Pivot Point as magnitude of a positive nature

CHAPTER 2 – FIGURE 12

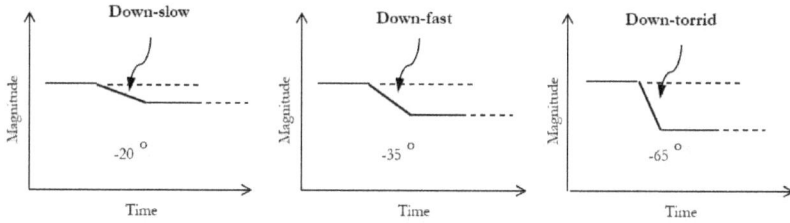

Paradigm of Pivoting: Magnitude of a Pivot Point

Down-slow

Magnitude

-20 °

Time

Down-fast

Magnitude

-35 °

Time

Down-torrid

Magnitude

-65 °

Time

Figure 13: Eliot – Pivot Point as magnitude of a negative nature

CHAPTER 2 – FIGURE 13

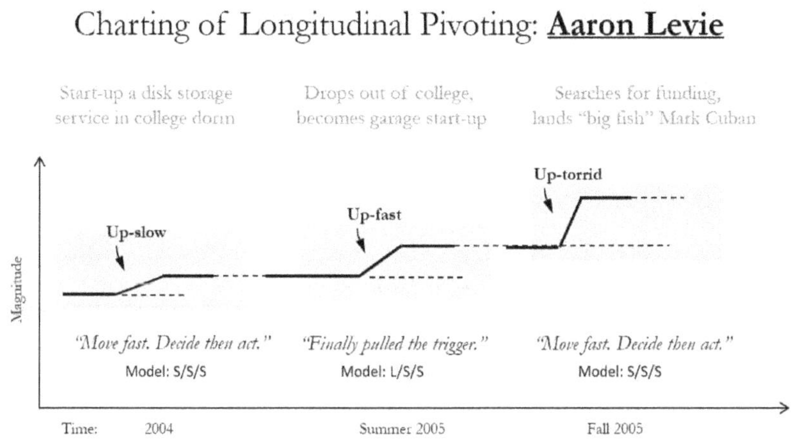

Figure 17: Eliot – Three early-day pivots of Aaron Levie and Box.com

CHAPTER 2 – FIGURE 17

Charting of Longitudinal: **Pivot Transparency**

Start-up a disk storage
service in college dorm

Searches for funding,
lands "big fish" Mark Cuban

Hidden: Drops out of college,
becomes garage start-up

Up-torrid

Up-slow

Hidden Pivots

Magnitude

"Move fast. Decide then act."
Model: S/S/S

"Move fast. Decide then act."
Model: S/S/S

Time: 2004   Summer 2005   Fall 2005

Figure 2: Eliot – Example of hidden pivot in early-day pivots of Aaron Levie

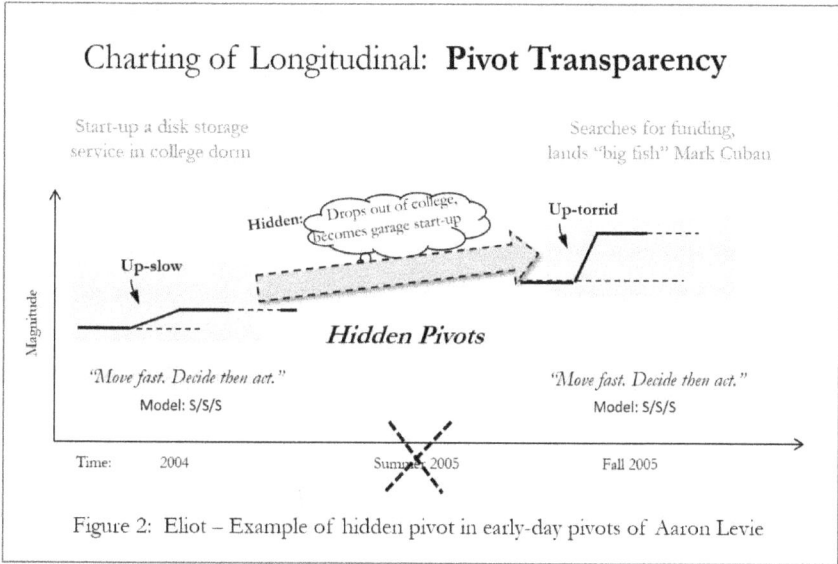

CHAPTER 13 – FIGURE 2

Charting of Longitudinal: **Pivots Saturation**

Example of pivoting saturation: Six pivots, back-to-back, upward and downward, seemingly endless and no true progress

Magnitude

Pivot "A" Pivot "B" Pivot "C" Pivot "D" Pivot "E" Pivot "F"

Time:

Figure 3: Eliot – Pivoting saturation over time and likely burnout

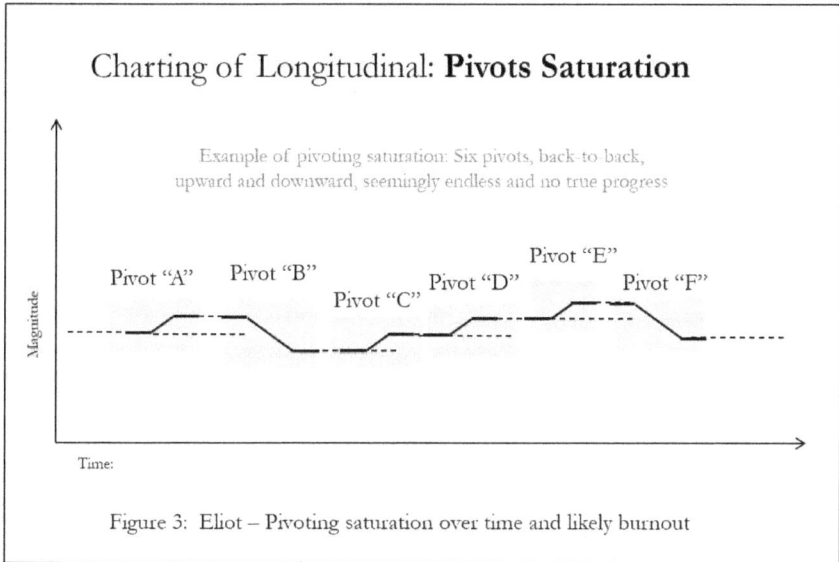

CHAPTER 13 – FIGURE 3

Lance B. Eliot

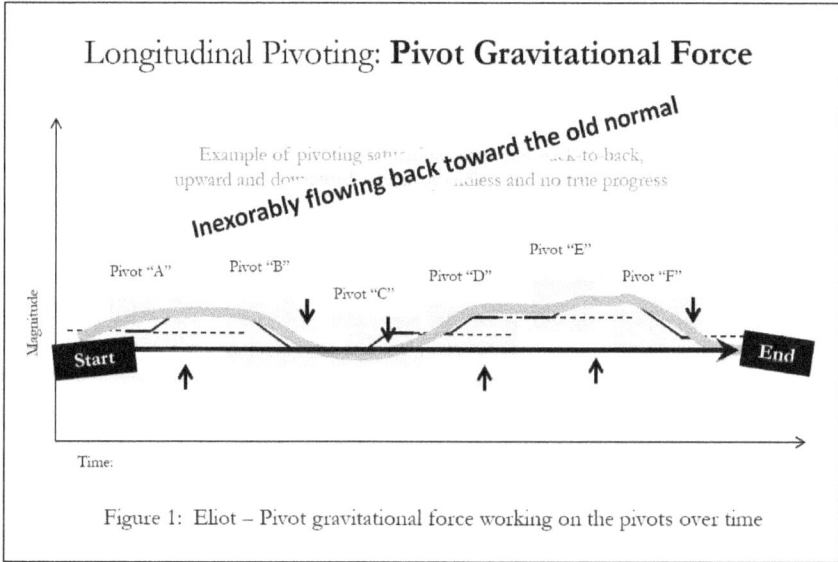

Figure 1: Eliot – Pivot gravitational force working on the pivots over time

CHAPTER 14 – FIGURE 1

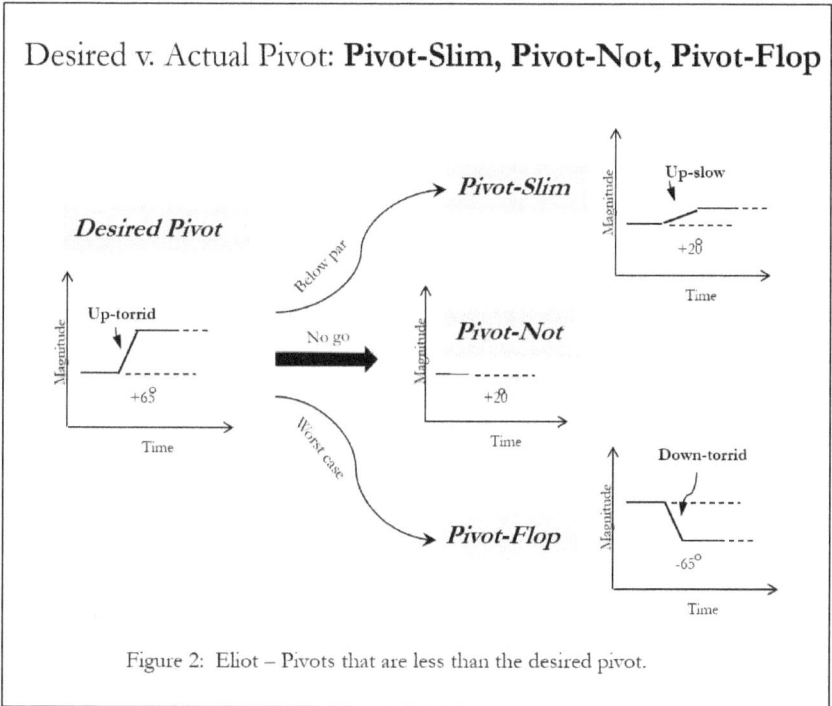

Desired v. Actual Pivot: **Pivot-Slim, Pivot-Not, Pivot-Flop**

Desired Pivot

Up-torrid

+65°

Time

Magnitude

Below par

No go

Worst case

→ *Pivot-Slim*

Up-slow

+28°

Time

Magnitude

Pivot-Not

+20°

Time

Magnitude

→ *Pivot-Flop*

Down-torrid

-65°

Time

Magnitude

Figure 2: Eliot – Pivots that are less than the desired pivot.

CHAPTER 14 – FIGURE 2

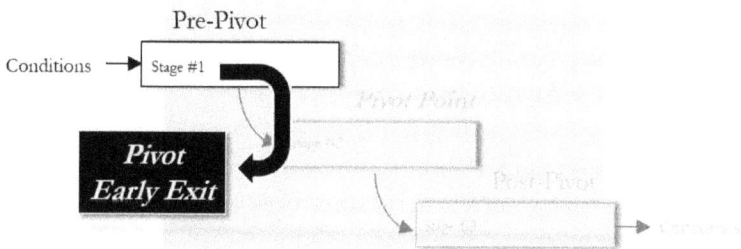

Paradigm of Pivoting: **Pivot Retreatment**

Pre-Pivot

Conditions → Stage #1

Pivot
Early Exit

Figure 1: Eliot – Taking the Early Exit to avoid going into the pivot fully.

CHAPTER 15 – FIGURE 1

317

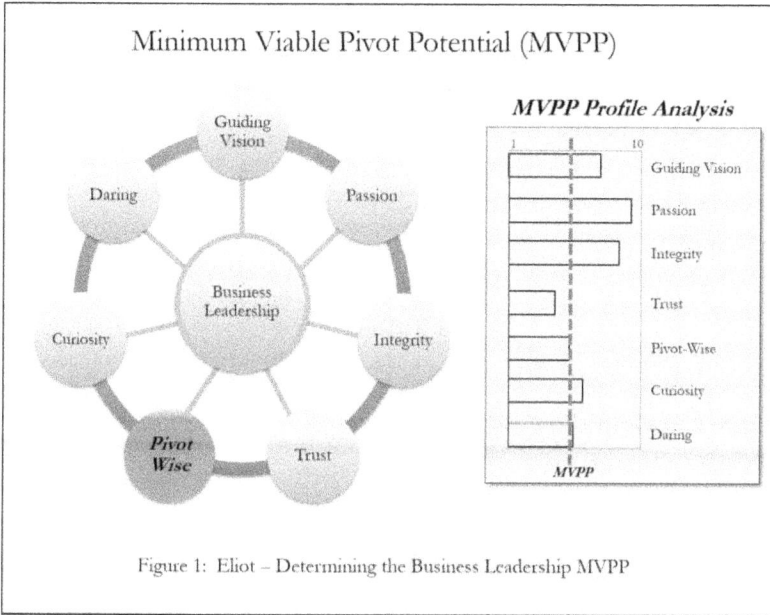

Figure 1: Eliot – Determining the Business Leadership MVPP

CHAPTER 16 – FIGURE 1

Minimum Viable Pivot Potential (MVPP)

MVPP Profile Analysis

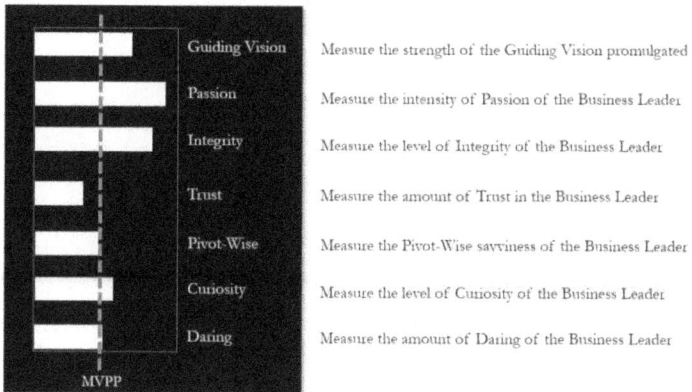

Guiding Vision	Measure the strength of the Guiding Vision promulgated
Passion	Measure the intensity of Passion of the Business Leader
Integrity	Measure the level of Integrity of the Business Leader
Trust	Measure the amount of Trust in the Business Leader
Pivot-Wise	Measure the Pivot-Wise savviness of the Business Leader
Curiosity	Measure the level of Curiosity of the Business Leader
Daring	Measure the amount of Daring of the Business Leader

MVPP

Figure 2: Eliot – Scoring of the Business Leadership MVPP

CHAPTER 16 – FIGURE 2

Business Leaders: Social Readjustment Rating Scale (SRRS)

Rank	Stress Inducer (LCU = Life Change Unit)	Score	Scale of 600
1	Death of spouse	100	17%
2	Divorce	73	12%
3	Martial separation	65	11%
4	Jail term	63	11%
5	Death of close family member	63	11%
6	Personal injury or illness	53	9%
7	Marriage	50	8%
8	Fired at work	47	8%
9	Marital reconciliation	45	8%
10	Other Major Life Event	45	8%

Figure 3: Eliot – Business Personal persona and Holmes & Rahe Stress Scale (variant)

CHAPTER 16 – FIGURE 3

Business Pivots: Business Readjustment Rating Scale (BRRS)

Rank	Business Pivot Inducer (BCU = Business Change Unit)	Score	Scale of 200
1	Pivot of Core Business Model	100	50%
2	Pivot of Company Vision/Mission	90	45%
3	Pivot of Primary Product/Service	80	40%
4	Pivot of Market Focus	70	35%
5	Pivot of Financing/Funding	70	35%
6	Pivot of Target Customer	60	30%
7	Pivot of Key Competencies	50	25%
8	Pivot of Partners/Suppliers	40	20%
9	Pivot of Operations/Production	40	20%
10	Pivot of Other Major Element	30	15%

Figure 4: Eliot – Business Pivot inducers on a rating scale referred to as BRRS.

CHAPTER 16 – FIGURE 4

Lance B. Eliot

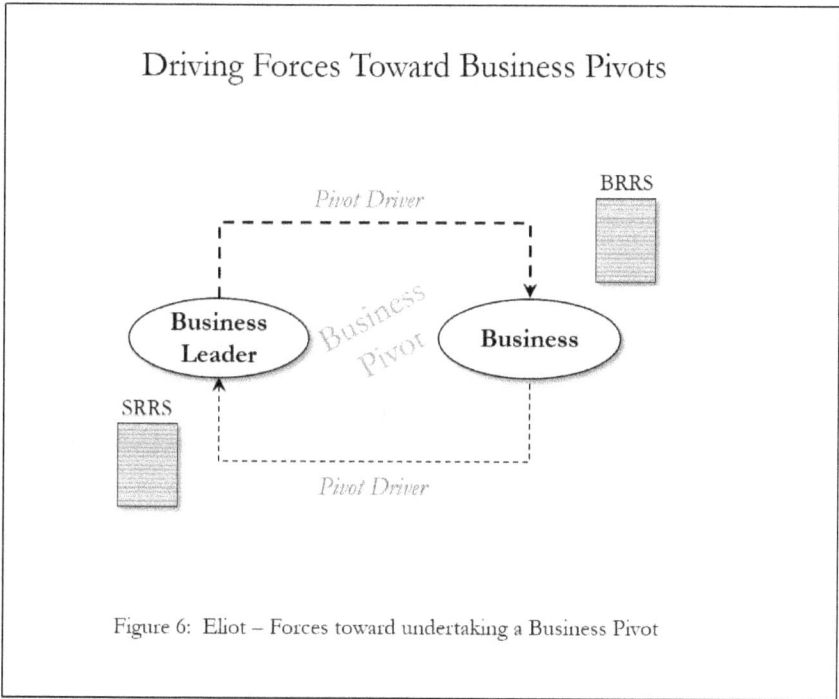

Figure 6: Eliot – Forces toward undertaking a Business Pivot

CHAPTER 16 – FIGURE 6

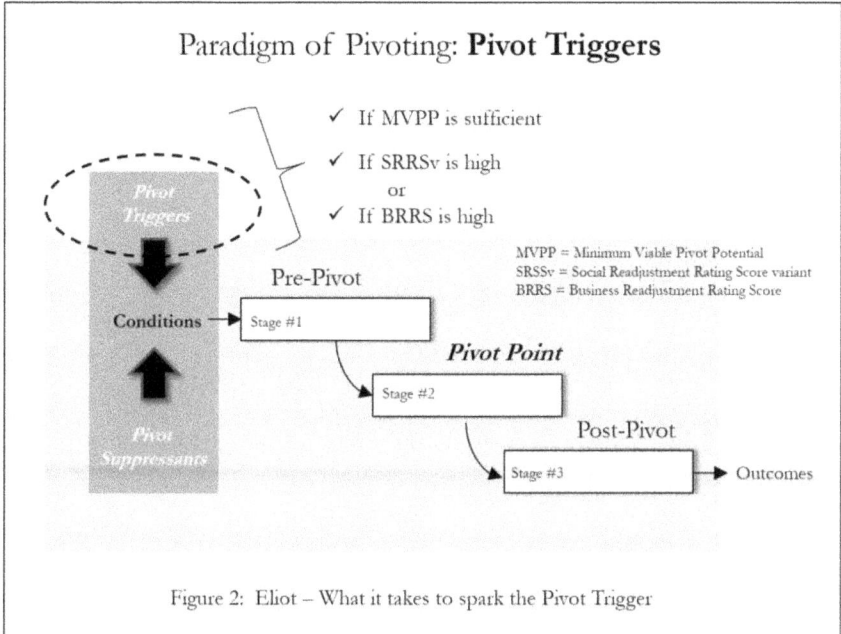

Figure 2: Eliot – What it takes to spark the Pivot Trigger

CHAPTER 17 – FIGURE 2

Lance B. Eliot

Paradigm of Pivoting: **Pivot Suppressants**

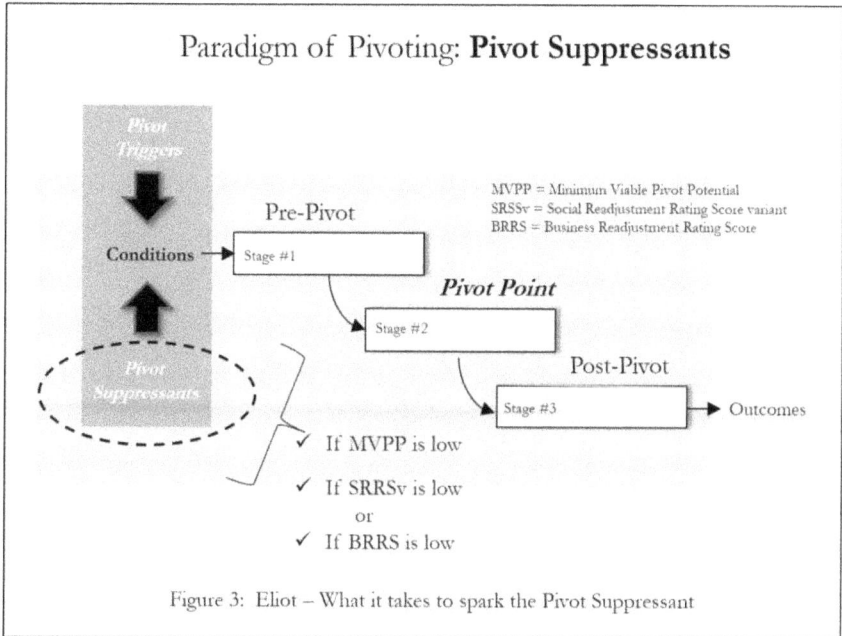

Pivot Triggers

Conditions →

Pivot Suppressants

Pre-Pivot

Stage #1

MVPP = Minimum Viable Pivot Potential
SRSSv = Social Readjustment Rating Score variant
BRRS = Business Readjustment Rating Score

Pivot Point

Stage #2

Post-Pivot

Stage #3 → Outcomes

✓ If MVPP is low

✓ If SRRSv is low
or
✓ If BRRS is low

Figure 3: Eliot – What it takes to spark the Pivot Suppressant

CHAPTER 17 – FIGURE 3

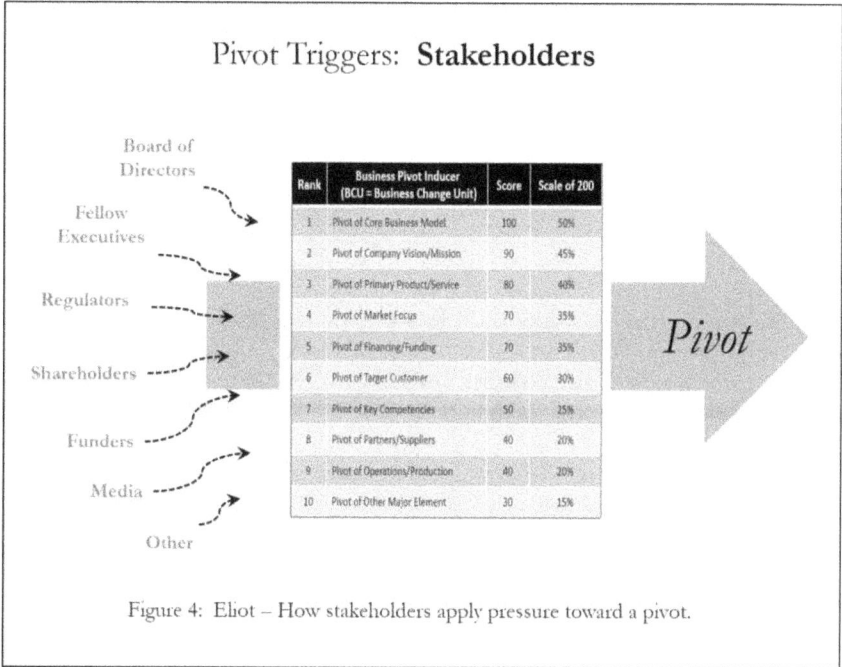

Figure 4: Eliot – How stakeholders apply pressure toward a pivot.

CHAPTER 17 – FIGURE 4

Pivot Suppressants: **Stakeholders**

Rank	Business Pivot Inducer (BCU = Business Change Unit)	Score	Scale of 200
1	Pivot of Core Business Model	100	50%
2	Pivot of Company Vision/Mission	90	45%
3	Pivot of Primary Product/Service	80	40%
4	Pivot of Market Focus	70	35%
5	Pivot of Financing/Funding	70	35%
6	Pivot of Target Customer	60	30%
7	Pivot of Key Competencies	50	25%
8	Pivot of Partners/Suppliers	40	20%
9	Pivot of Operations/Production	40	20%
10	Pivot of Other Major Element	30	15%

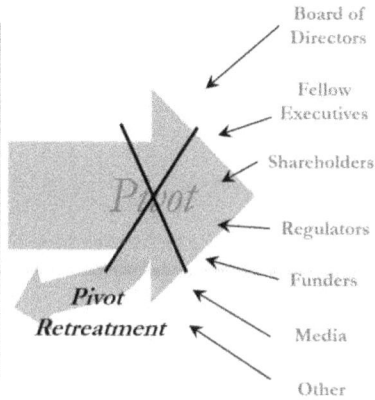

Pivot

Pivot Retreatment

Board of Directors

Fellow Executives

Shareholders

Regulators

Funders

Media

Other

Figure 5: Eliot – How stakeholders apply pressure suppressing a pivot.

CHAPTER 17 – FIGURE 5

Pivot Triggers & Suppressants: **Stakeholder Push/Pull**

Supporting Forces		**Opposing Forces**
Board of Directors →	Pivot	← Board of Directors
Fellow Executives →		← Fellow Executives
Shareholders →		← Shareholders
Regulators →		← Regulators
Funders →		← Funders
Media →		← Media
Other →		← Other

Figure 6: Eliot – How stakeholders apply pressures about a pivot.

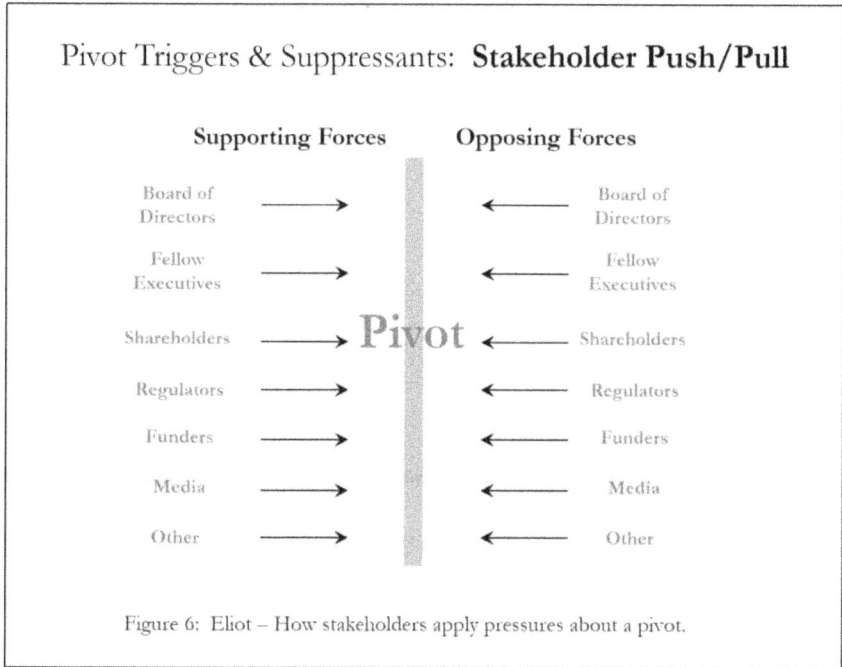

CHAPTER 17 – FIGURE 6

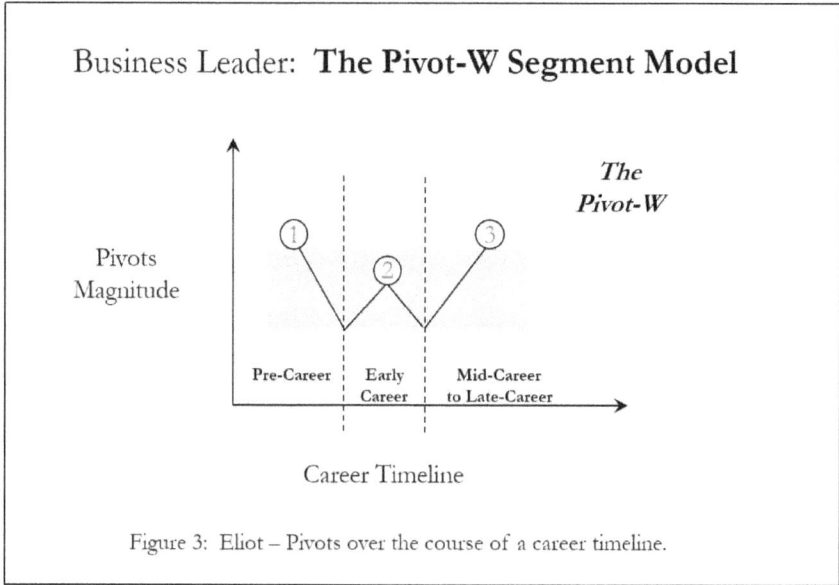

Figure 3: Eliot – Pivots over the course of a career timeline.

CHAPTER 18 – FIGURE 3

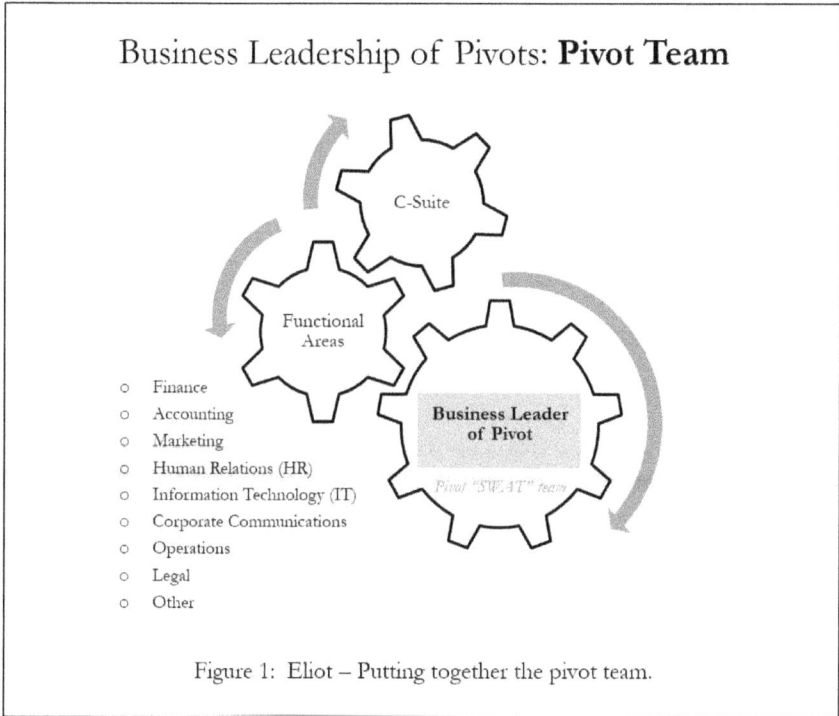

Business Leadership of Pivots: **Pivot Team**

C-Suite

Functional
Areas

- o Finance
- o Accounting
- o Marketing
- o Human Relations (HR)
- o Information Technology (IT)
- o Corporate Communications
- o Operations
- o Legal
- o Other

**Business Leader
of Pivot**

Pivot "SWAT" team

Figure 1: Eliot – Putting together the pivot team.

CHAPTER 19 – FIGURE 1

341

Business Leadership of Pivots: **Pivot Team**

Functional Area of the Firm	Explanation of Role on Team
Finance	Estimate value of pivot, ROI, obtain funding, handle financial aspects
Accounting	Identify impacts to the books, restructuring of accounts, procedures
Marketing	Ascertain market impacts, rebranding and refocus, channels assessment and adjust
Human Relations (HR)	Talent impacts, job roles and reporting relationships, people backlashes coping
Information Technology (IT)	Systems impacts, upgrades to legacy systems, put in place new systems
Corporate Communications	Internal and external communications aspects, ascertain per stakeholder
Operations	Operational impacts, changes in practices, new procedures, production
Legal	Legal impacts, new licenses or contracts, potential for lawsuits and protection
Other	Other areas of the business as needed

Figure 2: Eliot – Team across all functional areas and representations needed.

CHAPTER 19 – FIGURE 2

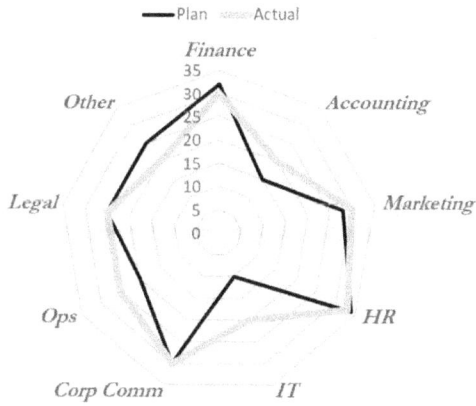

Business Leadership of Pivots: **Pivot Team**

Pivot "Radar" Chart of Representation on Team

Figure 3: Eliot – Gauging the effort of representation participation.

CHAPTER 19 – FIGURE 3

Lance B. Eliot

LBE Business Pivot Methodology

Stage 1	*Stage 2*	*Stage 3*
Pre-Pivot	**Pivot Point**	**Post-Pivot**

- Identify impetus for pivot (use MVPP, SRRS, BRRS)
- Assess pivot value and ROI
- Consider alternatives
- Examine Triggers, Suppressants
- Conduct Stakeholder analysis
- Prepare the Pivot Plan
- Assemble & ready the Pivot Team
- Readiness check for Pivot Point
- Retreatment if needed

- Pivot Point readiness check
- Engage the Pivot Plan
- Monitor pivot progress
- Update on stakeholders
- Adjust pivot as needed
- Retreatment if needed
- Prepare for Post-Pivot

- Post-Pivot readiness check
- Undertake Post-Pivot as planned
- Monitor progress of Post-Pivot
- Update on stakeholders
- Adjust Post-Pivot as needed
- Retreatment if needed
- Do lessons learned analysis
- Tout pivot completion as needed

Figure 1: Eliot – What to do during each of the stages of the pivot.

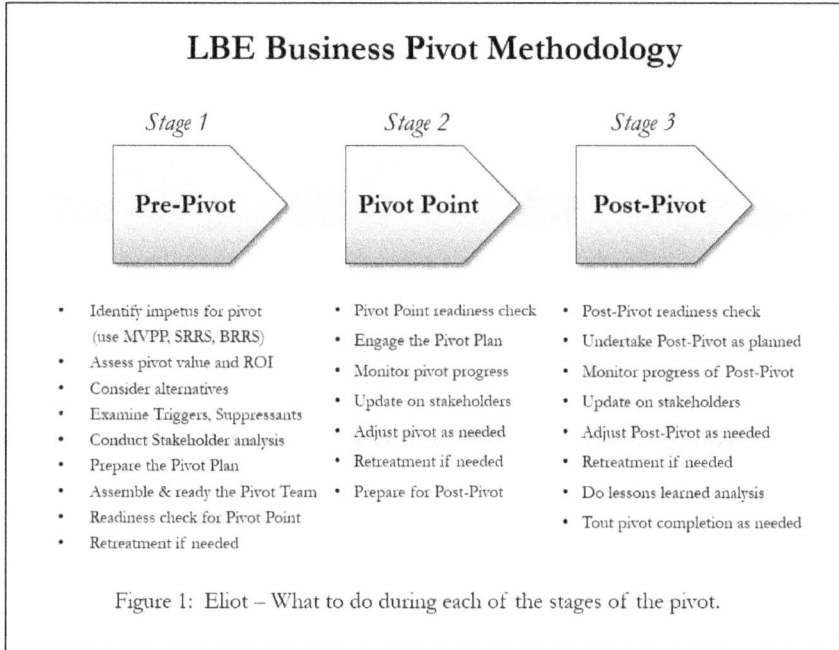

CHAPTER 20 – FIGURE 1

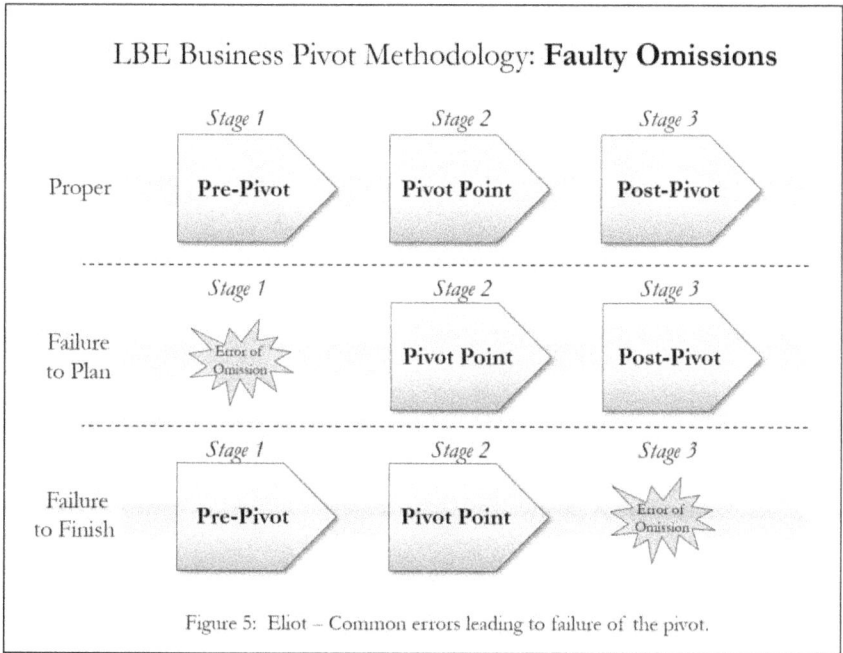

Figure 5: Eliot – Common errors leading to failure of the pivot.

CHAPTER 20 – FIGURE 5

Business Leadership Pivots: **Pivot Pitfalls**

Ref	Pivot pitfall	Explanation of problem
1	The pivot "one man band"	Business leader tries to go solo
2	Emperor has no clothes pivoting	Failure to recognize pivot concerns
3	Jumped the gun on the pivot	Lack of Pre-Pivot preparation
4	Train wreck ahead of the pivot	Lousy direction and Post-Pivot nightmare
5	Pivot stakeholder rebellion	Stakeholders lose faith in the pivot
6	The Pivot "scatter gun"	Wild shot pivot with no solid aim
7	Pivot bites off more than it can chew	Jam packed pivot is bulging at the seams
8	Mega-pivot is mega-disaster situation	"Big bang" pivot unsuitable in this case
9	Gravitational force wins over pivot	Status quo overpowers the pivot
10	Pivot is needed, but no leadership	Headless floundering and void of pivot

Figure 1: Eliot – Common ways in which pivots go awry.

CHAPTER 21 – FIGURE 1

Lance B. Eliot

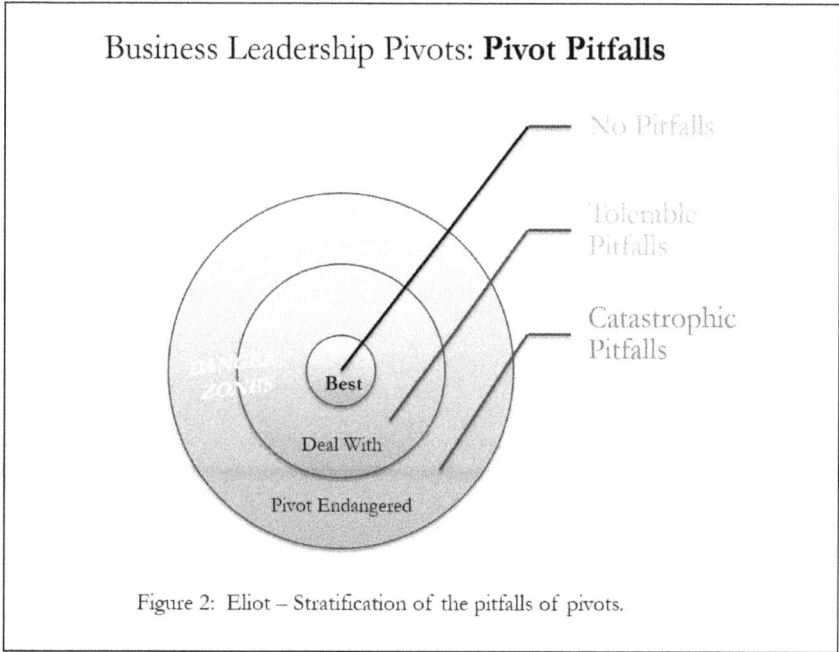

Figure 2: Eliot – Stratification of the pitfalls of pivots.

CHAPTER 21 – FIGURE 2

Business Leadership Pivots: **Key Principles**

Ref	Some Key Principles about Business Pivots
i	Any Business Leader will have 1 or more business pivots in their career
ii	Likely to be 3 pivots: *Pre-Career, Early Career, Mid-Career to Late*
iii	At least 1 business pivot will arise unexpectedly or unawares
iv	1 or more business pivots will go negative during the business career
v	The first-time pivot by a Business Leader will be least well-handed
vi	1 or more business pivots will involve a Pivot Retreatment (backing off)
vii	So-called "Dumb Luck" will be involved in at least 1 business pivot
viii	Opportunistic luck ("Made Luck") will be involved in 1 or more pivots
ix	Being Pivot-Wise will positively impact the business pivot success
x	Most Business Leaders are not yet Pivot-Wise

Figure 1: Eliot – Some guiding principles about business pivots.

CHAPTER 22 – FIGURE 1

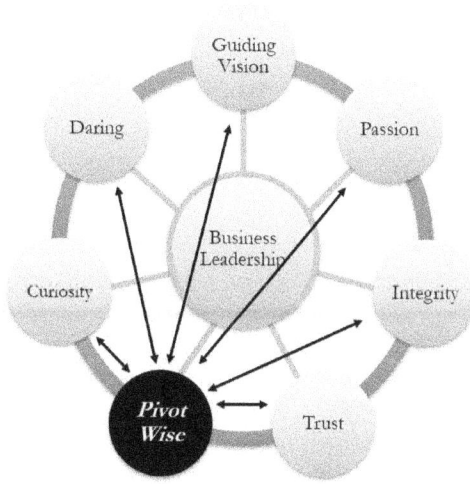

The Key Ingredients of a Business Leader

Guiding Vision

Daring

Passion

Business Leadership

Curiosity

Integrity

Pivot Wise

Trust

Figure 2: Eliot – Business Leadership with the new ingredient of being "pivot wise".

CHAPTER 22 – FIGURE 2

APPENDIX B

TEACHING WITH THIS MATERIAL

The material in this book can be readily used either as a supplemental to other content for a class, or it can also be used as a core set of textbook material for a specialized class. Classes where this material is most likely used include any business classes at the college or university level that want to augment the class by offering thought provoking and educational essays about business.

In particular, here are some aspects for class use:

o   Business Leadership. Studying the nature of business leadership, and use the mini-case studies of the various founders and CEO's that are analyzed in this book.

o   Business Pivoting. Exploring how business pivoting works, using the paradigm shown in this book as a starting point for discussing the inner workings of business pivots.

o   Business Change and Transformation. Focusing on the nature of change and transformation in businesses, of which this book covers a subset that is devoted to the business pivoting aspects.

o   Start-up's and Entrepreneurs. Gauging how successful start-up's adapt and adjust while trying to find their Darwinian survival place in the market, along with how the entrepreneurs that founded the firms were able to endure and succeed in the overwhelmingly harsh start-up gauntlet.

Specialized classes at the undergraduate and graduate level can also make use of this material. An MBA-seminar class at the graduate level on entrepreneurship is one such example of how this material has been used.

For each chapter, consider whether you think the chapter provides material relevant to your course topic. There is plenty of opportunity to get the students thinking about the topic and force them to decide whether they agree or disagree with the points offered and positions taken. I would also encourage you to have the students do additional research beyond the chapter material presented (I provide next some suggested assignments they can do).

RESEARCH ASSIGNMENTS ON THESE TOPICS

Your students can readily find a plethora of background material on these topics, doing so in the usual business publications such as the Harvard Business Review, Forbes, Fortune, WSJ, and the like.

Here are some suggestions of homework or projects that you could assign to students:

a) Assignment for Business Pivots topic: Research and prepare a paper and a presentation on the role of business pivots as described in the Lean Start-up literature. The paper should cite at least 3 reputable sources and analyze how business pivots are portrayed by those sources. Compare and contrast the business pivot characterization in those sources to how this book has portrayed business pivots.

b) Assignment for Business Leadership topic: Research and prepare a paper and a presentation on business leadership. Cite at least 3 reputable sources and analyze the model of business leadership presented. Compare and contrast the business leadership aspects to those described in this book, especially as indicated in Chapter 1.

c) Assignment for Business Change and Transformation topic: Research and prepare a paper and a presentation on business change and transformation. Cite at least 3 reputable sources. Compare and contrast the advice and techniques to those depicted in this book. Identify how business pivots fit into business change.

d) Assignment for Entrepreneurship and Start-ups topic: Research and prepare a paper and a presentation on entrepreneurship and start-ups. Cite at least 3 reputable sources. Compare and contrast to the start-ups and entrepreneurs depicted in this book.

You can certainly adjust the aforementioned research assignments to fit to your particular needs and the class structure. You'll notice that I ask for 3 reputable cited sources for each of the assignments. I usually steer students toward "reputable" publications, since otherwise they will cite some oddball source that has no credentials other than that they happened to write something and post it onto the Internet. You can define "reputable" in whatever way you prefer, for example some faculty think Wikipedia is not reputable while others believe it is reputable and allow students to cite it.

The reason that I usually ask for at least 3 citations is that if the student only does one or two citations they usually settle on whatever they happened to find the fastest. By requiring three citations, it usually seems to force them to look around, explore, and end-up probably finding five or more, and then whittling it down to 3 that they will actually use.

I have not specified the length of their papers, and leave that to you to tell the students what you prefer. For each of those assignments, you could end-up with a short one to two pager, or you could do a dissertation length paper. Base the length on whatever best fits for your class, and the credit amount of the assignment within the context of the other grading metrics you'll be using for the class.

I mention in the assignments that they are to do a paper and prepare a presentation. I usually try to get students to present their work. This is a good practice for what they will do in the business world. Most of the time, they will be required to prepare an analysis and present it. If you don't have the class time or inclination to have the students present, then you can of course cut out the aspect of them putting together a presentation.

If you want to point students toward highly ranked journals in business, here's a list of the top journals as reported by *Financial Times* (this list changes year to year, plus you might disagree with how they ranked them):

    i.   Academy of Management Journal

   ii.   Academy of Management Review

  iii.   Accounting, Organizations and Society

  iv.   Administrative Science Quarterly

   v.   American Economic Review

  vi.   Entrepreneurship Theory and Practice

 vii.   Harvard Business Review

viii.   Human Resource Management

  ix.   Information Systems Research

GUIDE TO USING THE CHAPTERS

For each of the chapters, I provide next some various ways to use the chapter material. You can assign the tasks as individual homework assignments, or the tasks can be used with team projects for the class. You can easily layout a series of assignments, such as indicating that the students are to do item "a" below for say Chapter 1, then "b" for the next chapter of the book, and so on.

a) What is the main point of the chapter and describe in your own words the significance of the topic,

b) Identify at least two aspects in the chapter that you agree with, and support your concurrence by providing at least one other outside researched item as support; make sure to explain your basis for disagreeing with the aspects,

c) Identify at least two aspects in the chapter that you disagree with, and support your disagreement by providing at least one other outside researched item as support; make sure to explain your basis for disagreeing with the aspects,

d) Find an aspect that was not covered in the chapter, doing so by conducting outside research, and then explain how that aspect ties into the chapter and what significance it brings to the topic,

e) Interview an business leader in industry about the topic of the chapter, collect from them their thoughts and opinions, and readdress the chapter by citing your source and how they compared and contrasted to the material,

f) Interview a relevant academic professor or researcher in a college or university about the topic of the chapter, collect from them their thoughts and opinions, and readdress the chapter by citing your source and how they compared and contrasted to the material,

g) Try to update a chapter by finding out the latest on the topic, and ascertain whether the issue or topic has now been solved or whether it is still being addressed, explain what you come up with,

h) Have the students role play as a business leader and ask them to consider the chapter material in light of being a business leader, and explain what they would say or comment in that capacity,

i) Have the students role play as the founder of a start-up and ask them to consider the chapter material in light of being an entrepreneur, and explain what they would say or comment in that capacity,

j) For students that work in a business, have the student describe how the aspects of this book takes place in their business and whether the issue or topic of the chapter is relevant to their firm or not, and say why,

k) Make use of case studies, such as a relevant case study from the Harvard Business Review library, and analyze the case from the perspective of this book and make use of the chapter material as a means to do so.

The above are all ways in which you can get the students of your class involved in considering the material of a given chapter. You could mix things up by having one of those above assignments per each week, covering the chapters over the course of the semester or quarter.

As a reminder, here are the chapters of the book and you can cherry pick whichever chapters you find most valued for your particular class:

Chapter Title
1. On the Key Ingredients of a Business Leader
2. The Essentials of Business Pivoting
3. Aaron Levie (Founder Box.com)
4. Peter Kim (Founder Hudson Jeans)
5. Jon Kraft (Founder Pandora)
6. William Wang (Founder Vizio)
7. Cindy Crawford (Founder Beauty Line, Supermodel)
8. Jenny Ming (CEO Charlotte Russe)
9. Steve Milligan (CEO Western Digital)
10. Chris Underwood (CEO Young's Market)
11. Frank Gehry (Renowned Architect)
12. Colonel Sanders (Luminary, Founder KFC)
13. Pivot Transparency, Saturations
14. Pivot Gravitational Force, Pivot-Flop, Pivot-Not
15. Pivot Retreatment
16. Ingredient Co-Influences, MVPP, SRRS, BRRS
17. Pivot Triggers, Suppressants, Stakeholders
18. The Pivot-W Segment Model
19. Your Pivot Team
20. LBE Business Pivot Methodology
21. Key Pitfalls that Wreck Pivots
22. Business Leadership's Pivot Principles

ABOUT THE AUTHOR

Dr. Lance B. Eliot, MBA, PhD is known as a Thought Leader in business, and has over twenty years of industry experience, including serving as a corporate officer in a billion dollar firm, and was a Partner in a major executive services firm. He is also a serial entrepreneur having founded, ran, and sold several high-tech related businesses. He previously hosted the popular radio show *Technotrends* that was also available on American Airlines flights via their in-flight audio program. Author or co-author of five books and over 300 articles, he has made appearances on CNN, and has been a frequent speaker at industry conferences.

A former professor at the University of Southern California (USC), he founded and led an innovative research lab on Artificial Intelligence in Business. He also previously served on the faculty of the University of California Los Angeles (UCLA), and was a visiting professor at other major universities. He was elected to the International Board of the Society for Information Management (SIM), a prestigious association of over 3,000 high-tech executives worldwide.

He has performed extensive community service, including serving as Senior Science Adviser to the Vice Chair of the Congressional Committee on Science & Technology. He has served on the Board of the OC Science & Engineering Fair (OCSEF), where he is also has been a Grand Sweepstakes judge, and likewise served as a judge for the Intel International SEF (ISEF). He served as the Vice Chair of the Association for Computing Machinery (ACM) Chapter, a prestigious association of computer scientists. Dr. Eliot has been a shark tank judge for the USC Mark Stevens Center for Innovation on start-up pitch competitions, and served as a mentor for several incubators and accelerators in Silicon Valley and Silicon Beach. He serves on several Boards and Committees at USC, including the Marshall Alumni Association (MAA) Board for Los Angeles and Orange County in Southern California.

Dr. Eliot holds a PhD from USC, MBA, and Bachelor's in Computer Science, and earned the CDP, CCP, CSP, CDE, and CISA certifications. Born and raised in Southern California, and having traveled and lived internationally, he enjoys scuba diving, surfing, and sailing.

ADDENDUM

On Being a Pivot-Wise Business Leader

The Secrets of Strategic Leadership
For Successful Business Pivots

By
Dr. Lance B. Eliot, MBA, PhD

———

For supplemental materials of this book, visit:

www.lance-blog.com

For special orders of this book, contact:
LBE Press Publishing
Email: LBE.Press.Publishing@gmail.com